better than fiction

better than fiction

True Travel Tales From Great Fiction Writers

Edited by Don George

LONELY PLANET PUBLICATIONS

Melbourne • Oakland • London

Better than Fiction
True Travel Tales from Great Fiction Writers

Published by
Lonely Planet Publications

Head Office
90 Maribyrnong Street, Footscray, Victoria, 3011, Australia
Locked Bag 1, Footscray, Victoria, 3011, Australia

Branches
150 Linden Street, Oakland CA 94607, USA
201 Wood Ln, London, W12 7TQ, United Kingdom

Published 2012
Printed by Hang Tai Printing Company, Hong Kong
Printed in China

Edited by Janet Austin, Kate James
Cover Design by Roberto Devicq
Design by Mark Adams
Layout by Margie Jung

National Library of Australia Cataloguing-in-Publication entry

Better than fiction: true travel tales from
great fiction writers / edited by Don George.

1st Edition.

978 1 74220 594 6 (pbk.)

Voyages and travels.
Travelers' writings.

George, Donald W.

808.8032

Don George has edited six previous Lonely Planet anthologies, including *Lights, Camera... Travel!*, *A Moveable Feast*, *The Kindness of Strangers*, *By the Seat of My Pants* and *Tales from Nowhere*. He also wrote the best-selling *Lonely Planet Guide to Travel Writing*. Don is Editor at Large and Book Review Columnist for *National Geographic Traveler*, Special Features Editor and blogger for the popular travel website Gadling.com, and Editor of Geographic Expedition's online magazine, Recce: Literary Journeys for the Discerning Traveler (www.geoex.com/recce). He has been Global Travel Editor for Lonely Planet, Travel Editor at the *San Francisco Examiner & Chronicle; and founder and editor of* Salon.com's Wanderlust. Don has received dozens of awards for his writing and editing, including the Society of American Travel Writers Lowell Thomas Award. He appears frequently on NPR, CNN, and other TV and radio outlets, is a highly sought-after speaker, and hosts a national series of onstage conversations with prominent writers. Don is also co-founder and chairman of the annual Book Passage Travel Writers and Photographers Conference.

Contents

Introduction

BY DON GEORGE

When I was preparing to settle in Greece for a year fresh out of college, in addition to my guidebooks, I packed two novels, *The Magus* by John Knowles and *Zorba the Greek* by Nikos Kazantzakis. As the year unfolded, in many ways the latter two proved to be the best guides of all, immersive, enlightening introductions to the landscape, people, and culture I was discovering.

As I have learned over and over in my wanderings, some of the best travel writing is fictional. And some of the best travel writers, going all the way back to Lady Murasaki, Homer, and the authors of *One Thousand and One Nights*, are the fiction-spinners who transport us to the worlds they create with their words.

This truth was the inspiration behind the anthology you hold in your hands. What would we get, we wondered, if we asked some of the planet's most acclaimed fiction writers to describe their most meaningful non-fictional journeys?

The answer is this treasure trove of surprising and inspiring tales: thirty-two stories that span the thematic spectrum from disorientation to revelation, disillusion to redemption, life-threatening risk to life-saving connection; in settings as varied as Antarctica, Alaska, and Argentina, Saudi Arabia, Sulawesi, and South Africa; written by a distinguished corps of contributors who have humbled us in their enthusiasm for this project.

Exhilaratingly varied in place, plot, and voice, these tales all share one common characteristic: They manifest a passion for the precious gifts that travel confers, from its unexpected but inevitably enriching lessons about other peoples and places to the truths – sometimes uncomfortable but always enlarging – it reveals about ourselves.

May your own life's journey be enriched and enlarged by these master storytellers' true travel tales!

Kurt Andersen is the author of *Heyday*, a *New York Times* bestseller and winner of the 2008 Langum Prize as the year's best American historical novel. His earlier novel, *Turn of the Century*, was a *Times* Notable Book and national bestseller, and his most recent novel is *True Believers*. Andersen is also the author of the nonfiction book *Reset*, about the 2008–09 financial and economic crisis. In addition, he is host and cocreator of *Studio 360*, the Peabody Award–winning public radio programme, and a regular contributor to *Vanity Fair* and *Time* magazines. Previously, he was a columnist for *New York* magazine and the *New Yorker*, as well as the design and architecture critic for *Time*. He also cofounded *Spy* magazine, and served as editor-in-chief of *New York* magazine and editorial director of *Colors*.

Going South

BY KURT ANDERSEN

I suppose it was inevitable. My family's annual vacations had always consisted of weeks-long summer driving trips, and almost exclusively *north,* to cool, tidy, familiar Minnesotas and Wisconsins and Manitobas. I had studied Spanish for ten years. I was 17 going on 18, out of high school a semester early, working a minimum-wage job and admitted to the college of my choice. And for three years my favorite book had been *The Electric Kool-Aid Acid Test,* Tom Wolfe's iconifying 1968 chronicle of Ken Kesey and his dozen friends' pointless and profound coast-to-coast-to-coast 1964 trip across America in an old school bus. It was a moment, for people my age, when high adventure seemed not only possible but easy, not only easy but obligatory.

And so in the summer of 1972, five other Omaha boys and I bought a stubby old yellow school bus. It got atrocious mileage, even by the standards of that era, but gas cost only 35 cents a gallon. We ripped out most of the seats, built some crude wooden storage cabinets, installed a cassette tape player and speakers, tacked down 100 square feet of gold loop-pile carpeting, bought some maps, and – cell-phoneless, internetless – lit out for the territory. We were headed south, due south, way south, beyond the frontier, to Mexico.

Two or three days later in Texas, at the end of I-35, we learned that anyone who looked like a hippie was being turned away at the border. Although not exactly hippies, we were a half-dozen teenage boys with longish hair, dressed in T-shirts and jeans and jammed into a funky school bus. (Also, it turned out, we were about to bring coals to Newcastle – that is, mescaline to Mexico. The most hell-bent of my companions, unable to abide throwing away perfectly good hallucinogens, swallowed his entire two-gram stash in Laredo.) At a Woolworth's in Laredo we bought a tube of Brylcreem, and for $3 apiece the squarest dress shirts we could find. Those of us with mustaches and sideburns shaved. *Voilà!* De-counter-culturalized, looking more like Mormon missionaries or *The Partridge Family*'s nerd cousins than Merry Pranksters or *Easy Rider* dudes, we were waved right across by two sets of border guards, out of America and into Mexico.

My recollection of most of the trip is strangely vague. I know we slept on the bus and ate mostly bread, cheese, cold cuts and fruit. I do remember certain specific, redolent neo-ugly-American moments – blasting Traffic's *The Low Spark of High Heeled Boys* out of our open door and windows as we rumbled through small towns, leaving scraped streaks of chrome yellow on masonry walls as we squeezed down streets barely wider than the bus. And I recall our route around the country – Monterrey, Guanajuato, San Miguel de Allende and Mexico City, then Cuernavaca, Acapulco, Mazatlan, Nogales. But forty years later, out of all those hot, dusty, windy weeks, one single day remains distinct and extraordinary.

It was the golden age of hitchhiking – a year earlier a friend and I had hitchhiked from Nebraska to the east coast and back to look at colleges – and as we approached Mexico City from the northwest, we stopped to pick up a kid, maybe a year or two younger than us, who had his thumb out. Between our shaky Spanish and his shaky English, a friendship was struck up. Standing at the front of the bus, holding on to the chrome pole next to the driver's seat, ducking to look out the giant windshield, for an hour our new pal, Fernando, guided us deep into the city and finally to his working-class neighborhood.

He *demanded* we come up and meet his parents and siblings. His mother *insisted* she was going to serve these six hungry young American strangers a late lunch. His father *required* that we each guzzle a *submarino,* a tall tumbler of Coke over which a shot glass of tequila was held with two fingers and dropped like a depth charge – and then another and maybe one more.

We talked about the last Summer Olympics, which had taken place in Mexico City, and the two black American medalists who had raised their black-gloved fists as 'The Star-Spangled Banner' played. And our new friends were still excited about the 1970 World Cup, also staged in Mexico, in which their national team had gotten to the quarter-finals. Fernando or one of his buddies who'd joined the party asked us, '*¿No es jugar al fútbol, fútbol mexicano, en los Estados Unidos, verdad?*' – *You don't play Mexican football in the U.S., right?*

He meant soccer, of course. And back in 1972, American kids did not play soccer – *except, providentially, the six of us.* I'd been the first to learn, at a nerdy international-themed summer camp when I was 12 and 13. Because soccer was foreign, it seemed cool, and because none of the real athletes in Omaha were any better at it than we were, a few of us freaks and geeks had organized a tiny intramural league in high school.

'*Sí,*' I said, '*en nuestra escuela hemos jugado en un equipo de fútbol mexicano!*' – *In our school we played on a soccer team!*

By means of phone calls and shouts, Fernando instantly assembled a local team of six. Minutes later the block was cleared of all parked vehicles, and a few empty oil drums – traffic blockades and goalposts – had been lined up at each end. The street was at the bottom of a ravine, the opposing hillsides covered with multicolored cinderblock and stucco houses from bottom to top. In other words, it was a kind of natural stadium, each terrace and porch its own skybox. Children and adults stepped outside, sat on walls, leaned on posts, opened Cokes and Coronas. And awash in the preternaturally perfect August light of six o'clock, the game began.

Until that day we had played only on grass, but years of school-recess asphalt kickball had prepared us, more or less, for the hyperspeed and crazy bounces of street *fútbol*. And the pre-game tequila probably made our pothole contusions and gravel-studded abrasions less painful. We had a goalie, but our positioning otherwise was highly ambiguous, with backs racing upfield to shoot, and forwards falling back to defend our oil drums.

The most glorious and dreamlike part of the experience was the spectator mob. There were 100 people watching, maybe 150, but the loud, happy chants and cheers – provoked by any and all dramatic action, whether committed by a local kid or a gringo – made it feel like a crowd of thousands. At half-time a *raspador,* a vendor of fruit-flavored shaved ice – an actual concessionaire! – wheeled his cart onto the block.

The game ended as sunset approached and church bells struck seven. I'm pretty sure we didn't play for a regulation 90 minutes. The thin air at seven-thousand-feet-plus was rough on us boys from the low plains. And we lost decisively – Mexico City 5 (I think), Omaha 2 – but we *scored,* twice, playing their national pastime on their street. We were breathless, sweaty, filthy, bloody, bruised and totally, deeply, existentially gratified.

We awoke at sunrise, performed quick ablutions in the family's single bathroom, ate Fernando's mother's breakfast of scrambled eggs and tortillas, offered money that was refused and refused again, reboarded the bus and headed out, on the road again, more than ever ready for adventures.

But nothing else on the trip – not our first visit to Las Vegas (Hunter Thompson's *Fear and Loathing,* published the previous fall, was a kind of sacred text), not our first visit to Disneyland (the Merry Pranksters had been headed for the World's Fair in 1964), not the archetypal young California blonde speeding around a curve in Big Sur and smashing her yellow convertible into our parked bus – was as wondrous as our impromptu soccer match in that ragged, random, impossibly hospitable Mexico City barrio whose name I don't remember and maybe never knew.

The process of recalling and reconstructing my faded and fragmentary memories of that ancient journey and heroic game has been as much like writing fiction as nonfiction. If it were fiction, I might have an unexpected and ironic and life-changing encounter years later, as an adult, with Fernando. Real life was not so obliging. In a piece of fiction, surely, the bonds forged over the course of 7000 miles on a bus – we few, we happy few, we band of brothers – would endure yet be tested and twisted over the decades. In fact, I haven't been in touch with any of my fellow travelers for more than 30 years; two of them died young, the mescaline-eater by his own hand at age 41. In a work of fiction, I might right now have the dusty, yellowed old *The Low Spark of High Heeled Boys* cassette in front of me, an elegiac artifact of my youth, as I construct a remembrance of things past. But I unsentimentally tossed out all my old albums long ago. I discovered on Google just now that that particular tape sells for between $60 and $500, depending on condition.

As it happens, however, I am in Mexico, at the end of a month-long stay, longer than I've spent in the country since 1972. I'm on the sunny rooftop of a house on a street called the Alley of the Dead, overlooking a hillside covered with a jumble of brown and white and yellow and red stucco houses. I hear afternoon church bells. And in the schoolyard at the bottom of the hill, children are kicking a soccer ball.

Sophie Cunningham has worked in publishing in Australia for twenty-five years. She is the author of two novels, *Geography* and *Bird*, and a nonfiction book, *Melbourne*. Her third novel (in progress), *This Devastating Fever*, is about Leonard Woolf's years in Sri Lanka. She is also currently writing a nonfiction book on Cyclone Tracy and extreme weather.

Kind of Blue

BY SOPHIE CUNNINGHAM

Once upon a time I lived in a turquoise-blue bungalow next to a vegetable garden planted at the back of a red-brick house. At the back of the veggie patch was a stand of bright-yellow sunflowers that stood tall as a human, faces toward the sky. On the ground lay pumpkins, their tendrils unfolding so fast that you could, I used to fancy, *see* them grow – if you were patient, if you watched closely enough. As it happened, my attempts to watch pumpkins grow didn't go so well – were as difficult as noticing those moments when you feel *yourself* grow. How often can we pinpoint when a conversation, a landscape or simply a gesture has stretched us, and broadened our view of the world?

The reason my bungalow walls were turquoise blue was that I'd been, just a couple of years before, to India and you can't go to that country and not have your relationship to colour change. In Australia, colour is, or was, a matter of taste, of restraint, of following rules. (Never wear pink and red together, my grandmother used to tell me. She's been dead 30 years but still I hesitate, if I'm wearing pink, as I lean in towards the mirror to put my red lipstick on.) In India colour was used with a flourish and confidence. It exploded around you. In fact I bought some of it home in little plastic pots, pots of powdered paints that I have, for

25 years now, carried with me from house to house. My talismans. The colours are as intense, as fresh, as the day I bought them from a market in Madras: golden yellow, bright grass green, cobalt blue, china red.

The story I want to tell, though, isn't about my improved colour sense. I'm digressing before I've even begun. As most travellers know, India is, in effect, one long, glorious digression, but what I want to describe is the moment when that country shifted things for me, ever so slightly, a moment over so quickly it wasn't much more than a flicker in the corner of the eye.

. . . .

I've never known exactly what is meant by the term culture shock but assume it refers to the intense disorientation you can feel while travelling. Recently, I read Allen Ginsberg's *India Diaries*: 'I slept all afternoon & when I woke I thought it was morning, I didn't know where I was. I had no name for India.' As I read Ginsberg, I thought, Yes! That's it! When you travel you can lose the names for things, and with the names, you lose meaning. You don't know where you are.

Certainly I felt some kind of shock when I saw India's beggars, their limbs tangled into impossible knots, or missing altogether. Or the blind women, eyes rolling in their heads or scars where their eyes once were, handing out printed statements explaining their situation and requesting financial help. Less alarmingly, some beggars wore saffron robes to indicate they were now living a life of a sadhu – that was more like it. That was what I'd expected.

I was a 20-year-old middle-class girl from Melbourne when I first went to India, and it was long enough ago that it was rare to see beggars on the streets of my own town. But I was diligent. I read books in an attempt to prepare myself for entering a reality very different from my own. On the flight over, to Bombay as it was then called, I read Gita Mehta's searing description of Americans stumbling around on misguided spiritual trips in India, *Karma Cola*. In that book she spoke of Americans taking advantage of the relative respect accorded to beggars by begging themselves, to subsidise their travels, or because they had joined some sect. She described Peace Corp workers attempting to save street kids and freaking out when those children attempted to repay that kindness with sex, or stolen goods. I read V. S. Naipaul's *India: A Wounded Civilization* and tried to wrap my head around the world he was describing. One where people's lives were dictated by caste. Where one's home might be a square metre of the Bombay footpath near the market you work in – and that small piece of territory may well have been passed down from father to son over several generations.

But even his vivid descriptions could not prepare me for the fact that lower castes weren't just physically smaller, they actually seemed to hold their bodies closer to the ground in an attempt to take up less space in the world while other, plumper, more confident souls would use their girth to push you out of a queue. All the while the taller, broader Brahmins carried themselves with pride. My reading certainly didn't stop me doing what most tourists – and possibly locals – do, which is looking through and around the beggars we came across. Learning to unsee them altogether.

So: I'd been in India for four months and was about to leave the country, from Calcutta, the city Ginsberg wrote so vividly about in his diaries. India hadn't been kind to me, but I assumed that my struggles were just another kind of culture shock. If the internet had existed then I would have known that the anti-malarial I was on, Lariam, was the problem, and that it caused 'neuropsychiatric effects' in 11 to 17 per cent of users. By 2002 the drug's labels and literature were clearer about what those effects might be: 'Mefloquine [Lariam] may cause psychiatric symptoms in a number of patients, ranging from anxiety, paranoia and depression to hallucinations and psychotic behaviour ... adverse reactions include ... tremor, ataxia, mood changes, panic attacks and rare cases of suicide ...' But there was no such advice back in 1984. I just thought I was going mad.

None of this boded well for that moment of growth I've been promising to describe. Certainly I'd given up expecting it. I'm not sure if the naivety of my hopes for India were why it had so disappointed me, though I felt, to more accurately describe my emotions, that I had disappointed India. I was embarrassed really. Like all those hippies Mehta was so scathing about in *Karma Cola*, I'd gone to India to *find myself* and found instead neuropsychiatric effects and giardia. It served me right. It was only once I'd left the country that I began to think of the latticework of dust I'd found laid out on my eiderdown after a dust storm, as a kind of blessing. Or that I realised the week I'd spent in Kashmir, a place of the most extraordinary beauty, was a rare honour. In fact it now seems the ways in which India changed me are too numerous to mention, but at the time I didn't see it like that at all. Well, until my last hour or so in the country.

I was sitting outside the hotel I'd stayed in for my last few nights in the country, reflecting on the fact that I found Calcutta – that plump, fetid, monsoonal version of a Victorian city – quite charming. I was, to my surprise, sorry

to be leaving. This is one of the things India does to you –
it's like a difficult, demanding lover who you swear you
never want to see again, only to find they've got under your
skin, and insinuated themselves into your dreams.

I was sitting on the ground, leaning against my backpack,
which in turn was leaning against a faded turquoise
concrete wall, waiting for that taxi. A few sprays of magenta
bougainvillea were waving in the wind, batting me in the
face, like sharp little kisses. The heat of the day had not yet
descended and I was revelling in the sun. A man – a beggar
– rolled up to me. His limbs were twisted up behind his
torso and he needed a skateboard to move around. Now I
realise he had polio, but at the time I didn't know what had
caused such distortion. He was strong across his shoulder
and arms and – it seems impossible that I remember this
detail, so perhaps it's my imagination – his hands were
calloused, and sat at sharp right angles to the rest of him, as
if they were feet.

I started feeling around in my pockets but I had no
money except rupees for the taxi left. I told the beggar this
and he shrugged, saying, 'No worries,' in near-perfect
English. After an awkward pause he asked, 'Would you like
some chocolate cake?' That was when I saw, with some
surprise, that he had a chocolate cake sitting in front of him
on his board. 'It's my birthday,' he elaborated.

I took the slice of cake I was offered and we started to
chat. He had a laid-back casual charm. He wanted to know
about Australia. I wanted to know where he got the cake. A
Japanese tourist had given it to him, he told me. He also
told me that he was married, he had kids, and the business
of begging was going pretty well. Over the next ten minutes
or so we were joined by several of his friends, all missing
bits of their bodies and all getting stuck into the chocolate

cake. A fairly animated discussion ensued about how certain territories attracted higher incomes. I was made to feel welcome rather than like the intruder I was, and after that initial approach, no one asked me for money. After a few more minutes the taxi arrived, so I said my farewells. As I drove off I waved out the back window at my new friend, who was resuming his post outside the front of the hotel. He waved back.

It embarrasses me now to realise how surprised I was to learn that this man, that most beggars, didn't see themselves as objects of pity. Pity was just the business they were in. They lived complex lives, like all of us. I realised, I suppose, just how ignorant I was. Having seen that, I hoped that I could begin to undo it, though I now see that learning is just a gradual revelation of how deep our ignorance really is. To give up to not knowing, to be uncertain of the name of things: that space is the place where possibility lives and in my mind it shimmers bright as a blue summer sky.

Arnold Zable is an acclaimed Australian writer and novelist, and one of the country's most-loved storytellers. His award-winning books include *Jewels and Ashes*, *The Fig Tree* and three novels, *Café Scheherazade*, *Scraps of Heaven* and *Sea of Many Returns*. His most recent book, *Violin Lessons*, a collection of stories, was published in 2011. He is the author of numerous columns, stories and essays, and is coauthor of the play *Kan Yama Kan*, in which asylum seekers tell their stories. Zable has been a visiting lecturer at Deakin, Melbourne, Monash, RMIT, La Trobe and Victoria universities. He is president of the Melbourne centre of International PEN and has a doctorate from the School of Creative Arts, Melbourne University, where he was recently appointed a Vice Chancellor's Fellow. Born in Wellington, New Zealand, Zable grew up in the inner-Melbourne suburb of Carlton. He has travelled and lived in the USA, India, Papua New Guinea, Europe, Southeast Asia and China, and now lives in Melbourne with his wife and son.

Huaxi Watermill

BY ARNOLD ZABLE

In September, 1984, I journeyed to Huaxi, a small town in Guizhou Province, in southwest China. For the following nine months I worked at the Guizhou Agricultural College, teaching English to research scientists. The red identity card the authorities issued had me grandly titled: 'foreign expert'.

The college was a world unto itself, the campus set apart from and above the township. Each day, I left my apartment to walk from the college out into the countryside. It was autumn when I began the walks. The valley and township were encircled in the near distance by steep limestone mountains. Crops of red chilli peppers and rice were spread out to dry on roadsides and village courtyards. Terraced rice paddies alternated with fields of yellow rape. Vegetable plots were ripe with cabbages, onions, turnips, potatoes and eggplant. All was on the cusp of reaping.

I found alternative routes, and extended my explorations along new ones. I became a familiar figure in the hamlets of the Miao and Buyi people, and was invited into their homes for toasts of *maotai,* the fiery liquor native to Guizhou Province. *Gam bei!* Drink up, they gestured. So I did. I was a novelty, one of the first foreigners to work in the province for decades.

No matter what route I took, I eventually made my way to a bridge over the Huaxi River. Eighty metres or so in length, the bridge was supported on concrete pylons. In the middle stood a brick shelter housing a watermill. The room was stacked to the rafters with sacks of grain waiting their turn at the grinding stone.

The miller knew no English, and I knew little Chinese. He filled his kettle and placed it on the coal stove. The whine of the kettle demanded attention like the insistent cry of an infant. The miller poured the tea, relit his long-stemmed pipe, and settled back on a stool opposite me. We sat in silence, broken occasionally by the chatter of passersby, and the laughter of children playing on the riverbanks.

From time to time a horse-drawn cart cluttered by, now and then a truck laboured past. Farmers came down from their hamlets with sacks of recently harvested grain. The miller added them to the stacks, returned to his seat, and resumed his silence. And all the while, beneath our feet, the steady beat of the watermill: *Thoom. Thoom. Thoom.* Round and round, an endless churning.

. . . .

At the time, China was emerging from the Cultural Revolution. As I got to know them, my students would come to my apartment and tell me tales of what they had experienced during that period.

I came to see that much of the country had descended into mass psychosis led by an aging pied piper – a self-serving potentate clinging, despite his waning years, to his power. That human capacity for slander and recrimination, betrayal and bullying, the settling of old scores and vendettas, was amplified many times over, as faction fought faction, and Red Guards roamed the countryside quoting the sacred homilies of their self-titled Great Helmsman.

The students had been assigned to years of hard labour in the countryside, or had seen their parents humiliated, imprisoned, or exiled to remote villages. Loudspeakers resounded with slogans and denunciations. *Bad elements, rich farmers, landlords, counter-revolutionaries, right-wingers* made up the five 'black categories' – with *capitalist roaders, traitors* and *spies* additional felonies, and *intellectuals* completing the roll call as the 'stinking ninth'.

The denounced were paraded in the streets or forced to kneel for hours. Placards hung from their necks, dunce's hats perched on their heads. Mobs jeered and beat them, and performed the loyalty dance. 'Mao is the red sun that shines in our heart,' they chanted, as they tore apart the lives of former comrades.

The fate of one student in particular encapsulated the madness. I shall call him Y. An earnest man in his mid-twenties, he was forever lost in thought, questioning, contemplating. He chose his words carefully, pausing to weigh up their meaning before releasing them.

'We were all caught up in it,' he said. 'Sooner or later, we stepped into the quicksand.' His father worshipped Mao. A Red Army soldier in the 1940s, he studied law after liberation, and rose to a prominent position in the bureau of public security. 'He was a kind and decent man,' Y assured me, 'and he had faith. Even now he has faith, though it has been so shaken.'

At the outset of the Cultural Revolution, Y's father followed Mao's injunction and criticised old cadres whom he believed had become corrupt. Inevitably, the wheel turned, the accuser became the accused, the interrogator the victim. Y's father was denounced and imprisoned. His son had followed his own trajectory, as a teenage member of the Red Guard and the son of a cadre, to his fall from grace as the son of a prisoner. Cut off from his father, he was reared by his grandmother, a kindly woman, fiercely protective of her grandchild.

As a child Y had dreamt of becoming a soldier in the People's Liberation Army. 'At that time I was shy, a person of few words,' he said. 'Their heroic image impressed me. I saw many films about them. I imagined I would give up my life on the battlefield, and my heroic deeds would be known far and wide by the people.'

After his father was imprisoned, books became Y's solace. He read voraciously, furtively, so as not to arouse suspicion: intellectuals were the 'stinking ninth' and their pursuits deemed counter-revolutionary. He developed a passion for ideas, sought out thinkers, read Rousseau, Voltaire, Hegel and Goethe in Chinese translation. He read Gorky and Hugo and became addicted to novels.

'I would lose myself in the characters. They remained imprinted in my mind a long time after I finished reading. They taught me how to live, how to observe the world around me. I revered the authors who created them, and wished I would one day become a writer.'

His life-experiences, and reflections upon them, led Y to believe that the most difficult challenge in life was how to be kind, yet strong. 'To be kind is not enough,' he would say. 'You have to be strong to give to others, and strong to withstand life's fluctuating fortunes.'

The wheel turned. The Cultural Revolution was over. Mao was dead, the Gang of Four imprisoned. At Party gatherings cadres pronounced the new slogans. The Cultural Revolution gave way to the 'Four Modernisations'.

'Extreme Leftists' were out and 'The Three Bad Types of People' were the new enemy. After years of self-imposed isolation, the doors were opening. Y seized his opportunities, studied agriculture, and became a research scientist and teacher of biology and horticulture; and he continued his reading and contemplation.

. . . .

Every evening I continued my walks. The farmers were bringing in the harvest as they had for millennia; and every evening I made my way to the watermill to sit with the miller. I left towards nightfall and made my way back along the riverbank, past darkening fields to the township.

The narrow streets were crowded. Teams of bullocks and horse-drawn carts trundled by. Jeeps and trucks whipped up dust, as they wove their way through competing traffic. I ate at roadside food stalls, the Huaxi teahouse and in basic restaurants. My favourite snack was a slice of fried bean curd with a filling of chilli and hot spices. *Nian-ai-dofu* it was called, 'love bean curd'. It was invariably dark when I arrived back at my campus apartment.

For two months the harvest continued, dawn to dusk, seven days a week. Bent over in rain, wind and sun, farmers shielded in conical hats drained the fields of rice and corn, sunflowers and rape, and leached the valley of its colour.

Then it was over, the fields reduced to fallow strips of dirt strewn with hayricks. The rice had been threshed, husked, bagged and carted, the trees denuded of their fruit and foliage. A collective sigh descended on the valley. The relief could be sensed in the temporary stillness. The seasons were turning, and still I continued to make my way to the watermill.

I walked as the countryside sank into the damp, walked as smoke curled day and night from village chimneys in below-zero temperatures. Walked until the entire valley was lost under thick layers of cloud and incessant drizzle, lost in its own thoughts in the depths of winter.

In the township, boys dragged wooden carts weighed down with winter fuel, their faces blackened, fingers charred, their clothes covered in coal dust. At the street stalls vapours rose from huge woks. The noodles and rice dishes were spiced with extra doses of oil and chilli. Vendors in fat padded jackets hung on till after dark selling pumpkin and sunflower seeds, while I retreated to the teahouses and surveyed the night scene through windows and doorways.

Through it all, the mill continued churning. The massive wheels could be seen beneath a trap door, turning incessantly, grinding the yields of the harvest into flour, taming my mind into stillness, and subduing the noise of the day into silence.

. . . .

The students continued to recount their stories. Y was a regular visitor. He loved nothing more than to allow full rein to his contemplations. His talk often turned to his grandmother. He had spent his earliest years in a remote mountain village.

As a child he was a dreamer, and very curious. The countryside spoke to him. In his eyes, the stalks of grain in the breeze were nodding their heads, extending their greetings to the labouring farmers. He roamed the fields, stole into orchards, ate his fill of fruit, and returned home with his stomach bloated. His grandmother admonished him for overeating.

Y's mother could not handle his relentless questions, but his grandmother listened to them with great patience.

She called him 'my little treasure' and told him stories, fables, and epic tales of the rise and fall of successive dynasties. She recounted her stories by the open doorway on summer nights, and by the stove in winter. She sidestepped the terrors, protected herself from the storms brewing about her, and did her best to answer her grandson's queries.

When a funeral procession wended its way past the doorway, Y took fright at the sight of the corpse and the sombre faces of the mourners. 'Why do we die?' he asked her. 'Don't worry,' she replied. 'The wheel of life keeps turning. Life gives way to death, and death paves the way to renewal. You have a long and bright future.'

. . . .

Still I walked. Walked until the skies began to crack open. Walked as the farmers stirred from their slumbers. Walked until they returned to the paddies, to transplant their rice seedlings. Walked until the spring was heralded by processions of dragons, snaking out into the countryside.

In the township and hamlets, in the rooms and courtyards, and on windowsills and doorsteps, candles and incense were burning. Lanterns, shaped as fish and lions, geometric shapes and dragons, hung over doorways and from balconies. Crackers heralded the last collective binge before the season of backbreaking labour returned in earnest.

'Grandmother, why do people fire so many crackers in the Spring Festival?' Y asked. 'My treasure, the sound of crackers can keep ghosts from the door and drive bad luck away,' she answered.

. . . .

Entire families were back in the fields hoeing, planting and transplanting. The valley heaved with their exertions. Spring and winter vied against each other for a while longer until winter was overtaken by peach, orange and pear blossoms, fields of fertile greens and the scented yellow flowers of the rape plant. Sharp winds gave way to intimate breezes interspersed by wild rainstorms. The Huaxi River overflowed its banks, rice paddies swelled to their limits, and the limestone slopes were thick with dark foliage.

The townsfolk emerged from their tiny rooms and apartments, weaned from the coal stoves they had huddled around all winter. Artisans and tradesmen took their work into the streets and alleys, while from my customary seat in the mill I listened to the return of farmers' voices drifting from the distance.

Yet the distance was deceiving. From a distance all was colour and harmony, symmetry and movement. From a distance the countryside was an idyllic tableau of farmer and buffalo, peasant and plough, all reflected in flooded paddies. But at close range, the beasts could be heard snorting and rasping. Farmers, thigh deep in mud, pushed their wooden ploughs, exhorting horse and buffalo to keep moving. Pleading, cajoling, they willed them to turn and return, at times lovingly, at others, whipping and shouting. From a distance all was placid, all serene and interdependent; close up, it was mud and shit, brute force and raw labour.

'This is how it is,' Y said, when we discussed it. 'This is why we are driven to revolution. This is why we now study. Why we bend our backs to our books, perform our experiments, and search for a way to ease the burden.'

· · · · • • • · · · ·

As with the countryside, so it was with the entire country – but in reverse order. Viewed from afar, the revolution had been betrayed and reduced to base accusation. Yet close up, I began to see that which had remained constant, the subtle understanding and resilience which had come out of years of struggle. Close up, listening to and getting to know my students, I began to comprehend the nuances – the enduring humanism reflected in their tales of love and exile, of struggle and renewal – embodied in Y's universal dream in childhood:

I saw a big bird flying. My arms turned into wings. I flew towards a tree and perched there. I saw several boys playing on the grasslands. I shouted to them. They heard my voice and told me to fly down to play with them. I didn't want to do this. The boys were upset. They picked up stones and threw them at me. To avoid them I flew back into the skies. I flew for a long time. I wanted to fly back home but I was too tired. I fell back to earth. My back hurt. I woke up and found myself lying on the floor beside my bed. I stood up, felt my feet on the ground. And kept moving.

. . . .

My stay in Huaxi was coming to an end. The full turning of the seasons was within sight; summer was well on the way, the harvest nearing. I planned to leave the valley within weeks and to embark on several months of travel in China. I asked Y to accompany me to the watermill.

The miller greeted us in his customary fashion. He poured the tea from his ever-ready kettle. We sat back and gazed out through the open doorway. A jeep careered by. A boy urged a pig past the shelter; a farmer led a bullock by its tether. The noise subsided. All was still in the windless valley.

'Tell the miller,' I said through my interpreter, 'that I am leaving, and I want to thank him for the many hours I have spent here.'

'Tell the foreigner,' the miller replied, 'that I want him to write a couplet that sums up our many conversations.' I was overwhelmed by the miller's remarks. We had barely uttered a word to each other, yet his observation rang true.

Y would translate the couplet into Mandarin, and as was customary the characters would be painted in black ink on red banners. The two lines would descend vertically, one line on either side of the doorway, while the title would extend horizontally over the lintel.

I spent hours trying to find the words that could do justice to the task the miller had set me. To write a book on my stay in Huaxi would have been easier, but two lines? The couplet is an exacting art form, an exercise in compressed language. The lines have to be of corresponding length, made up of the same number of words. Each word had to be precise, and each line had to suggest many nuances of meaning.

The completed couplet would have to convey my journey and arrival, the landlocked eternity of a province buried deep in the Middle Kingdom. And at its heart, it would have to hint at the presence of the miller and the foreigner, engaged in silent conversation to the churning of the waterwheel.

In time the couplet began to take shape. The heading was obvious: *Huaxi Watermill*. The sentences, nine words in each, eventually formed:

I come from a distant place to Huaxi Watermill

Here I feel at peace, my mind becomes still.

I had deliberated over each expression, and one in particular. Should I write my 'mind' becomes still, or my 'heart'? I finally had chosen 'mind', but I felt that the word did not represent the fullness of the meaning intended. 'Mind' would not have been enough. It could not convey my engagement with the people and countryside. It could not convey the intimacy of the experience, the kindness of the miller and the students. Yet, when Y translated the couplet into characters, I learnt that in Chinese 'heart' and 'mind' were one and the same.

The completed banners were glued above and beside the mill entrance. When we were done, we returned inside, the three of us, and sat back in silence. Punctuated by the rhythm of the waterwheel: *Thoom. Thoom. Thoom.* Round and round, an endless churning.

Known as much for youthful scandal as for books, Australian-born **DBC Pierre** was an artist, photographer and designer before writing his first novel in 2001. The debut *Vernon God Little* went on to be published in forty-three territories, leading to a further two novels – *Ludmila's Broken English* and *Lights Out In Wonderland*, in a loose trilogy of comedies. Pierre was the first author to win a Booker and Whitbread prize for the same book, and his work now appears on school and university curriculums in a number of countries. He lives in County Leitrim, Ireland, where he continues to write.

Shooting Pompeii

BY DBC PIERRE

Every brand of bottle on the shelves of the Bar El Mirador contained the same clear firewater. If you ordered rum, you got firewater from a rum bottle. If you ordered Scotch, you got firewater from a Scotch bottle, but it cost more. Nobody ordered much Scotch.

The barman was cross-eyed. Then he got drunk, then his name ended up being Pompeii, and those motifs started gathering which attend the kind of journey you can't explain back home. I was lit up, and didn't grasp the motifs until Pompeii pulled out a pistol and started pointing it around. It wasn't the revolver you'd expect, but a rakish European job, more *Longest Day* than *Treasure of the Sierra Madre*. Stylish, and he wasn't hostile with it – he was just bragging, playing. But he was cross-eyed, and drunk. And then there was a wooden cross nailed to the wall at the end of the bar, at stool height. The local next to me looked at it just as I did, and tutted – a memorial.

The will to live, in its mysterious ways, made me pick up my camera. I levelled it under the forty-watt bulb and stole Pompeii and his gun and our moment. For me it defined why to travel, why to live. It said be stripped to good nature and wits as often as possible, and survive by them. Leave the reach of embassies. Leave the myth of rights.

It was my first trip to Pahuatlán del Valle, in central Mexico. A coming of age. I tasted my first joint on that trip, prompted by the mentor I never told was a mentor, and for seven years the smell of damp wood-smoke pulled me back, over the high plain and through the Sierra Madre to this shambling town, thousands of feet below in a micro-tropic of its own, a river valley seething with orchids, bananas, ginger lilies, weapons and ferns, lost somewhere between the fall of the Aztec empire and the transistor radio. It was a journey that erased the world in stages, and if night fell as you corkscrewed down the track through the clouds, flaming torches might bob on the opposite mountain, as people gathered in the cemetery there.

A funeral workshop in Pahuatlán rented three upstairs rooms. Sawdust from coffins fed an old burner in the courtyard, which in turn heated an open-air shower. And after a shower the options for tourism were many: you could lie on a dangerous bed and listen to cockerels and mule hooves; you could wander to the plaza and eat tacos from old women with trestle tables and hotplates; you could visit the other lady who served food in her kitchen, and whose mother would pass you unfinished scraps from her plate; you could write a dissertation on ethno-botany; you could explore the river and fondle the beautiful plant which infested you with itching poison, compulsive enough to make you want to drag a fork through your flesh; you could visit the healer and discover the traditional remedy for the itching plant, which is a cream from the pharmacy; you could guess if the trail of blood leading to the pharmacy came from someone who survived; you could buy a machete, or a hat; you could trap a possum; you could visit Pompeii. Or you could share the back of a pick-up truck and bounce up the track to San Pablito, the Otomí village high up the facing mountainside, where the flaming braziers bobbed. The town was said to be full of witches and warlocks who could clean your soul, or cast a curse.

I gave a curse some thought, but in the end opted to have my soul cleaned. Pahuatlán folk regarded witches with suspicion, perhaps due to the crossfire of curses and counter-curses that wove through their town, or perhaps because you couldn't refuse a witch anything, and didn't know if it was even unlucky to look at one. But once you climbed off the truck in San Pablito, everyone looked like a witch or a warlock. Otomí men were tiny and strong, in white cotton suits, with car-tyre sandals, machetes, and curiously sage features; women were shy, hidden up to their eyes behind shawls as rich as tapestries. The culture still struggled with Spanish, their remoteness having delayed the Spanish Conquest by four hundred years; and the mountainside still clacked with amatl bark being beaten into sacred paper, an industry that peaked in Aztec times when the emperor's court ordered tons of amatl for use in state magic.

In the end I went into a shop to ask after a witch. They pointed me along a cliff-edge of track, past the cemetery, where I found a senior witch in a shack of sticks and earth, her face a cornfield of furrows. It was a serious business, and arrangements would have to be made. Musicians would have to play strange music through the night, she told me. Firewater would have to be drunk, chickens would have to be sacrificed, and a number of dolls would have to be cut from amatl paper, to be fed with cigarettes and grog. I already liked the dolls. They would embody a quorum of powerful spirits, most brandishing machetes, some with animal heads, or black noses, or dogs for arms. A baby Jesus would also be there, for His cigarettes and firewater, without a machete.

But as it happened I didn't give the gods their smoke. I saved a pair of chickens up there in the clouds, because I didn't go back to be cleaned. The day after my last visit in that seven-year spell, I left Mexico for good. The coming of age had turned into a coming of life, and I swept out on it.

Unclean, I suppose.

A lunar eclipse fell on my last night in Pahuatlán.

Nineteen years passed before I could return. Nineteen years to the day, by coincidence. Going back felt like returning to a previous life. And as I drove through the chill sierra to begin the descent, mountain peaks formed islands above the cloud, and a full moon rose between them. Another eclipse. This time I would get cleaned. When I asked after a witch in the shop, they sent me along the same cliff-edge, past the teeming cemetery. But sticks and earth had turned to concrete; the town had become a slum, a favela of unplanned storeys and niches with a view. Some clacking of paper still ricocheted out of yards, some Otomí still shuffled on retreads, in white, carrying bundles twice their weight; but now the clacking was matched by reggaeton beats, the retreads by Nikes, the whites by football shirts, the machetes by guns. At least as big a community of mountain folk now lives in Chicago, and the umbilical cord between the two has added a hectic, nervous edge to this home of gods. Children are drinking, some barely old enough to lift a full beer, and the mountains boast a score of 'coyotes' – fixers who smuggle humans into the USA, or promise to smuggle them.

The cemetery is jam-packed.

Civilisation has come.

The shop sends me to a witch who asks for four hundred dollars, and any bartering is quelled by a threat of curses. And so my musicians play their strange music, my dolls have their smokes and drinks; my chickens die, and I am cleaned, but the pain of passing time on this rare place weighs more than dirt. I tell my witch that I had a date with an elder of hers many years ago, and didn't make it back. I show her a picture.

It was her grandmother.

Down the mountain in Pahuatlán, things don't look so different. They already had concrete. A pleasant hotel with a lookout tower now graces the main street; opposite sits a café and cocktail bar called the Magic Sierra, run by the second Hispanic I know who is named after Malcolm Lowry of *Under the Volcano* fame.

Before I explore the new, though – I have a date with old life.

I wander past the plaza to El Mirador – but when I round the bend it overlooked, from its perch above the square, I see it shuttered and overgrown.

'What happened to Pompeii?' I ask a man.

'You remember Pompeii? Dead, long time,' he says.

I watch a Beavis & Butthead shirt move past, hear Britney through the palms, and I ponder the aspect of travel that is time, that is once-in-a-lifetime experience. I wonder about those who say you can never return, wonder if I've returned somewhere or simply come to a new place.

Because I was there, and have the picture. I lived it.

I was there and I am here, and I'll live something else; and that's travel, that's life.

So if you happen upon the town where Pompeii once waved his gun, if you see my second Malcolm Lowry before I do – tell him I'll be back.

Tell him I'll return.

Carol Birch was born and grew up in Manchester, England, which she left when she was seventeen to go to Keele University. Her twenties were spent in London, mostly in the Waterloo/Kennington area, and it was her experiences there that led to the writing of her first novel, *Life in the Palace*. She had various jobs – working in stores, libraries, offices, and with young children and teenagers with special needs. At the beginning of the 1980s she went to live in West Cork in Ireland, where she started writing. She returned to London when her first marriage ended. *Life in the Palace* was published in 1988 and won the David Higham Award. Nine more books followed, including *Turn Again Home*, which was longlisted for the Man Booker Prize in 2003, and *Jamrach's Menagerie*, which was shortlisted for the Man Booker in 2011. She lives in Lancaster with her husband, and has two grown-up sons who come and go.

The Mountain Mine

BY CAROL BIRCH

This was West Cork in the late '70s, in the days before health and safety. The mountains at the end of the Beara Peninsula were an open warren, the landscape dotted all around with huge gaping shafts that plunged sheer into the earth.

Allihies was a quiet little humpbacked village with a half-bowl of mountain at its back and the sea in front. It had an old cobbler's, just a house with old tools and lasts and boots waiting to be picked up in the window, and one shop that sold everything. You went in and waited in the queue to be served by Mrs Terry, who was always patient, always unhurried.

There were three or four waiting so it was a good half-hour before I could buy myself a strong flashlight and head off up to the old mine. The track ran up the mountain, and a path led off on the left to a flat stony area where heaps of cylindrical drill cores lay about, mineral bores of swirling greys and greens. One semicircular brick wall on a rectangular foundation was all that remained of some kind of building. The main entrance into the mine was a black door-shaped hole in a high rock face. I sniffed around it for a while, peering into the darkness and wondering if I was brave enough to go in now that it came to it. You couldn't see very far but it looked safe enough, just a bit wet, so I turned on the flashlight and found myself setting off.

The rock was grey above my head but stained copper-green from the level of my eyes downwards, and there were water-filled holes on the left, some with ladders fixed flush to their sides, going down into darkness. The tunnel stretched straight ahead into the heart of the mountain, rough and uneven underfoot. A couple of times I stopped to stand still and think, checking to see if I was feeling scared, but I didn't seem to be. If I stretched out my arms I could just about touch the walls on either side. The thought did occur to me that if I got the creeps when I was inside there'd be all this way to come back, but I was feeling quite elated, and carried on with a growing sense of wonder at the fact that I was actually doing this.

I knew it would open out at some point, and it did. The tunnel emerged at a massive rock chamber, high-ceilinged, with a lumpy, rubble-strewn floor and a wooden hut standing over to one side. The hut had a window with, I think, a sill, and there were corrugated-iron sheets lying around, and passages going off to the side. I looked into the shed, just a shell, then wandered around shining the flashlight into other cave-like places, one that was like a big circle, another low and poky and full of rubble. A wheelbarrow had rusted away to lace. A big beam of wood about eight feet long lay across the floor, and there were traces of narrow tram lines, dusted over, heading away into some dark side place. It was surprisingly unclaustrophobic. Where it was high, it was like being in a cathedral; where it was low, I didn't go. And mostly it was safe, as long as you didn't do anything stupid. Some parts were clearly off-limits, places where water took over and the ground gave way. There was a wide slanting passageway, deeply flooded, spanned by thick wooden supports. The water was surprisingly clear. A ladder was visible down there, and a ledge big enough to stand on. The passage ran towards a far opening, low and overhung, like the mouth of a dragon's lair.

I kept oriented by constantly bringing myself back to the big open chamber where the hut was. Wherever I shone my torch, the rock walls were streaked and smeared with green copper.

I saw light ahead and went towards it. It was falling from up high onto a rock wall, a bright triangular patch of sunlight that threw the jags of rock into high relief. I turned off the flashlight and approached with awe. A green cave landscape was illuminated, a copper lake of turquoise water that glinted in the sunshine, a small shaly beach, a far-flung outcrop of rock, almost white in the glare. You could get to the outcrop by going round the side and crouching low where the rock hung out over the water, but the ground there was scree-like and sloping and the water looked deep.

I was underneath one of the big open shafts. The walls glittered. The water flowed out of the lake, round the rock and away down a channel about three feet across, meandering towards a grand arched darkness in the distance. I'm bad at judging distances, but you could have swum in the lake, rowed a boat.

My exploration into the mine was the culmination of three days and nights of road-trip horror. Two warring couples in a car. All the campsites we'd stayed in were full of all-night revellers and I hadn't had a decent sleep in days. It was so peaceful in there. I found a nice little spot and sat down to look at the lake for a while. I'd never realised how lovely a cave landscape can be. It was so still and quiet, and so light and bright even though I was deep underground. No moaning or arguing. Nothing to do, nowhere to go, no comings, no goings, no bother. Now that I knew I was not going to be scared, it was wonderful to be in there alone. I ate some Morlands Munch and drank some orange juice and got comfy with my head on my bag.

I hadn't intended to fall asleep.

When I woke up it was not quite dark. You could still see the light on the wall opposite but it had lost its glow. I knew where I was immediately. There was no confusion, but I did feel strange, and it took a moment to realise that the strangeness was the fact that I had just come wide awake from the best sleep I'd ever had. Sleep has always been full and crowded for me. I wake exhausted feeling as if I've been fighting a battle. Sometimes I feel I have to go back to sleep to get over the trauma I've just come out of, even if I can't remember what it was. But this time there was only a lovely blankness. This is what it must be like to be normal, I thought.

The light on the wall was waning. I had to get out quick before it got dark outside. I don't know why, because away from the lake it made no difference at all, but I just didn't want to be in the mine after dark.

The flashlight made everything black around its glow, and what it illuminated was mysterious. But there were no problems. I got back to the hut. From there the way was clear in my mind. I did imagine taking the wrong tunnel and wandering deeper and deeper into a maze, deeper and deeper underground, but the thing about fear is to just carry it along with you and let it be, and soon I was walking back along the straight track out of the mine. With every step the darkness increased at my back and I felt more and more impressed with my own bravery.

When I emerged at last on the hillside it was with a great rush of elation. There was a light rain and the sun and the moon were in the sky together, one coming up from behind the mountains, the other going down over the crags at sea. A light on the biggest crag winked steadily on and off. The heaps of mineral bores all around the mine entrance shone. When they were wet they changed completely, the colours came alive and glowed. I picked one up to take with me and walked down the hill to the chaos I'd left behind, only to find that it had dissipated in the hours I'd spent in the mine, as if some malign shadow had passed away while I slept.

. . . .

A few years after this I went to live in Allihies. I went into the mine again several times but always with other people, and it was never quite the same. Sometimes there were children whooping and shouting, or people running up the mountain to drop things down the open shaft while their friends stood below cheering when something splashed into the water.

I returned to London after eight years, having learned that moving to a place you fall in love with on holiday can be like falling for someone you'll always love but can't live with. Things have changed a lot. The village has turned into a beautiful rainbow of fresh paint, and the tourists come. Folk-music sessions sound from the pubs and spill outside on summer evenings. The bars have modernised, and Mrs Terry's shop is now a supermarket. You get a trolley and push it up and down the aisles.

The main entrance to the mine has been closed off. There are tough barbed-wire fences round all the big open shafts. On the edge of the village there's a ruined chapel that's been turned into the Allihies Copper Mine Museum. You can pick up a map and walk the two-mile mining trail, taking in the ruined village, the two big engine houses and the powder magazine.

But you can't go in the mines any more.

Tom Carson is the author of the novels *Gilligan's Wake* (a New York Times Notable Book of The Year for 2003) and *Daisy Buchanan's Daughter*. A two-time National Magazine Award winner during his stint as *Esquire* magazine's 'Screen' columnist, he has been nominated twice more in his current day job as *GQ's* culture critic. He was formerly a staff writer at the *Village Voice* and *LA Weekly*, and has written on pop culture, politics and other topics for publications ranging from the *Atlantic Monthly* to the online edition of the *Encyclopedia Britannica*. He lives in New Orleans with his wife, Arion Berger, and their cats.

The Tin Can

BY TOM CARSON

The first dislocation was landing at Tegel, which had been in the French Sector and no one's idea of glamorous thirty-plus years earlier. In my childhood – in my *day*, I almost wrote, certifying my possessive dementia – our airport had always been Tempelhof.

Back then, it had been mobbed year-round by the Cold War's human equivalent of Christmas ornaments: US Air Force blue and Army green, gladdening proof to my then ten-year-old eyes that home was where our military was. But Tempelhof was in disuse by 1999, severing a link to not only my own past but Berlin's. It bugged me unreasonably that the Luftbrückendenkmal, commemorating the 1948-49 Allied airlift and equated by my ten-year-old brain with a three-fingered rebuke to the Hitler salute, now arched forlornly in a spot not many non-Berliners had much reason to visit.

At least the Airlift Memorial still existed. Not so Pan American Airlines, in my youth such a symbol of Uncle Sam's might that I had a terrible time wrapping my head around its having been a corporation run for apparently unreliable profit. To a State Department brat in the 1960s, it was cradle and church combined. 'The captain has turned off the NO SMOKING sign' was the only *Dominus vobiscum* to which my father loved giving the liturgically proper answer.

Yes, arms and Pan Am I sing. Not my idea; it could so
easily have been baseball or stamps. But as Germans know
better than most, most tykes dote on allegiances. My
confused identification with the very Googleable
'Panzerlied' sequence in 1965's *Battle of the Bulge* – a
fabulously crummy WW2 epic I saw in a US Army theater in
Berlin as a child – troubles me to this day.

Coming back to Berlin was my default choice, not that
reality had any options on tap. Given my imagination's
druthers, I'd have much preferred to be revisiting *West*
Berlin, officially a non-place since reunification. When we
Carsons had been stationed there in 1964–67 – in Foreign
Service families, it's always 'we' – it had been as arbitrary
(geopolitics is like that) but concrete (well, I'll say) as
Disneyland. My love of Disneyland in adult life may not be
totally coincidental. Neither is how it drives me nuts
whenever they install something new there.

Unlike my wife's and my return trips to the Magic Kingdom
– in the vein of Napoleon overdoing demonstrations of his
Frenchness, I'd proposed to her there and married her in
Vegas – Berlin wasn't just a sentimental journey. For some
months, I'd been brewing an absolutely grand novel based on
my upbringing in what I've since grown fond of calling the
superpower diaspora: Kipling Americanized by John Cheever,
say. But postmodernized by Günter Grass.

Because I soon learned that I am none of those writers,
let alone all three – I'm still not sure whether Cheever or
Grass hurt more – that book never did get finished. But at
the time, I was sure *The Tin Can* (yes, I'm joking) would be
electrifyingly goosed by a return trip to what I kept catching
myself casually calling the scene of the crime.

Our cab trip through a perversely jolly, utterly unfamiliar
city wasn't exactly frothy with epiphanies. By the time we

unpacked in our *pension* off Kurfürstendamm, I was feeling panic about what came next. Considering I'd once spent three years here in an identical state of mind, that should have been the past's first wink that not everything had changed. But it felt different now that my itinerary was up to nobody but me.

Luckily, it wasn't quite. To be a child of the Foreign Service is to be a nugget in a charm bracelet of helpful oldsters. Partly to keep company with *eine alte Berlinerin* we'll call Marlene Richdiet, my dad's dapper onetime colleague Alex March (OK, so that alias is a bit Jamesian) had retired to Berlin. Hearing that Jim and Ginny's fortysomething son was in town to do the Mairzy-Doats-against-the-current bit, he volunteered himself and his car.

On our first night, he took us to the reunited city's idea of the *ne plus ultra* in chic pizza. Considerate of tourism's ideal – exoticized familiarity – was he trying to soften our landing? No idea. But as I tucked in, it crossed my mind that I'd never had pizza in Berlin before. I'm not even sure I'd known what it was.

That wasn't because my years there had been short on American or even 'American' food. I ate more baloney in Berlin than I ever will again. But at the PX cafeteria, my big sister's and my idea of genuine (like we'd know) back-home treats were Sloppy Joes and milkshakes. I love telling anhedonic lefties that the US Army makes the best milkshakes in the world.

Between gentlemanly recollections of my childhood I'd just as soon my wife hadn't heard – 'God, how you loved playing soldier. All those guns! What did they call those miniature fatigues the PX sold, "Just Like Dad's"?' – Alex filled us in that we might have to cope on our own for a day or two. But now I could handle it. Anyone who read *Kim* and *The Jungle Book* young enough to know they're two versions of the same story will understand that all I'd needed to hear was 'Bagheera loved thee.'

So we set out. I had to see the Brandenburg Gate – see *all* of it, I mean. My 1966 view had been obstructed by the Wall, my diminutive height and my mother's ushering gestures for her Kodak's benefit. Imagine how superstitiously I touched one of its columns as I walked *through* it for the first time. Yet myriad bustling Berliners seemed already inured to that miracle.

My wife was more interested in the flea market in the Reichstag's shadow. But I scored the best find: a cigarette case delineating the old Allied sectors. Pretty cheap, too, since no one else wanted it.

A Wall-belted no-man's-land in my youth, Potsdamer Platz was where either the present's surrealism or my past's ur-surrealism sank in. More construction cranes than I'd ever seen in one place were turning the sky into trigonometry lessons. Unmarked, *natürlich*, was Berlin Mitte's version of 'The Princess and the Pea' – the site of Hitler's bunker.

We were proceeding fishhook fashion, bringing us next to Friedrichstrasse. But there was nothing I recognized from my nervous back-seat rides through Checkpoint Charlie past our MPs' beckoning versions of Christmas Yet to Come. I had to settle for a museum.

Said museum – the Haus am Checkpoint Charlie – did kind of put my nose out of joint until I moved it back. Its exhibits kept me aware of how the Cold War seemed to Germans to be one more thing that had happened to Germans. Not Americans – or Brits, or even French. Or our WW2 allies turned rivals, save only an alcove exhibiting priceless but cheap Soviet schlock.

The retrospectively mocking reproductions of the USSR's war memorial in Treptow gave me mixed feelings, since the original is kitsch that stills mockery. A ridiculous 80-foot-high allegorical statue of Stalin's knightly Russia saving baby (East) Germany after stabbing the Fascist beast, it overlooks the mass graves of 20,000 Russian dead. If my childhood fixation on all things warlike eventually mutated into a lifelong fascination with 20th-century history, credit my accidental kindergarten.

Nearer my family's old Zehlendorf neighborhood, I soon found myself on Clayallee, gazing upon the now pointlessly huge headquarters of U.S. Mission, Berlin – my version of *The Shining*'s Overlook Hotel. The concrete sentry boxes once manned by silver-helmeted MPs were still technically ours, but empty. So far as I could tell, the final commander of the Berlin Brigade might as well have been General Boo Radley.

Across the street was the Outpost Theater. There I'd popcorned my imminently four-eyed way through not only *Battle of the Bulge* but the forgotten likes of *Up from the Beach*, *The Young Warriors*, and *Flight from Ashiya*. The latter are three very real 1960s movies you can't Netflix, because Hollywood's dregs were what we got and we didn't know it. Is it really any wonder that I've ended up making my living as a movie critic? But the Outpost was the 1999 site of the future Allied Museum, inaccessible except for glimpses behind fencing of snub-nosed old planes from *Lüftbrucke* days in its former parking lot.

It wasn't all *This Was Your Life*, though. Because my wife loves German Expressionist painters in general and Kirschner in particular, we had to go to the Brücke-Museum in Dahlem. That put us near the villa where the Final Solution had been decided upon in 1942, so we made a spousal afternoon of it. When we had tea with Marlene Richdiet, Alex's *Berlinerin*, our coos about the Brücke-Museum all but had her reaching for the chloroform. Hearing we'd visited the site of the Wannsee Conference impressed her more: 'Not many do.'

Puzzled, I bit my tongue. What was there to care about in Berlin, I'd almost asked, *except* history? Kirschner's, Adolf Eichmann's. Willy Brandt's and JFK's. Mine. The city's obstinate pretense that its present tense mattered more chafed me like seeing one-size-too-small lederhosen on an elderly cheerleader. As Nick Lowe once put it, I knew the bride when she used to rock and roll.

I also needed Alex March's help with my two Grails. First, I wanted to see my old school. Second, if at all possible, I wanted to not only see but get inside our old house.

So I'd better explain about my school: the *Lycée Franco-Allemande de Berlin*, right next to Tegel. Mom and Dad's claim that pride in their kids mastering French in our previous post in West Africa made them eager to preserve our command of the language was a half-truth at best. My self-made parents were the worst kind of snobs – namely, inept ones. They purely hated the idea of us mingling with the GI enlisted men's roughhouse kids in our own sector.

That's one way Kipling comes in, I guess. One of my favorite stories in *The Jungle Book* is 'Her Majesty's Servants,' all about various camp animals bickering over who's got pride of place. The Kiplingesque joke is that they're all identifying themselves with their various masters; the Kiplingesque cruelty is the equation of India with a zoo. But Foreign Service children are always somewhere in between. Not long ago, I was speechless with envy when I met a fellow State Department brat who'd done time in Lahore – and who had, therefore, actually straddled the great cannon known as Zam-Zammah, as Kim did in his eponymous novel's opening scene. I mean, to most of us – Berlin alums included – sitting astride Zam-Zammah is a *metaphor*. Maybe the ultimate one for our kind.

Anyhow, my miseries at the *Lycée* had been so unspeakable I still can't talk about them. (Yes, that's my attempt at channeling Sam Goldwyn.) I used to literally barricade my bedroom door in vain attempts to stop my mom from breaking in and dragging me there. After yet another day of stammering hell, I'd give myself over to the quasi-maternal consolations of Petula Clark crooning 'Downtown' on the Armed Forces Network. Of course I wanted to see my blacking factory.

Alex's car dutifully put-putted Tegelward, but then we got lost. Alone among the Western Powers, the French had rechristened all the streets in what they called – how vengeful can you get? – the *Quartier Napoléon*. Now they'd been de-christened again.

When we found what seemed to be my *Lycée*, it was just another dreary 1960s building without a purpose. Shuttered and inaccessible, no doubt bound for demolition. My wife and Alex were both polite as I grasped after some sort of full-circle emotion and found none. Stupid waste of a morning, really. The only way I could have reconnected with my past was by getting mugged there, but that didn't happen either.

Picture my anxiety as we re-put-putted toward Zehlendorf. What if I came up blank twice? I took it for granted our Kleiststrasse house was no longer in the US government's hands, the main reason I wanted Alex along. My own command of German is a memory of a sport I went out for and turned out to be no good at long ago.

We knocked and some chunky kid aged about 12 came out. Feet mimicking mops with a sibling rivalry, hands stuck in pockets to hide their itch to get back to a video game. My inner Mowgli should have known right then he was American: 'We be of one blood, you and I.' But Alex valiantly spouted a paragraph or so of *Berlinerisch* to the effect that I'd once lived here and would like to see the *Titanic*'s engine room.

The kid just rolled his eyes. 'Can't you say it in English?' he said in the voice of a pubescent Jonah Hill. Looking at the 1999 edition of myself, I envied his confidence.

His dad was CIA, I think. Alex learned later that our house had been considered such a plum that the American community protested at relinquishing it – but to whom, I wonder? Whichever mid-level Nazi panjandrum we'd evicted in 1945 to take it over wasn't coming back. Neither was the well-to-do family in some minor Thomas Mann tale I'd always imagined building it in the first place before young, newly plumed Ernst rode off to the Battle of Tannenberg and didn't return.

Yet here it all was, unchanged. (Yes, my plump CIA-brat doppelganger let us in to rove.) The Jugendstil luxury of the dining-room picture window that lowered at the touch of a button to let in the garden's smells. The bizarre little *Bierstube* in the basement, just down the cement corridor from the massively iron-doored bomb shelter.

Here Cold War diplomats had once boozily swayed in the ornate front room, singing along to my father the song parodist's masterpiece: 'Meet Me at the Checkpoint, Charlie.' Here a bespectacled young me had puzzled to mysterious words on the radio: 'When you're alone and life is making you lonely, you can always go ...'

Too Freudian: I couldn't find my old bedroom. Knew it must be one of the three on the third floor, but something went blank. This one, that one? Which door had I barricaded to stave off going to the *Lycée*? Which floor had I painstakingly covered with toy soldiers jammed into plastic landing craft to recreate D-Day? As Kurt Vonnegut once put it about his own homecomings to Indianapolis, 'Where is my bed?'

Much as I hated the thought that all of Alex's help had been for nothing, it may have been then and there that *The Tin Can* bit the dust. I'd never master my past, a prerequisite for turning it into fiction. All of a year later, I found myself writing a slapstick novel that featured the characters from TV's *Gilligan's Island* explaining their preposterous purchases on the 20th century. That was the one that got published instead, and Berlin never appears. A shrink would no doubt say it's omnipresent.

We flew out the next day. When we fastened our seat belts, the clicks reminded me of a joke I'd made long ago: 'Foreign Service castanets.' As the plane revved for takeoff, I glanced out the window – and there, yellowly glowing, was my *Lycée*, distant enough to look like its old self at last. I know it was an illusion, but it was as if it had crept up to the fence to say goodbye.

Keija Parssinen was born in Saudi Arabia and lived there for twelve years as a third-generation expatriate. She is a graduate of Princeton University and the Iowa Writers' Workshop, where she was a Truman Capote fellow. Her debut novel, *The Ruins of Us*, for which she received a Michener-Copernicus award, was published by Harper Perennial in North America, and by Faber & Faber in the UK, Ireland, South Africa and Australia. It is forthcoming in Italy from Newton & Compton. She lives with her husband in Missouri.

Among Saudi Sands

BY KEIJA PARSSINEN

I learned how to leave home from a young age – how to pack a suitcase, how to do a final scan of the small room I shared with my brother. The rituals of departure came easily to me; I was an expatriate child. Where I was from and where I called home were not the same place.

I remember the European vacations that served as stepping stones in my family's yearly journey across the ocean from Saudi Arabia, where we lived, to Southern California, where my grandparents lived, and where my parents were technically from. Though first you'd have to trace them back through the valleys of Lebanon and the bustle of Tunisian souqs and the wadis of Jordan, and of course, through the salt-ridden Gulf town where they had settled their family.

On the interminable flights to the States, we children made nests of thin airplane blankets on the floor where we were supposed to put our feet, but where instead we put ourselves, tucked away like carry-on luggage.

The rhythms of that multi-legged trip, which spanned three continents, reverberated in me so that I came to define my year by that annual departure, when our family left on 'repat' – short for repatriation. And of course, there was always the return trip to the desert peninsula that had been my home since birth, which I and my siblings loved, but which my parents met with dread, passing the in-flight hours on the KLM flight by recounting events of the previous six weeks – the bottles of Italian wine imbibed beneath fragrant grape arbors, the walks in the foothills of the Alps, the electric-blue swimming pools and churning coastline of California.

But I longed for the blast of humid air against my face when I descended the plane in Dhahran. To me, the pleasures of vacation never outweighed those of home, perhaps because I had a child's limited appetite, or perhaps the desert had worked its way inside me – its dust and oil-flare air coating my lungs, giving me both asthma and the feeling that I belonged to the place.

There was one voyage out, though, that did not involve return. In July 1992, Dad took early retirement. In a photo from that time, I'm looking out across the water, my face twisted up with the realization that these are the days of 'lasts' – last time swimming in the Arabian Gulf, last time racing up the giant dune at the end of the beach, last time seeing a camel crammed in the bed of a tiny Datsun truck, last time eating a shawarma on the dusty streets of Khobar.

'Leaving for good' was part of the contract of life in the Gulf – an understanding that Americans were only travelers in the holy peninsula, not permanent residents. When I arrived in Texas, I did what anyone would do when told s/he can't have something: I yearned for the denied object, obsessed over it. Finally, after fifteen years of fostering nostalgia for my home, I was able to go back. My father had returned for work and could sponsor my visa.

The return trip both excited and terrified me. September 11th had happened in my family's absence, darkening my gilded memories. Now I recalled with clarity the armed men guarding the compound gates, the roar of fighter jets dividing the sky overheard. As a child, I had failed to connect these suggestions of violence to my narrative.

In January 2008, as I stepped from the plane in Bahrain and felt that familiar blanket of humid air wrap itself around me, I wondered if I wasn't inviting pain by attempting to return home. Would I even recognize the land of my childhood?

For three weeks, I rotated between the households of Saudi friends. The trip marked my first extended stay in a Saudi household. I was welcomed heartily, spoiled with lavish meals and the generous attentions for which Arab homes are famous. And yet each family's way of life was distinct. In the home of our more conservative friend, I sat down on the carpet and took a traditional meal with the women of the extended family, while the men gathered in a nearby room; in the Westernized home of another friend, we watched reruns of *Grey's Anatomy* and sat around cracking jokes with no regard for the Kingdom's strict sex segregation rules. Proximity proved to me that, for all its mystery and complexity, Saudi Arabia was a country filled with people trying to live their lives – to work, raise their children, and enjoy life in accordance with their beliefs.

Certainly, tension lingered. One friend recounted where she was the day of the Khobar Towers bombing, and how she had felt the blast reverberate in her stomach, even at a distance of several miles. We drove by the Oasis compound, where twenty-two people had been killed in a 2004 hostage-taking, and observed the heavy concrete fortifications that had been put in place around the building.

Additionally, I hardly recognized the city. When I was a child, there were no shopping malls, Italian coffee shops, or gourmet restaurants – only a few downtown stores that sold gaudy dresses and droopy restaurants hidden away in still droopier hotels. Like me, the Kingdom had grown up.

One place remained nearly unchanged by time's passage: the compound where we lived. It had always possessed a suburban neutrality, with its neat landscaping, cookie-cutter houses, and children playing in the street. I borrowed a bike from a friend, feeling my way around by instinct. I went to the hobby farm, where I'd owned an old Arabian horse named Xanadu, and to my school. Finally, I went to my old home, P-304 Prairie View. A woman gardened outside on the empty street. I told her I'd lived there once, as a girl. She invited me in, gave me water, showed me the backyard. The house and yard were smaller than I remembered. I thanked the woman and left.

As an adult I found the compound to be less riveting than what lay beyond the barbed-wire fence – the pulsing, polylithic, complicated country of Saudi Arabia, with its ancient geography, tribal customs, outrageous wealth, and resolute faith. In the face of so much change and so many memories, I took comfort in the timeless desert and sea. My story of Arabia was a grain of sand nestled among a million more.

In my novel, *The Ruins of Us*, one of my characters says, 'The cure for nostalgia is return.' Since my trip home, I don't cling as ardently to my memories, don't ache to reclaim the vanished land. I understand that while our homelands shape our story, they cannot be possessed. Ever forward we keep moving – people and countries, the world over.

Frances Mayes had written six books of poetry and *The Discovery of Poetry* before she bought a house in Italy and spontaneously began writing prose. *Under the Tuscan Sun, Bella Tuscany, Every Day in Tuscany*, two photo texts, the novel *Swan* and *A Year in the World followed*. The books are translated into over forty languages. Recently she gathered together the recipes from many feasts and published *The Tuscan Sun Cookbook*. She and her poet husband, Edward Mayes, live in North Carolina in a community of writers and artists, and in Cortona, Tuscany.

Quetzal

BY FRANCES MAYES

As a Latino man stops next to me at the museum, I breathe in a scent that makes me turn toward him. I never knew if Carlos splashed himself with cologne or if he naturally smelled of lime, sugarcane, cloves, and some tropical yellow flower I imagined to be hibiscus until I smelled a hibiscus. The man near me also has black hair slightly curling over his collar, so I look at my shoes until the surge of memory subsides.

The first time I saw Carlos, he, his wife Ingrid, and baby Marienöelle were getting out of their Mercedes with umpteen suitcases, parcels, umbrellas, toys, and garment bags. A young woman in a crumpled uniform, who turned out to be the nanny, carried the baby, while Ingrid scooped up as much as she could. Carlos looked at a key on his ring and started toward the door. He carried nothing but a sleek briefcase.

I was sitting in a lawn chair with two new friends while our tiny children played in a wading pool. They'd found a turtle and were teaching it to swim. 'Well, look at that,' Michaela said softly. 'Is this the prince of the realm?' Carlos nodded to us as we took in his fawn-colored suit with over-stitching that announced the suit as Italian and tailor-made. Later, I'd see that he had twenty-seven others in his closet.

As they all neared, we stood up and said hello, welcome to Lawrence Court. Did they need any help? Frances.

Irene. Michaela. We've just moved in, too, late August, in time for fall semester. We were the first to live in the new graduate student apartments at Princeton. The Mercedes, the fine Italian suit, the nanny – my god, where would she sleep in the small two-bedroom apartment? My husband was on a scholarship in math and computer science. We planned to borrow what the generous funding didn't cover. The others we met were in similar situations.

I went inside to direct them to apartment #2, across the hall from mine. As Carlos opened the door, I caught a scented breeze of the tropics.

'He smells like something to drink at the beach,' I said as I sat back down. 'Something with a twirly umbrella.' The turtle lay upended, forgotten in the grass. Its legs worked but it could not right itself. 'Sweetie, put the turtle back on the rock in the water. She's very unhappy.'

Ingrid brought the baby out and deposited her in the wading pool. Ingrid was monochromatic – pale, no-color hair, no lipstick, and with those glasses that darken. They'd come from Paris, where they'd both studied at the Sorbonne. Carlos had other degrees, she mentioned, one from the University of Bologna, another from the Escorial in Spain, where he was a classmate of the heir to the throne. While Carlos pursued a Ph.D. in economics, she would be studying theology at the seminary.

'Is your husband Spanish?' Irene asked.

'Oh, no. He is Nicaraguan.' Ingrid blew her nose into a tissue and crammed it into her pocket. 'Allergy,' she explained, waving her hand with a glance that included the whole apartment complex. Irene helped her haul in more luggage and Carlos did not come out again.

. . . .

The last time I saw Carlos, he stood by his green Mercedes limo on the tarmac at the Managua airport. 'Your book has traveled too far with me.' He handed me my long-lost copy of Yeats's poems as I was climbing the stairs to my plane to Panama. He'd mentioned on the way that he was worried about skirmishes along the Honduran border. He was wearing a white shirt, immaculate as always, jeans and crude huaraches. His hair, combed back and wet from the shower, began to curl. As I turned back to wave, he squinted. I couldn't tell whether or not he was smiling but as I look back from here, he stands starkly alone and I think he is biting his lower lip.

. . . . . • • . . . .

Brand-new Lawrence Court was a ring of two-storey apartment buildings around a grassy center. We could see the 'dreaming spires,' as Scott Fitzgerald described the university, across the fields where the children hunted for baby rabbits. Under the powerful force of propinquity, we made friends quickly. We organized a baby-sitting pool because most of us were intensely social and ready to party and to explore New York. The air seemed charged. The grad students (male – Princeton was just on the brink of allowing women) came from Iraq, Ireland, England, Germany, Sweden, Japan, and all over the U.S.

Only a few of the women worked while the men studied. We volunteered at the university's nursery school. We had a common room where we could gather for dinners. Often a couple would house-sit for major professors, so we entertained each other in the book-filled faculty houses as well. Although in our twenties, we already cooked with a vengeance. If you had the flu, someone brought over dinner. If you wanted to go to the city, someone always could pick up your child, who hardly would notice when you returned because so many children were around. My daughter, three, had an immediate best friend. Frank, my husband then, like most of the other men, felt on the verge of stepping up to an incredible future. So much brilliance in this druidic circle of red brick buildings.

Without such a promised-land future, I nevertheless felt as though I'd landed in paradise. For my whole life, I'd wanted *abroad*. I felt exhilarated to meet Ann from Ireland, with her severe chiseled face and wry wit; Grete from Norway, with her apartment furnished with ceramics she'd made, and Turkish rugs from when her husband Ralph had taught at Roberts College in Istanbul; Michaela, from Nuremberg, with ethereal blonde beauty and family secrets from World War II; Lauren, a California dreamer with a radiant warmth. And Ingrid, sniffing into her tissue, carrying a tome on Heidegger or Kant, never participating in the parties. She would come outside while the baby played, and I'd ask her about Italy, where she'd studied and met Carlos. 'We'd hike above Verona to a hut and make love,' she said. *My, my*, I thought. *How exotic for this critique-of-pure-reason, standoffish woman.* If others joined us, she'd soon tuck her tissue into the pages of Reinhold Niebuhr and wander off.

I, too, always had a book and that was how I got to know Carlos one afternoon when he arrived home from class. 'Ah, William Butler Yeats.' He began to quote: *We sat together at one summer's end / that beautiful mild woman, your close friend / and you and I, and talked of poetry* ... The lines were from 'Adam's Curse,' one of my favorite poems. He sat down, took my book and began to read aloud. Now and then he'd look up and I saw a sweetness, maybe just a little reaching out toward someone else who liked what he did.

He was already considered odd and remote. 'Could I borrow this sometime?' he asked. 'I'm without my books here. I do have some. Would you like to read Rubén Darío, a very beautiful poet of my country?' He took a thin leather book out of his pocket and read. The Spanish was mellifluous (later I read him in translation and was not so enamored). I'd never met anyone remotely like Carlos. He spoke fluent Italian and German, as well as Spanish and English. His way of saying *my country* seemed more intimate than if I'd said the same. He was not at ease like the other guys, who came out and threw a football or shared a beer in the afternoons or met for pool, hitting the ball very hard if the subject of qualifying exams were in the air.

On occasional afternoons we talked under the pines outside our building. 'Garcia Lorca, Francesca, is the poet of the *corazón*.' I had not heard of Neruda then. He knew poems by heart. He brought me the just-translated *One Hundred Years of Solitude*. It's hard to write how this affected me, a secret aspiring poet. Talking to Carlos, I had the (very bad) image of myself as a dry sponge suddenly dipped in spring water. By the time I finished reading Gabriel Garcia Márquez, I had a magnetic pull toward Latin America. Or Latin America as embodied by Carlos.

Of all the superb, bright people at Lawrence Court, he was the most mysterious. Frank was totally tolerant of this friendship. Maybe an economist/poet from Central America just posed no threat to his secure self-image. Besides, he liked Carlos, too, more than others did. Frank thought he was very smart, and Ingrid as well, though her lack of interest in the day-to-day world drove us both nuts. Frumpy and disdainful of those who were not, she lived in an intellectual cloud. Everyone knew that the people we were meeting would go home to become important figures in their worlds, and Carlos, with his over-the top, world-class education would be major in Nicaragua.

We invited Carlos and Ingrid for dinner, leaving their door and ours open when the nanny was out. They never invited us, and I wondered what they ate. Ingrid was no cook, though she appreciated good food. Over candles and Julia Child's Beef Bourguignon, Carlos quietly told us that he would return to León, where his family came from, that he would wrest Nicaragua from Anastasio Somoza Debayle.

Poet with smooth bronze skin and eyes the color of whiskey. Revolutionary. And lover of a book that began: *Many years later, as he faced the firing squad, Colonel Aureliano Buendía was to remember that distant afternoon when his father took him to discover ice.*

When they went home, I'd sing, while we washed up, *Managua Nicaragua is a wonderful spot, with coffee and bananas and a temperature hot ...* Some song from my mother's era, all either of us knew about Carlos' bruised spot of a country down in the crook of land between the U.S. and South America.

. . . .

In 1974, it was raining the day we drove to León, a golden Colonial city and Carlos' liberal birthplace – the early capital and the center of opposition to Somoza. On the horizon, two pyramidal volcanoes pierced the sky. Carlos took us to meet his relatives, who lived in narrow row houses of Greek-blue, ochre, dead white, saffron. Inside, rooms with no doors splayed around a courtyard. I thought the houses were the most felicitous architecture I'd ever seen, the shiny tile floors that looked as though they'd been waxed for a hundred years of solitude, the seamless connection of indoors and out, big long windows open to shifts of air.

I imagined a lifetime there: a skinny schoolgirl who played the piano in the corner, tried to perfect French, dreamed of Europe while swimming in Lake Nicaragua, the only freshwater lake with sharks. My room would have been across the courtyard. Bare, except for a hammock, cot, and a chest painted with parrots. A room with eight rocking chairs in a circle around a low table opened to a courtyard. What brilliant simplicity, arranged like that for centuries, austere and voluptuously tropical. The old aunts offered guava and pineapple juice and called Carlos 'little one.' I was narcotized by the shadowy room banded by panels of light, banana leaves rustling in the slight breeze. A time-skimming image came to me then: Gnarled hands, thin as a heron, dim eyes dim, I am still sitting in this circle.

Carlos attended university in León first, before he embarked to Europe. How did he accomplish this? It did not seem likely – these were not rich people.

The largest cathedral in Central America dominates León. There's a statue of Rubén Darío, who lived there and walked through the dusty plaza with lion statues and the gaily painted outdoor restaurants where he was not wary of the iced drinks. León, a luminous city of bells. Years later, I dreamed that a woman looked down at me from the bell tower of the cathedral. 'You don't get it, do you?' she asked. 'When you get it, I will ring the bells.'

. . . . . ● ● . . . .

At Princeton, when I was offered the chance to audit art history and architecture courses, my days expanded exponentially. I sat in the back of the museum auditorium, silent. The real students, all boys, were seven or eight years younger; I, the interloper. The professors dazzled me. Every lecture seemed a revelation. I was completely alight with interest in Renaissance art, medieval and modern architecture – but, who understood? Well, yes, Carlos. He talked about Sainte-Chapelle in Paris, Picasso's *Guernica*. The Piazza Navona in Rome used to be flooded for races. The tomb of Augustus is actually an Etruscan shape. 'There's a piazza in Verona with a statue of Dante, *muy simpático*. I will meet you there one day.' He bought art books that I couldn't afford and we sat in the grass looking at Giorgione and Titian. He discounted Memling and the northern painters. Too constrained. In his apartment he had a pre-Columbian figure made from lava stone, a squat, thick-lipped seated humanoid. Ugly, but with silent power. It was wrapped in newspaper on a closet shelf. That's when I saw the twenty-seven bespoke suits in fine, thin wool, and silk, and linen.

In those years, you heard the term *soul mate* a lot. My husband seemed that to me then, though not later. We had a child, we had a plan, we were a great match. Still, I understand now, decades later, the magnetic pull between an overly romantic Southern girl and the secretive, worldly student from the tropics. Reading Márquez then, I was struck with the similarities between my South and the territory of that novel. Violent, hot countries, seething with tensions, perhaps promote stronger longings for aesthetics. Or maybe it simply was my pull toward the *not known*, his pull toward – what? I was literary but unformed, socially adept like most Southern girls, and beginning to feel my way toward being a writer.

Over the months, our connection flourished. The books flew back and forth. Picnics with both families along the lake, walks, bocce. Carlos adored my daughter and lost his reserve when teasing her, making her stuffed animals talk, and asking her serious questions that she seriously

answered. He had a timetable: He, and several of his
friends, would overturn the regime in Nicaragua within
three years. We were shocked that he felt bitter toward
America for foisting the Somoza family onto his country.
'But you came *here* for education ...' We thought then, as
many still do, that everyone envies America.

'So did Somoza.'

Mostly he described his country. 'Green, green, how I
want you green ...' he quoted from Lorca.

'Greenest green I've never seen,' I countered.

'When you come to my country, we will go to Granada.
There's a convent painted the color of the bluest sky. The
cathedral is yellow. And the houses – they're like fruits:
pineapple, green apple, pomegranate, peach. All lined up
with doors always open. The lake is so large that there are
waves and you can see the very small islands. The most
perfect architecture – houses with arches around the
bottom and upstairs porches. You have never before thought
of Nicaragua as a place for architecture, yes?' He often
added on a 'yes?' where most would say 'no?' I didn't say
that I'd not thought of Nicaragua, period.

. . . . . • . . . . .

I did not think of Nicaragua but when I arrived there I
recognized a place I always would remember. Frank, Ashley
and I were en route to Peru, where Frank would teach
seminars on computers in Cuzco, where there were none.
We had almost lost touch with Carlos after he moved back
to Managua. In a few calls, he'd said that he was working
for the government. 'But you understand,' he'd say, leaving
what, where, when, and how dangling. When I told him we
were going to Peru, he insisted that we stop on the way.

He picked us up in a luxury car with a driver. My first image of Managua was the only tall building, which the earthquake of 1972 cracked down the side. Vines scaled the walls – surreal – up to about the fifth floor. What a mighty force from the earth pushed up those vines. The rest of the city seemed made of tin and scrap lumber. We crept, parting crowds. The street was full of poor people, full. Some were shirtless, with ragged pants. The first question I asked in Nicaragua was, 'Why aren't they stoning us?'

Carlos looked out with a bemused expression. 'Because, *cara*, they don't know to.'

Just then one angry, toothless man shouted something and banged his fist on the hood.

'What the hell did he say?' Frank asked.

Carlos pursed his lips. 'Mmnn, he said something like "You're enjoying life, aren't you, you son of a bitch."'

· · · · · · · · · · ·

I would like to have lingered at Princeton but my husband raced through grad school and was handed his Ph.D. in two years. We were off to larger spaces guaranteed by the visionary choice of a computer science degree in 1970, the cusp of the changed world. Carlos, too, was leaving. We'd experienced a close connection without ever becoming physically involved. One kiss, that was it. He was in our apartment returning a box of books. He couldn't find my Yeats. When I offered him a glass of water, he followed me into the kitchen and put his arms around me from behind. I turned, and there, finally, we kissed, a kiss of longing and loss, not passion. 'I have something I want you to keep,' he said. From the box, he took a newspaper-wrapped package. He gave me the pre-Columbian figure. I wanted to give him something too.

'Wait.' I went to my room and opened my jewelry box where I kept my father's gold cuff links monogrammed with his initials.

The next day Carlos left for New York and onward to Nicaragua and his destiny to overthrow the dictator. He called from the hotel. 'Will you come with me? Will you live with me in my country? I will make it happen if you will come.'

Head-over-heels romantic I was, but I knew I was not leaving my family.

'I told Ingrid how I feel. She found the cuff links and threw them out the hotel window.' I saw them falling, catching glints of light, bouncing on the sidewalk.

And that was the end of Princeton, where we all had loved our lives and where we began to grow in different directions.

. . . .

When the Peru trip came up, I'd lost touch with Carlos, except for a few calls. One day he said, 'Some workers on my farm saw this rare quetzal land on a shed – a magnificent bird with a turquoise head and green wings and a scarlet breast.'

'Oh, how marvelous. Did it stay or fly away?'

'They did not know what to do with such beauty and they stoned it.'

We arrived at Carlos' house to find baby Marienöelle a lively daddy's girl speaking three languages. How Ingrid had changed! No more dowdy clothes and snuffling allergies. Her hair upswept, her dresses bright, her nails polished, she thrived in Nicaragua. Their house reminded me of Gaston Bachelard's idea: *A house should protect the dreamer*. It *was* a house to dream in. They built it on a rise, the hazy lake in the distance. The rooms opened off one side of a long curved loggia. The other side – all shutters – swept open to a jungle garden. I looked for quetzals. The ceiling made of bamboo, shining tile floors, beds draped in white gauze, the dark library, the warm rain falling along the open loggia – the house seemed to have been formed by a hand like the one that made the pre-Columbian figure Carlos gave me: *sui generis*, totemic, spell-binding. Three women worked in the enormous kitchen and I loved the noises of pounding, laughter, rattling, and their dialect that lulled like the hum of cicadas and tree frogs. The electricity scared me. It often crackled and the lights blinked rapidly then went out. For hot water, you had to turn on a switch above the showerhead, get blasted by cold until suddenly the water was too hot and sparks flew.

The first night, we drove out on rough roads. One Land Rover kept ahead of us, another stayed behind and we jounced along in the third. 'They're carrying extra tires,' Carlos explained. 'We're bound to blow one along the way but it's worth all that.' We had two flats. Frank nudged me and nodded toward the drivers as they changed the tires. Two guards back in the shadows carried rifles. We'd seen a pistol in the glove box. Then we arrived in the dark, dark at the edge of a volcano. We stepped out on sharp black lava and walked to the lip: over the edge, earth on fire. The sound, a washing, hot sound, could be an old god laughing. From the ferocious orange inferno way below, sulfur singed the tropical night. Everyone in such a place must imagine sacrificial victims. Ashley grabbed her father's hand; she was as mesmerized and horrified and awed as I.

At an outdoor restaurant, a line began to form at our table. People came to Carlos, even to Ingrid, petitioning them for a favor. *My cousin needs a license, my son lost his job, I need a permit.* This is when we learned that Carlos' job was 'something like you'd call secretary of state' under Somoza. I didn't ask questions, assuming this was his plan, to subvert from within.

We grew used to guns. Everywhere we went we were guarded. *Just a precaution.* Ingrid invited three witches to a session I joined. The women, who looked like well-to-do matrons, performed a ritual in a dark room. The five of us sat around a table. Ingrid asked the question, 'Will there be a revolution?' In dim candlelight, the women began moaning. The table lifted and began to spin. We rose and circled with the table, which then crashed to the floor. I suppressed a laugh. Did they really think the table spun with spirits' force? One witch flung open the window. 'No. No revolution.'

We drove far into the rain forests. At one house we stopped and Carlos paid the coffee-farmer something. He dragged a homemade marimba into the chicken yard where we sat on stumps while he played mournful melodic tunes that sounded like music beating on our ribs, like the jungle if it could sing. Farther into nowhere, we stopped at a worse shack and a small girl came out. She was amazed at car headlights, which she'd never seen, and by the dresses Ashley and Marienöelle wore. Her shift of cotton sacking hung straight. At another, deeper and deeper in, a family of a dozen lined up on porch rockers, and as we rode by Carlos said, 'Each of them has his own philosophy.'

Our connection, as it had been, was broken but still there was something everlasting.

Frank and I talked at night about whether Carlos still was the revolutionary meliorist poet or if he'd sold out to live the lavish life of corrupt government powerbrokers in a banana republic. I saw that he could not have been kinder to people we met and that they liked him. While he was remote at Princeton, here he clasped hands everywhere and threw his arm across people's shoulders.

We traveled to the coast to visit Carlos' colleague Cornelio Hüeck, always addressed with the honorific 'Don,' the head honcho of the legislature. I expected grandeur but the merely large white house on the sea was sparse and tacky; the bedrooms were like prison cells. Ashley slept in a hammock and our beds were bunk-sized and damp. We met for dinner in a covered pavilion. The wife looked like a kitchen worker, not the partner of #2 in command. She sat by Don Cornelio's side and tasted everything before he did. Was she his poison detector? He was a compact man, mean looking. I thought he might be one of those escaped Nazis who had landed in the Americas. He paid the slightest attention to us, concentrating on Carlos. Two grandchildren played around the table. Each boy carried a real pistol.

At breakfast, Don Cornelio slurped turtle eggs, dozens of them, raw. (Even then they were endangered.) We loved the big rice and black bean breakfasts in Nicaragua, the fried plantains, fried pork, and red fruits we'd never seen. Carlos told Don Cornelio that Ashley liked to ride. As he finished breakfast, he said, 'The horses are saddled. Ride down the beach as far as you like. I own all the way to Costa Rica.' Another imprint experience, that ride, galloping down a completely empty beach. Empty, that is, except for the men with machine guns. Don Cornelio kept four Land Rovers and we were more than uneasy to learn that he did so because no assassin possibly could wire four with explosives. A Russian roulette solution. No one could know which he'd select when we drove to secluded beaches.

Not long after, when the revolution ignited Nicaragua, Cornelio Hüeck hid up to his neck in that balmy sea, I read, until he was found and castrated, his testicles stuffed in his mouth. Hands tied, he was buried in a ditch. Whether or not he'd ordered the execution of the newspaperman Pedro Joaquin Chamorro in 1978 that jump-started the revolution, he was reviled for his outrageous land deals *(all the way to Costa Rica)* and doomed.

Carlos did not go on the horseback ride, and we wondered what they discussed all morning. I read years later that the American ambassador, Mauricio Solaún, thought Hüeck wanted to overthrow Somoza. Were he and Carlos co-conspirators?

We never met Somoza, though Carlos said that he wanted to meet the American visitors. Our five days passed quickly. Carlos was hospitable, generous, so very happy to show us his country. We had only one private talk. He told me that change was a scent on the wind and that the wild could smell it.

'What will you do?' I asked.

'I am sending my family away. Maybe for good. Maybe not. I will be here.' As we headed for the dining room for our farewell dinner, he said, 'Always you must be happy, *cara*. That is a talent I can't have in my country.' His lips glanced across my bare shoulder.

We were off to Peru and then to start the rest of our lives. Frank and I would live together for many good years, then part. Ashley always yearns for the pace and taste of the tropics. I keep my love for that place *as it was revealed*. Years from then, I will live in a foreign country with a poet, a different paradise, without the marimba, the quetzal, the empty beaches, or witches who did not smell the gathering firestorm.

Carlos disappeared during the revolution. He's untraceable. Did he give the Sandinistas sealed information, money, anything they needed to succeed? Did he take the last plane out? Run across the weedy tarmac with a satchel of filched money? End up in Paraguay with Somoza? Is he in Miami, working in a lamp store? Will he someday publish poems more beautiful than Rubén Darío's about the golden light of León? What of Ingrid with her righteous theology books, and bold, babycake Marienöelle? Memory cuts and comes again. Where are the Italian-seamed suits – on the back of the petitioner who needed a license? And the house built out of dreams?

· · · · · · · · · · ·

The plane to Panama looks rickety. 'Say a prayer!' There are no seats, just benches along the sides.

'This thing is a box kite.'

'Isn't this fun?' I say to Ashley.

When I sit down, I see beside my foot a hole in the floor, and as we take off, through the rusty oculus I look down at the green, green sublime and dangerous country widening into a blur. I open my old copy of Yeats that Carlos handed me in the car. Slowly I translate what he scrawled across the frontispiece:

After all, there was some exchange.

Marina Lewycka was born of Ukrainian parents in a refugee camp in Kiel, Germany, after World War II, and now lives in Sheffield, Yorkshire. Her first novel, *The Short History of Tractors in Ukrainian*, was published when she was fifty-eight years old, and went on to sell a million copies in thirty-five languages. It was shortlisted for the 2005 Orange Prize for Fiction, longlisted for the Man Booker Prize, and won the 2005 Saga Award for Wit and the 2005 Bollinger Everyman Wodehouse Prize for Comic Fiction. Her second novel, *Two Caravans* (published in the US as *Strawberry Fields*), was shortlisted for the George Orwell prize for political writing. *We Are All Made of Glue* was published in 2009, and touches on the property boom in London, the conflict in the Middle East, epilepsy, cats, bondage and glue. Her fourth novel, *Various Pets Alive and Dead*, published in 2012, is the story of a family who lived in a commune in the '70s, whose children have grown up with different aspirations: one has become a banker, one is a schoolteacher, and the youngest daughter, who has Down's syndrome, just wants a place of her own.

Off the Beaten Track in Malawi

BY MARINA LEWYCKA

It's easy to get off the beaten track in Malawi. In fact it can be difficult to stay on it, as we found one early evening in July three years ago, when we were driving up the lake road from Salima towards Nkhata Bay for a week's holiday, in my daughter's old low-slung Nissan Bluebird, her boyfriend at the wheel.

It was that dangerous twilight time when the roads are swarming with villagers, their children, chickens, runaway piglets, wayward goats, workshy dogs, all dashing to get home before nightfall; drivers of vehicles without functioning lights or brakes career around potholes, also hurrying homewards. For twilight is short, in Malawi, and when night comes, the darkness is absolute. Road accidents are frequent in this dusky light. Children are often the victims. It's also the time of day when disease-vector mosquitoes come out to feast on human blood.

By now it was obvious we weren't going to get to Nkhata Bay and we'd have to stop somewhere overnight. We tried a couple of up-market lodges on the way, but they were closed, or full, or they just didn't like the look of us. We were directed to other, more remote places, which either didn't exist, or were also full; we were beginning to get worried. Suddenly, out of the dusk, a crooked hand-painted wooden sign flickered across our headlights: Maia Beach Cafe Accommodashon. We let out a cheer, executed a U-turn, and set out down the sandy track signposted towards the beach.

After a kilometre or so, the track divided into a number of less distinct tracks. The tracks were definitely not beaten – they were hardly more than faint trails. There was no light ahead – in fact there was no light anywhere, apart from the stars, which hung so close and bright you almost felt you could reach up and pick them out of the sky like low-hanging fruit.

Suddenly, our wheels hit a patch of soft sand, skidded, and sank in. The tyres were spinning, but not gripping. We were stuck. Getting out to assess the situation, we saw it was even worse than we had imagined. Three wheels were hopelessly churning up the sand; the fourth was spinning free, perched over a sandy bluff with a four-foot drop beneath. If we slipped down there, we would never ever get the heavy car out again. Beyond the narrow beam of our headlights, it was pitch black. All around us were prickly bushes, their vague menacing shapes blocking out the lie of the land. Swarms of mosquitoes smelled our fear, and swooped.

While my daughter and her boyfriend took turns at the wheel of the car, vainly trying to get it moving, I hunted desperately through the bags for some mosquito repellent. It was my first time in Africa. What happens in a situation like this, I wondered, without the AA or even a farmer with a tractor to call on? We held our breath and listened to the silence. Somewhere far away there was a sound of drumming, and we could smell wood smoke. There must be a village – but where? Then we heard voices, coming from somewhere beyond the bushes.

The voices drew closer, and two boys appeared, followed by an older man. They greeted us, grinning. In fact, they might have been laughing at us. We didn't care. Greetings were exchanged. People are very polite in Malawi. My daughter had been living in Malawi for six years, and speaks Chichewa, though the dialect is different along the lakeshore; still, it didn't take many words to explain what had happened. The three of them and the boyfriend all got behind the car and started to shove, and slowly, slowly, the car inched onto firmer ground. We gave them some money, and asked for directions to the Maia Beach resort. It had closed down last year, they said. But someone in a nearby village had a key.

We left the car on safe ground and followed them down a series of dark winding tracks, without knowing who they were or where they were taking us. I felt alternating waves of panic and resignation, for I realised that if they wanted to rob or kidnap us, they could have done so already.

At last we came to a small hamlet, half a dozen thatched mud-wall houses, all closed up for the night. They called, and a man emerged from one of the houses; he was tall, and blind in one eye. We asked whether we could stay at the Maia Beach accommodation. 'You are welcomed,' he smiled, apparently unsurprised by these three pale strangers who'd turned up on his doorstep in the middle of the night. He fetched a bunch of keys, and we followed him as he set off again down a winding track through the bushes. The other man and the boys tagged along too, and a few villagers who'd come out to see what was going on. We were the best entertainment they'd had all week.

After a while the bushes thinned out and I could see the soft star-lit glimmer of Lake Malawi spread before us like a wide swath of grey silk, so still you'd never have guessed it was water, apart from a faint ripple that wrinkled its surface when the breeze stirred. And there, along the shore, was a cluster of small bamboo huts. One was opened up for us. A torch was found. A price was agreed. Bedding was brought – three thin stained pieces of foam, and ancient and musty sheets that smelled as though they hadn't been washed since the last visitors, whoever they had been. The mosquito nets were full of holes, but I had a sewing kit, and the kindness of our hosts more than made up for any discomforts.

This beach resort, we were told, had been created by an English couple from Birmingham, who intended to use the proceeds of this tourist venture to fund a school and a health centre in the village. But few tourists had ever made it here. There was the wooden skeleton of a restaurant and lodge, still unbuilt, and a scattering of decrepit huts, gradually returning to nature. The Birmingham couple had not been back for a while. No one knew whether they would ever come again. Our rescuers smiled and shrugged, and vanished into the night. After they'd gone, we spread out our malodorous bedding, stitched up the biggest holes in the mosquito nets, and fell into a deep sleep.

Bright sunlight woke us, needling through the cracks in the bamboo wall, and the sound of children's voices. I pushed open the door of our hut, and gasped at the sheer beauty of our surroundings. After all the trauma of the previous night, we'd landed in paradise. There, just a few metres away, was a crescent of silver sand lapped by the crystal water of the lake. A couple of palm trees waved lazy branches against the sun. And, as in paradise, there were angels: a gaggle of ragged smiling children had gathered at our door, chattering excitedly. As I stepped out into the sunshine, they fell silent for a moment, then burst into a chorus: 'Good afternoon. Good morning. How are you? Do you speak English? What is your name? Manchester United! Give me money!'

I smiled back and chatted for a while. Gradually more and more children arrived. There must have been at least twenty, staring curiously as I tried to wash and clean my teeth (the electric toothbrush drew squeals of delight) and following me to the hut which served as washroom and toilet.

'Please, that's enough. Go away now,' I pleaded.

'Gowayno,' they echoed, smiling angelically.

I retreated into our hut and closed the door, hoping they would go away. They didn't. Little hands pattered on the walls, and little voices outside persisted, 'Do you speak English? What is your name? My name is David Beckham. Merry Christmas!'

Sometimes even angels can get a bit irritating.

In the end, we surrendered. We emerged from the hut in our swimming gear, ran down to the beach and into the water. Some little boys who could swim followed; others hung around the hut, peering curiously inside. We played splashing games and beach football with them. They did somersault dives from the rocks, and brought us mangoes. Later, fishermen came by with fish to sell, which we cooked on an open fire, thanking the good luck that had brought us to this place; others appeared with vegetables and fruit. Our good luck was also theirs – a few extra kwachas to boost the local economy.

At dusk we walked along the shore to the village, and watched the fishermen setting off with lamps in their unstable canoes carved out of hollowed-out tree trunks to fish for the teeming cichlids. Lake Malawi is up to 700 metres deep, 75 kilometres wide and 560 kilometres long, with treacherous submerged rocks and violent storms that can blow up out of nowhere. But while we were there, there was hardly a cloud in the sky – apart from a great black swarm of hatching lake-flies pluming over the water one morning, a natural wonder and a local delicacy when caught and fried. Lake Malawi is also home to snails that carry the debilitating bilharzia parasite, and locals who swim in the lake regularly are likely to be infected; but for tourists like us, a dose of Praziquantel usually clears it up. Anyway, such thoughts were far from our minds as we splashed in the water or let our feet sink into the warm sand.

Next day was exactly the same: sunlight, sand, water, heat, shade, fruit and fish, nightfall, starlight, sleep. And the day after. We gave up our other plans and decided to stay. Without electricity, the batteries on my toothbrush, phone and laptop gradually ran down, and I let the slow rhythm of the sun reorganise my workaday brain. I became lazy, dozy, sunburned, forgetful. I started to take our paradise for granted, and I even snapped at the angels to leave us in peace. They ignored me or pretended not to understand.

At last our money, our anti-malarials and our drinking water were running out, and it was time to go. When we packed up our things in the car, I found my dog-eared copy of *Middlemarch* by George Eliot and the electric toothbrush were missing. Maybe some of the angels were not so angelic after all, but given the unimaginably huge disparities in income between them and us, it was a small price to pay. And I think George Eliot would have been rather pleased.

· · · · · • · • · · · ·

Recently I visited my daughter in Malawi again, with a bit of time to spare, and we took our camping gear and drove up the lake road thinking to spend a few nights at Maia Beach. We drove north from Salima, past Nkhotakota, looking out for the crooked painted sign, but it had disappeared. At Chinteche we turned around and drove back slowly, seeking a turning off the road, a track towards the lake, but there was no opening, not even a gap between the prickly bushes where the track should have been, only the same unremitting vista of low trees, bushes and sand.

We stopped some passing locals to get directions, and asked at a couple of stores near where we'd first spotted the sign.

'Maia Beach?' They shook their heads. 'There is no such place around here.'

Had we imagined the whole thing? I remembered the terrors of our previous visit, the spinning tyres, the loose sand, the mosquitoes, the dark trail through the bushes, and my heart pounding with fear that the villagers would kidnap or rob us. That's when it occurred to me that maybe, in their own gentle way, they actually had.

Mark Dapin's Australian debut novel *King of the Cross* won the Ned Kelly Award for First Fiction in 2010. His short story 'Visitors' Day' was chosen for the anthology *Best Australian Short Stories 2011*. His second novel, *Spirit House*, has been nominated for the 2012 Miles Franklin Award, Australia's most prestigious literary prize. A journalist, editor and lecturer, Dapin compiled the *Penguin Book of Australian War Writing*, and has worked on magazines from *Penthouse* to the *Australian Women's Weekly*, and written for newspapers including *The Times* and the *Guardian* in the UK, and the *Sydney Morning Herald* and *Dubbo Weekender* in Australia.

Adrift in the
Solomon Islands

BY MARK DAPIN

In 1990, I kept a diary of a six-week journey through
the Solomon Islands, a bracelet of emeralds between
Papua New Guinea and Vanuatu, east of Fiji in the South
Pacific. My journal was handwritten in a spiral-bound
notebook and, after the trip was over, I gave it to my
friend Chris, who had travelled with me and my partner,
Jo. Chris was to keep it for six months, then return it
to us. Half a year later, we would give it back to him.
It was communal property, the shared record of our last
great adventure.

But I didn't see the notebook again for twenty-one years.
Soon after I came home to Sydney, I found my first job in
journalism and, from then on, every intense, crowded year
passed faster than the last. I split up with Jo and, although
Chris and I met in pubs and bars in Sydney, Dubai,
Singapore, Malaysia, Bahrain and France, I hardly thought
about the Solomon Islands, and lost all my photographs
when I moved house in 1997.

Chris finally gave the diary back to me in December 2011.
I read it with amazement. I had forgotten the people we
used to be.

Back in 1990, I was working as a typesetter and Chris, my friend from university, was an accountant with a short-term contract in the Solomon Islands' capital, Honiara, on the island of Guadalcanal. Jo and I flew out to meet him, travelling by Air Nauru, and stopped over for a night in Nauru's de facto capital, Yaren.

I remember parts of that first day. The Australian at the Air Nauru counter at Sydney Airport sniggered when we checked in, and said, 'I presume you haven't flown Air Nauru before,' as if anyone who had wouldn't do it again. He warned of 'trouble' in the Solomon Islands and assigned us window seats, although he said 'locals' would probably be sitting in them already.

When we passed through immigration, an official said our arrival had doubled the number of people he had ever cleared for Air Nauru flights. (The airline regularly ran at 20 per cent capacity, and most passengers boarded in Melbourne.)

The 737 was crowded with people, plants and food. There were indeed Nauruans in our seats, hulking men with heads and fists like great brown boulders, blue tattoos, and rails of silver rings climbing their ears, so we chose another row. Belted bolt upright in the seats behind us were two trees. Behind them, the furniture had been removed to accommodate tinned tuna fish.

Soon after take-off, an inaudible announcement came over the tannoy. From the reaction it provoked, it must've been something like, 'Will all Nauruans please stand, light cigarettes and move to the rear end of the aircraft. There will now be a competition to see who can drink the most Foster's.'

Five minutes into a conversation with a red-eyed tank of a man named 'Rommel', we were invited to a party to celebrate the return of his Nauruan darts team from a competition in Melbourne. They had won about half their matches and come home with a trophy and a shield, which were jubilantly passed up and down the aisle. We said we'd join Rommel after we'd checked into our hotel – but it didn't seem likely, as he had no address.

The darts team had all bought Australian khaki bush hats with dangling corks to keep off the flies in Victorian hotels. They intended to wear them en masse as they stepped off the plane, but only three of them remembered.

I accidentally walked through customs and out of Nauru International Airport while looking for the baggage carousel. The only man who had his luggage examined was Rommel, who insisted on opening his bags to show off the trophies.

The next day, we woke up early so as to have the time to explore all the delights of the Republic of Nauru. We were out of the hotel by nine, but unfortunately our bus back to the airport was scheduled for ten o'clock, so we had half an hour too long. Nauru is one of the world's smallest independent nations. Decades of heavy phosphate mining had left it with a surface like the moon's, and a population only slighter larger. Yaren had a post office and a bank, a couple of Chinese restaurants, and a gift shop. We bought stamps and postcards from the post office and nothing from the gift shop, which had nothing in it.

· · · · · • · · · · ·

Chris picked us up from Honiara International Airport in an old Holden Kingswood. I am relying on my diary now, because I remember none of this. We drove down a road lined with coconut palms to his timber house a few kilometres from the city. Chris had to get back to work, but he managed to cram in a short tour of Honiara, including such interesting features as the Solomon Islands' only set of traffic lights.

At night, we drank at the Point Cruz Yacht Club, where wealthier Islanders shared the bar with expatriates, but only black women sat with white men.

We drove to the La Perouse Restaurant to pick up Chris's Islander girlfriend, Estelle, who worked there as a waitress. She was dark, pretty and shy. She didn't have much to say, possibly due to Chris's choice of conversation – the early mortality of the indigenous people.

Chris, Jo and I planned a ferry trip to villages in the Western Province, to visit some of Estelle's wantoks, or family. They lived in leaf huts on islands in Marovo Lagoon, with no local telephone service, so we couldn't warn them of our arrival, but all the Islanders were supposed to be traditionally hospitable and proud to accommodate visitors, especially if they brought with them rare supplies from distant towns. At Consumers supermarket in Honiara, we spent $60 on navy crackers, tinned corned beef, tinned tuna, tinned mackerel and Two-Minute Noodles.

That night, two of Chris's Islander workmates came to Chris's house to smoke my cigarettes. I asked them about village life, and what sort of things we might be able to buy in the trade stores.

'Navy crackers, tinned corned beef, tinned tuna, tinned mackerel and Two-Minute Noodles,' they replied.

But we were worried about finding toilets on the islands, because we were told there weren't any.

Chris threw a party, and we got drunk with some of the Solomon Islander women who had relationships with expatriates. One in particular, named Sheila, was beautiful, all dressed up like African hi-life, supposedly a princess in her home province. She gave Jo a pair of shell earrings, and told how she'd been beaten up and raped in Brisbane while she was pregnant. I remember she asked why white people hated blacks. I don't know why, but I didn't write that down.

The MV *Compass Rose* took about fifteen hours to reach New Georgia. Jo and I travelled 'deluxe class', which meant our seats were upholstered. Chris chose to go 'second class' and ended up sleeping on a web strung across the deck. It looked like a big hammock, but the other passengers used it as a garbage net, and at night somebody threw fish bones over him.

A teacher called Charles introduced me to a young Islander named Ben, who had a rest house near the ferry stop at Seghe. We agreed to stay there for a couple of days, even though we'd never heard of the place or its owner.

We reached the jetty at 3.30am, and had to wait hours for a motor canoe to come and collect Ben. In darkness lit by shooting stars, the canoe's engine failed on the lagoon. Jo sat closest to the paddle so she was designated as auxiliary boatman. I took the role of motivator. Every time she seemed to be flagging, I offered a hearty 'Come on, Jo' to encourage her. I was very successful and we soon reached Ben's parents' general store, where we fell asleep on the outside decking.

By daylight, the Marovo Lagoon, the largest saltwater lagoon in the word, was one of the loveliest places on earth, with water like sheets of beaten silver surrounded by brilliant green rainforest and teeming with riotously vivid fish.

Ben's rest house was one of only two buildings on Matikuri Island. We had been warned what to expect – a leaf hut with no bedding, furniture or plumbing, and only an ocean to shit in. In fact, Ben had installed a mattress, running water, an enclosed shower and, incredibly, a classic vitreous ceramic-bowl flush-style toilet. It didn't actually flush, because it wasn't connected to anything, but the sight of the seat made my heart hula.

We tried to fish for our food. I caught a few stones, a leaf and the boat.

Ben took us around the lagoon to meet Estelle's wantoks, who were friendly but stunned at our arrival. They really did sleep in leaf huts and shit in the sea. They showed us their gardens, their waterfalls and the village crocodiles, which they kept in bamboo cages and fattened up for skinning. Most people owned nothing apart from their clothes, their hut and a canoe. We did not hand out our tinned food until we were ready to leave, to ensure they didn't cook it for us. We stayed two nights in their villages, and Chris eventually waded out waist-deep in the water and, I assume, emptied his bowels.

I say 'assume' because, when I asked him what it was like, he said, 'I am never, ever going to tell you,' and he never, ever has.

I didn't record his pledge in my diary, although I remember it more clearly than any other part of the trip.

More than ten per cent of the population of the Solomon Islands had been converted to Seventh-day Adventism, and did not eat pork or shellfish, drink tea, coffee or alcohol, smoke tobacco or take drugs. They abstained from most non-religious activities on a Saturday, but this was no great strain since the majority of Solomon Islanders didn't do a great deal anyway. The two most popular pastimes in the villages were sleeping and going to market.

The majority of people were Anglicans, Catholics, and South Seas Evangelicals. Uninvited, we turned up at a Christian wedding, where a Gilbertese man from Kiribati was to marry a local woman. We stood outside the church during the service, but the pastor was quick to point out that this happy occasion had brought two families together 'and also the whitefella has come to watch'.

We sat down on palm leaves and joined the wedding party for a feast of dried fish, yam bread, tapioca and cassava. Jo made a speech on behalf of the whitefella, and the crowd applauded both before and after she spoke.

We caught the *Compass Rose* on to Gizo (population about 6000), the capital of the Western Province. On board, I met a New Zealander called Sean. We all found places to stay in Gizo, and Chris and I drank beer in the 'world-famous Gizo Club', where the barman claimed his name was Barman.

Chris had to fly back to Honiara because one of his cheap running shoes had disintegrated, and his feet were rotten with infected coral cuts, open sores and mosquito bites. I took a walk around the island with Sean. At the top of a hill, the road split into three. Sean asked a woman sitting outside her house if she knew the way to Titiana, the first village on our route. The woman replied in the Marovo language, but pointed out a direction.

'That woman's an idiot,' said Sean. 'I can't understand a word she said.'

Sean knew that Titiana couldn't possibly be where the woman, who lived less than two kilometres away from it, thought it was. We found two young men, who were strangers to the area but could translate the woman's Marovo into English, and they gave us the same advice. Sean would have none of it, so all three Islanders went into conference and decided it was possible to take another road but it would be a long way around. They refused to choose the route Sean was keen on, though, so he ignored them. He was adamant that he had memorised the map in his guidebook, and we spent an hour trailing dead ends before he agreed to follow the road to Titiana.

'Well, that's one up to you, Mark,' said Sean, cheerfully.

I resolved not to speak to him again.

Jo and I flew out of Western Province on a five-seater plane operated by Western Pacific Air Services, the airline of the Seventh-day Adventist Church. From 4000 feet, the islands were heartbreakingly gorgeous, like a lover who shows you a perfect body but lies too distant to touch.

. . . .

The old religion had no name and it certainly didn't have an airline, but in the province of Malaita, there were still communities who worshipped the dead. In 1990, almost a decade before the civil war that set the Malaitan Eagle Force militia against Guales in Guadalcanal, Malaitans were feared as the fiercest fighters in the islands. Their homeland was hardly visited by travellers, but when we met a Malaitan briefly in a bar, and he gave us his address on an artificial island in the Lau Lagoon, we accepted his invitation to visit with an enthusiasm I now find baffling.

Once again, we boarded an inter-island ferry carrying nothing much but a scrap of paper, a few tins of fish and a Lonely Planet guidebook. On board, I quickly met Jack Kii, who spoke good English and lived in Funafou where, he said, custom was strong and the people still believed in the old religion.

In his village, he said, they had a devil priest who could conjure up 'small Satans'. The guidebook mentioned the possibility of visiting the area, but only to note 'this would be a heavy experience. Not for the average sightseer.'

We fell asleep but Jack woke me at 6am, drinking gin from a Coke can, possessed by the idea that we should come to stay at Funafou where, he insisted, no white man had visited in his lifetime.

'Sparkmaster,' hissed a passing Malatian. ('Sparko' was pidgin for 'drunk'.)

There was nowhere for our boat to dock at Funafou, so we were met by a flotilla of small canoes that unloaded the passengers and their bags of tobacco, tinned food and rice. One of the canoes was paddled by a tall, thin white man wearing glasses.

At Funafou, an island built of stones brought from the mainland and piled up on the reef, we were taken to see the chief, a handsome man in a lava-lava, and his bent-backed, white-haired father, who was the devil priest, his face a moko of blue tattoos.

Funafou was divided by invisible taboo lines, most of them marking areas forbidden to women. Chris and I paid the devil priest ten dollars to take us to the tabu stones and beu (men's house) while Jo was shown the bisi, where women were sent during menstruation and after childbirth.

The space around the beu was taboo to everybody but the devil priest, although the village children who followed us hopped in and out of it whenever the old man turned his back. The beu itself was a hut which had partially collapsed. Inside, the devil priest showed us some old spears, which he needed to keep himself propped upright. The skulls of their former owners were kept in a mound behind the building.

The tabu stones marked the place pigs were sacrificed, to find out the will of the ancestors. The names of the dead were chanted over the body of the dead animal, along with a question with a yes/no answer. If the pig bled through the snout, the ancestors' response was negative. If it didn't, their spirits were pleased.

Many of the Funafouans' wantoks, who didn't follow the island's pagan ways, lived in the larger neighbouring island of Sulufou, where they worshipped at the Seventh-day Adventist church, which had recently been blown away in a cyclone. In order to annoy their pork-averse relatives across the water, the Funafouans kept their pigs – sacrificial and otherwise – in cages raised on stilts over the water, all of them facing Sulufou.

· · · · · · · · · · ·

My diary only hints at how bad tempered and exhausted we had all become by the time we caught the copra boat back to Honiara. I hardly mention that our calves were studded with ulcers that subsequently took years to heal. On our last night at the yacht club, I noted that 'everybody was equally pissed off with everybody else' and we drank at separate tables. I wrote 'I don't remember much about the evening and I have deliberately tried not to dredge much up ... Apparently, I fell asleep in the car. Apparently, Jo wanted to leave me there.'

Now, that evening, like so many others, is lost and forgotten. What comes back to me is an overwhelming feeling of angry, hungry, constipated nausea – dampened then inflamed by Spear tobacco smoked in exercise-book paper – and a growing concern that Chris might be going mad.

There are a lot of drunken nights in my diary and I can hardly bring any of them to mind. I'd thought I never argued with Jo, but we seem to have been fighting at least half the time. While images of the journey have faded with impressions of our relationship, the hardest part to believe is the people we used to be.

What did I think I was doing, boarding boats to isolated islands, trusting in the kindness of strangers and the promises of drinkers (let alone the directional sense of New Zealanders)? I remember the diary but not the author. I don't recognise him at all.

Steven Amsterdam's *Things We Didn't See Coming* won the Age Book of the Year (Australia) and was longlisted for the Guardian First Book Award (UK). His most recent novel, *What the Family Needed*, has been published in Australia and the UK, and will be released in the US in early 2013. Born in New York, he has lived in Melbourne since 2003, where he works as a writer and palliative care nurse.

Confessions of a Coconut-Soup Eater

BY STEVEN AMSTERDAM

The sign was handwritten in English: there was going to be a meditation session at a community hall in two hours, locals and tourists welcome. The hall was in the middle of Surakarta, Java, as was I. After three weeks on my own, waking up every morning to the 4.50 call to prayer, the thought of something that might settle my mind for the evening had appeal. I've never been prone to stillness, but it was worth a try.

Twenty or so of us, in all shapes and shades, sat in folding chairs. The maroon-wrapped ringleader instructed us in Bahasa, while his grizzled white sidekick, who had clearly been in-country too long, followed up in English. Every thirty seconds we were led to contemplate a single word – *egg, lake, soil, leaf,* and so on. Rather than leaving my mind to wander off into a fog of associations, the steady prompts kept me moving forward. As the words flowed onwards, a rhythm filled the room. Without getting too spiritual about it, the distractions seemed to matter less than the beat of our shared path. It was deep.

(Relevant: I was in my late 20s and prone to revelations. Additionally, I was on an anti-malarial drug called Mefloquine. Its list of side effects included vivid dreams, hallucinations and psychotic reactions. I wasn't aware of this. The intensity of the side effects was cumulative. In a few days I would take my fifth tablet.)

After the session, the crowd sorted itself out, with the locals walking home and the travellers – mostly other loners – hanging out for conversation before going back to their mosquito-netted beds and, if they paid extra, a lazy ceiling fan. A South African woman dressed all in white started chatting with me. She had a breathy kind of voice, as if all of her possessions would be white too. She opened with, 'Are you planning to go to Toraja? You'd love it.'

Funny that she should know me so well. Toraja already occupied a space in my imagination and a few pages in my Lonely Planet *Indonesia*. The people who lived there had some interesting notions of the afterlife and what to do with dead bodies. They hung them in baskets, from high branches, or left them in caves. The young ones were inserted into tree trunks and tarred in. If the family could afford it, effigies of the deceased were placed in balconies built out of cliffside caves nearby. Obviously, this had huge appeal, but I had researched it and getting there required a flight to Ujung Pandang on the southern tip of Sulawesi, and another to Rantepao, in the middle of Toraja. It seemed like a lot of trouble to perve at another culture's burial practices.

The woman went on, 'I had to leave last week because of a plane ticket, but I felt like a fool. Funeral season is just starting. Don't think about it. Just go.'

This was a challenge. It had always been my fantasy to *just go*. Momentarily Zen, I knew the only way to achieve flow was to step into it. It seemed that I could follow the

truer path of my life, or something. Leaving behind the
detailed plans for temples and trails that I had researched
for weeks, I booked my flights to Toraja. Two days later I
was on my way.

The twin-engine hopped through cloud level for the
entire connecting flight, so I only caught glimpses of what
was below. Here was a farming village hiding in the
rainforest. There was a white expanse of sandy coastline
and a couple looking up at an airplane. In-between, I
imagined a freakish zoo of the animals I had briefly read
about – dwarf buffalo, pig deer and birds that nested in
volcanic vents.

The choppy flight amplified the Shangri-La effect as we
descended through the mist into the regency of Toraja. The
greenest of valleys was composed of concentric rings of
terraced rice paddies, winding dirt roads and broad
pastures, all ending at the steep cliff line and spirit-filled
caves that encircled the area. Below, rows of traditional
houses peeked out from the canopy. Each one had an
exaggerated roof that sloped dramatically upwards at the
long ends, as if the canoe of a grand tribal chief had been
balanced on a thatched hut. From the plane, the settlements
looked like an armada pushing through the trees.

Towards the flat centre of the valley were the concessions
to modernity – the meeting of connecting roads, a central
market, a dozen afterthought buildings, and a dull grid of
streets surrounding it all.

The only other passengers on the plane were a German
couple. They were rugged and fresh faced, with clean,
ingeniously pocketed backpacks. Everything about them
was competent. We shared a lawnmower/taxi into town.
They were going to camp at the edge of the jungle for a few
days before stocking up for a big hike into the bush. Then

they would trek south and photograph fauna for a few weeks before reaching a sacred diving spot on the coast. This was their honeymoon. I had been feeling mildly intrepid about arriving without reservations at a hotel, but their schedule sucked that right out of me: I was a coddled, underequipped softie. When we said farewell at the central market, I was certain they would plague me for the rest of my stay, continually turning up with breathless reports of deep connections with local ghosts and just-missed views of pig deer, all of which I would have experienced if I weren't such a wimp.

After traipsing around for an hour, I found a place to stay that had Christmas lights in the common areas (in May) and waterfall-like rock features plastered into the bathroom. In the front of the hotel, there was a small dining area, which smelled of pork and wine that had been cooking in bamboo all day. That dinner and my book comforted me past any feelings of lameness. Going to sleep on my single bed, I clung to a minor bravery: against my usual habit, I had no set plans for the next day. I just took my weekly dose of Mefloquine and went to sleep.

The muezzin's call didn't wake me – Sulawesi is more Christian than Muslim – but the equatorial sunrise did. I ventured out, making it as far as a corner shop that had truly local coffee and wholegrain toast with coconut jam. This was my kind of journey into the unknown. And it got easier. The store's proudly English-speaking owner told me that I was in luck, a funeral was starting that morning. It was some village big shot with lots of children, so they would have to put on a good show. At least ten water buffalo would be slaughtered by relatives of the deceased to aid his journey to the afterlife. Rather than rocking up with, say, a ham, his friends and neighbours would bring 100 pigs for the feast.

What was the etiquette for crashing a funeral in Toraja? The guidebook had been thin on guidance. The shopkeeper wasn't. Fortunately, a steady stream of morbid travellers had eased my way and an inoffensive solution had been worked out. I would be led to a viewing area from which I might be invited in to participate. If I hurried, I could see the funeral parade and score a good lunch.

A square of land a little smaller than a football field had been cordoned off with a simple fence. A narrow, elaborately decorated, three-storey wooden tower was set up in the centre, with the coffin on the top level and a stream of respect-payers filing up and down wooden staircases on either side.

Some of the animal offerings were penned into one corner of the large square; others, already slaughtered, were lying in pieces in another, or being delivered to an organised squadron of cooks busy stewing them in big vats under a thatch-covered walkway. All of these crowds, plus recent torrential rains, left the entire area muddy and bloody. As for the tourist area, there was only the honeymooners and myself, the three of us in Birkenstocks.

It may have been the invitation up to the coffin tower or it may have been the Mefloquine kicking in, but I believe it was around this point that things began to go strange. In my moment alone with the deceased, I gazed at his coffin. It looked like a boat with scales or a dragon with a prow. I was hypnotised by the paint on it. Sniffing its hand-carved grooves, I thought, or possibly said out loud, *Whoa, that is so gold.*

I remember being given some meat to eat on a paper plate and a cup of sharp dark wine. I remember a crowd of us holding the coffin over our heads and trotting in circles to spin it, ensuring that its inhabitant would lose his way and never return to haunt us. I remember thinking that I would suggest this ritual at the next funeral I attended.

I remember an afternoon organised by my new best friends from Deutschland. We visited burial trees and caves, looked into the balconies packed with effigies that were looking at us. I remember piles of bones and baby-filled trees. I have no idea what we said to each other but I have a feeling I talked, a lot. I remember feeling special.

The next morning, feeling even more special, I checked out of my cinderblock hotel. The mountains on the edge of the valley were my destination. They were dotted with tiny settlements, most reached only by footpath or pack animal. The clerk was content for me to park most of my belongings behind the front desk, as long as I intended to come back for them.

My clothes, my passport, my wallet, the guidebook, my book, my paper and my pen all stayed behind. My journey needed to be pure if it was going to be honest, right? With a daypack, some water and a little bit of cash, I set off.

As indicated earlier, I am not the *Into the Wild* type. I had started the trip with a typed itinerary and travel insurance, intent on spending my days wandering the big-ticket sights and my evenings in dimly lit rooms, reading and writing. This walkabout was the Mefloquine talking, and it wouldn't shut up. Each step into the mountains brought greater splendour. Passing a donkey on the narrow footpath became an otherworldly pleasure. The mirrored rice paddies seemed to be painted by the gods. In the nearby shuffling leaves around me, it was easy to see a dwarf buffalo following my progress with a sly grin of approval.

Although nearly out of my mind, I knew I needed to sleep indoors. Somehow, I negotiated a bed from a woman whom I passed on the trail. Her house had been constructed from scavenged parts of other houses, with walls of different materials fastened together. Inside, the plaster hearth beckoned. In one pot there was coconut soup and in another there were coconut fritters. Would I like some? Three cats sat on the fireplace, making sure I gave the right answer. The coconut was like none other, before or since. It was caramel and woody and milky and floral and sublime.

The window in the tiny guest room had a scrap of fabric nailed across it. This, I thought, with evangelical fervour, was all I needed.

With no light except the moon and nothing to read, I fell asleep listening to the noise of the jungle, making up a name for every creature I heard until I drifted off. An epic thunderstorm woke me in the middle of the night, soaking the fabric and my bed. I didn't move to get out of the way. It was preordained that I would get wet. Forgetting about my ticket home, I vowed to stay in these hills for a month, just being.

I stepped out the front door to inspect the new day. Vivid. The jungle cascaded down one side and lush farmland terraces stepped down the other. After a breakfast made from reheated dinner, I headed for the next ridge, bold and victorious.

It was around here that my lizard brain switched on to save me. I realised that instead of feeling invincible, doubt was setting in. All the thrilling thoughts of supreme self-sufficiency and better-than-German-traveller fearlessness were now matched with an uncomfortable fullness in the chest and stomach. From the most distant switchback of my brain, this protective pulse overrode my desire to conquer the jungle. With urgency that I am still grateful for today, it turned me back toward Rantepao.

Still Magellan-ish though, I searched for shortcuts. Sweaty and wild-eyed, I climbed fences, pushed through leech-ridden lowlands and trod along the edges of rice paddies. Curious locals and every variation of chicken watched me take the longest route back to town.

Eventually there was the comforting sound and scent of diesel trucks. It was market day and the central area was teeming with water buffalo. In a flicker, I calculated that I could buy one and take it with me on my trek, but my cautious conscience marched me back to the hotel and my stuff.

The cook was there. He offered me more marinated pork. No thanks, I said, closing the door and falling onto the bed.

The coconut soup began to curdle in my mind. It had been warm, not hot. Warm. My host's fireplace had been comfortable enough for the cats to curl up there: The soup had never boiled. With this realisation, I began to erupt. The next hours were spent in the bathroom. I wasn't brave enough to venture far between bouts, and minutes passed with me hazily tracing my fingers along the rock sculptures above the tub. When I was able to seize a moment to advocate for my health, I wrapped myself in a sheet and crawled out to the desk to beg for toast. The increasingly patient owner escorted me out of the common area and soon delivered my request. Which my body quickly rejected.

By the next night, I was empty. There was still the occasional contraction, but there was nothing left. I stretched out on the bed and let the moon illuminate what was left of me. This is when the children's choir began performing Christmas carols. They were sweet songs, not quite recognisable, but harmonised with a homely imperfection that could only come from dutiful children in bright matching uniforms. I hauled myself to the door and opened it for a look. Outside, the night was quiet. I closed the door and the choir returned.

My first thought was not that it was unlikely there were carollers in my room, as it was the middle of the night in the wrong month. My first thought was that I needed to determine where in the room the choir was hiding. I was certain I could help them. The solution was to circle the perimeter on all fours. They were vexatious, this choir, and, in between trips to the bathroom, they kept me stumbling around trying to pinpoint their secret location for hours.

The next days followed similarly, with me distracted by hallucinations and unable to eat anything with the confidence of retaining it. In the middle of extreme exhaustion and this drug-induced fog, I resigned myself to continuing like this until my body gave up. I would live out my days jabbering in a corner of the village. I would waste away and then contract some equatorial infection that had long shiny teeth. Finally, the choir and their siren song would lead me in front of a bus.

From this funk, I wondered if my travel insurance would know that they had to make good on the repatriation of my remains or if I should send a postcard home advising my family that it would be covered. In the more exuberant moments, I decided that I wanted my body to stay there, that this was a lovely place to die. With planning, there could be an effigy of me on one of the hillsides.

As you may have gathered, I survived. The psychiatric symptoms eased up enough for me to link them to the Mefloquine and I skipped the last tablet (and didn't get malaria, either). The local chemist had a good stock of Imodium, which provided all the gastric security I could hope for, enabling me to endure the flights to Ujung

Pandang, to Denpasar, to Jakarta, to Singapore, to Frankfurt, and home to New York – not the best 36 hours of my life. It would be months before the coconut-soup parasites were identified and treated, and almost fifteen years before the makers of Mefloquine stopped marketing the drug in the United States. It's still available elsewhere in the world.

That I didn't die may be something of an anticlimax, like when the bomb is defused at the end of the movie. I don't mind. The whole detour stays together for me, from the meditation class to the long trip home. It doesn't linger as a bad travel story as much as an adventure. I did what I wanted to do: I got myself lost. The fact that I didn't stray deeper into the jungle or ingest something more lethal is largely due to luck. That is enough of a lesson for any traveller, with or without an itinerary.

On my last day in Toraja, the German couple showed up at the corner shop, as I was girding myself for the long trip ahead. They were flying back to Ujung Pandang too. We shared another lawnmower/taxi. I wasn't feeling nearly as vivacious as the last time I'd seen them, so they talked. They'd had a change in plans. The jungle was uncomfortable, they hadn't found the animals they'd set out to see, they'd underestimated the difficulty of their hike and didn't think they could make it as far as the diving site. They'd had enough of travel, they said, and were ready to go home.

In January of 1982, **Joe Yogerst** quit his job working for a sports magazine in the San Francisco Bay Area, sold his car, took all of his money out of the bank and bought a one-way airplane ticket to South Africa. Truth be told, he was chasing a woman, a relationship that (like so many born of travel) didn't work out in the real world. To get his mind off the breakup, Yogerst began taking ever-longer and riskier trips – backpacking solo through the African bush, hitchhiking to northern Namibia, where a furious border war was then in progress, and then undertaking an epic Cape-to-Cairo journey that included his ride on the Scarface Express. That was the start of thirteen years overseas, during which Yogerst worked as a newspaper reporter, magazine editor and freelance writer on three continents. He returned to his native California in 1995 and continues to write about his travels across the globe. He is the author of two novels, *White Tiger* and *Fortunate Son*.

Sudan: The Scarface Express

BY JOE YOGERST

F ive of us stumble through the streets of Kosti in the middle of the night, trying to put as much distance as possible between ourselves and the thugs who are chasing us. I can smell the mulchy aroma of the nearby Nile, feel the grit of Sahara sand beneath my feet. But this is no time to contemplate the local geography, because we are literally running for our lives.

I have just done something amazingly brilliant or incredibly stupid – depending on the outcome of our current escapade. I have told the scar-faced sergeant of the platoon protecting a train that's just brought us halfway across Sudan that we are not going to cave to his extortion. Under no circumstances are we going to pay the bribes that just about everyone else on the train has been shelling out over the past four days. Not only that, but we have confronted him openly in front of the locals – people who normally don't see anyone challenge his venomous authority – causing a loss of face that no doubt outweighs the value of the cash he was trying to scam from us.

And once that die was cast, the only thing to do was abscond. Run as fast as we could, find a place to hide until first light, and hope that Scarface and his men would tire of the chase, crawl back onto the train and chug away. Because the alternative – getting caught – was unthinkable. We'd seen how Scarface and his men had dealt with Sudanese passengers who didn't comply – beating them with leather strips and rifle butts, tossing them off the train in the middle of nowhere. And we had no illusions that they would deal any less harshly with us, five young foreigners traveling across their country.

Gasping for air, we came upon the darkened bus station. The front doors were padlocked, but we shook them all the same, hoping to rouse someone inside who could tell us when the next bus was leaving – for anywhere, really. Destination didn't matter at this point. An elderly watchman poked his face through a crack between the doors. 'Inshallah, six o'clock,' he told us. Another four hours.

We looked around, back up the street that had brought us from the river. Nothing but silence and a stray dog shuffling across the road. But then in the murky distance, half a dozen men running our way. Scarface and his troopers, armed to the teeth and bent on revenge.

Opposite the bus station was a large open-air café. It was closed for the night, the tables upturned, and that's where we took refuge. Where we decided to make our last stand. If they found us, so be it. But we couldn't keep running forever. Hunched behind one of the tables, all sorts of thoughts ran through my mind. Nobody in the outside world had the faintest idea where I was at this point in time. Scarface and his men could do pretty much anything they wanted to us – torture, prison, even death – and nobody would ever know the difference. You hear about people disappearing without a trace during their travels. And it suddenly occurred to me that the five of us might soon be among those gruesome statistics.

There was a rush of footsteps into the square. Scarface and his men, speaking in Arabic, pointing up and down the street, no doubt trying to figure out which way we had fled. The sergeant barked orders and they began to fan out in different directions. One of them looked around at the café where we were hunkered down, took a tentative step our way ...

. . . .

It was my 'year of living dangerously' in Africa, an overland journey from Cape to Cairo by any means I could find or afford – trains, boats, buses, walking, hitching. I knew the 2000-mile leg between Nairobi and Khartoum would be the most difficult because there wasn't any public transport and not much in the way of private vehicles that might be willing to give me a ride. Southern Sudan wasn't an independent nation yet and the country was still plagued by its long civil war. But there was a temporary ceasefire and I decided to take the chance of venturing across Sudan.

I rode buses to northern Kenya and then hooked up with an overland truck and a handful of other young Western travelers headed north. Crossing the Turkana Desert was a breeze, and other than getting stuck in the mud a couple of times – and having to dig out the truck – we managed to make it across the Sudd swamps without major incident. Reaching the town of Wau on the northern edge of the wetlands, we figured the worst (in terms of road conditions) was behind us. What we hadn't counted on was freakish weather. Heavy rains had washed away both the road and the rail line between Wau and Khartoum, creating a 150-mile-wide flood zone that was virtually impossible to cross. The local cops estimated it might be a month before anyone could get through.

Stunned by the news, we retreated to a campsite on the grounds of the Catholic mission to discuss our options. We could try to make an end run out west around the flood zone, but that would take us through Darfur and its notorious bandits. We could backtrack 400 miles to Juba and hope the Nile ferry was running. Or we could sit tight in Wau and wait for the water to recede.

Wau was the lesser of the evils, but not by much. Founded by slave traders in the 19th century, the town had grown into a market and administrative center for much of central Sudan. Most of the buildings were shabby cinderblock or mud-brick, the streets so covered with sand, dust and cow manure it was hard to tell they were paved. The terrace in front of the hospital was littered with used hypodermic syringes and other medical waste. And there were vultures everywhere: picking at the garbage beside the Arab and Greek shops, haunting the rooftops around the market square, perched ominously on the branches of a barren tree behind the Wau police station and prison, tearing frantically at an undefined carcass in the high grass behind the city hall.

With its Italian padres and towering red-brick cathedral (modeled after the Duomo in Florence), the Catholic mission proved a welcome refuge. But even that was short-lived. The Dinka caretaker killed a poisonous snake beside the well. One of the other travelers discovered a foot-long worm inside one of her feet. Adding to our misery was persistent heat, humidity and insects. There was no way we could spend a month here without losing our minds.

On our fifth morning in Wau, the caretaker came running into the orchard shouting, 'The train, the train – it is here!' Having had so many false alarms, we didn't know whether to believe it or not. But as we walked into the center of town, it became obvious that something was up. People with handcarts, pack animals and bags were rushing toward the station. There must be a train, we thought. And then lo and behold, there it was: a raggedy line of box cars and passenger coaches behind an old General Electric diesel. The stationmaster told us it would depart for Khartoum in precisely three hours.

Figuring the train couldn't possibly be any worse than what we were already enduring, five of us decided to ride the rails rather than stay another night in Wau – myself, three young Brits and a Greek-Lebanese law student by the name of Philippa who spoke fluent Arabic. We'd come up from Kenya together and were well acquainted by now.

Gathering our things together, we rushed back to the station – and utter pandemonium. Hundreds of Sudanese had laid siege to the ticket windows; soldiers with rifles were trying to keep them at bay. Mayhem broke out when the signal was given that tickets were finally on sale – people jumping over one another, screaming, punching, clawing like animals, anything they could do to get tickets and get the hell out of Wau. But even then, the panic wasn't over. After buying their tickets, the passengers made a mad dash to secure their spots on the train, crushing through the train doors, forcing their baggage through windows and crawling up to the roof, until there was a solid line of human beings along the crest of the train and faces hanging out of every window.

By the time we elbowed our way to a ticket window, the train was nearly full. The stationmaster told us that one of the better carriages was reserved for army and police personnel. Perhaps we could convince the officer in charge (a certain Major Hassan) to let us sit in that car. With her good looks and easy charm, Philippa was able to ingratiate herself to the young major within minutes. Readily agreeing to our request, he personally escorted us to the military carriage and enough empty seats to fit us all.

We slumped into the hard wooden seats to enjoy our grand departure from Wau. A locomotive whistle shrieked and the train lurched forward. Up and down the train, passengers screamed with excitement as the journey began. Children ran beside the windows trying to snatch one last sale of guavas or peanuts. Soldiers around the station cheered and waved their guns in the air as a salute to departing comrades. We slowly chugged past the grass huts and millet fields on the north edge of town and suddenly Wau was gone.

. . . .

The view out the window was endless savannah, grasslands speckled with the occasional tree and patches of muddy water. There was much more to watch *inside* the carriage. This being the military car, there were indeed soldiers, half a dozen grim-faced troops in dark-green uniforms, clutching banana-clip machine guns or old British .303 rifles.

But most of the passengers seemed to be people like us who had somehow talked, begged or paid their way into the special compartment. A short Arab man in a white galabieh, another with a white fez and prayer beads. A dark woman with a turquoise thoub that she wore down around her chin, so that you could see the tribal scars that marked her face. There was a crippled man with an ebony and ivory cane, and next to him a mother with an infant suckling at her breast. A couple of kids had a live chicken tied to a leg of their bench, and there was a pair of Dinka warriors with spears and dark-blue balaclavas rolled up to their foreheads.

Two hours into the journey came the first of many stops: a thatched-hut station with no sign to indicate its name and a dirt platform thronging with the wildest-looking people I had seen in all of Africa. The men were barefoot and completely naked but for loin cloths. They carried wooden maces and spears, and around their necks hung square lockets that appeared to be made from animal hide. Their women were spangled with metal: nose studs; ornaments hanging from chains suspended through their lower lips; beaded chin straps, head bands and necklaces that fell across their naked breasts. But the crowning glory was their tribal scars: geometrical patterns carved deep into the ink-black skin of their chests, stomachs, faces and upper arms.

Who were these people? Nobody on the train seemed to know. At first I thought they were going to climb onto the train with us. But they were only trying to sell us peanuts and fruit through the open windows.

That night, Major Hassan invited Philippa and me to his private compartment in the first-class section. It was a marvel of convenience with running water, electricity, a ceiling fan and room service, and it was difficult to disguise our envy. The major told us he was the head of the police post in Wau – the one with all the vultures – and that he was traveling to Aweil to quell a mutiny by local administrators who had gone over to the rebels.

'And how will you deal with these men when you find them?' asked Philippa.

Hassan's reply was cut and dry: 'I will kill them.'

'I thought there was a policy of national reconciliation,' she retorted.

'They would do the same to me. I must travel with plainclothes policeman on this train because the rebels have many spies and they might try to kill me if they learn about my mission.'

A room boy delivered mint tea and the three of us launched into a long and spirited conversation on the Sudanese civil war, the differences between north and south, between Muslims and Christians, and how to unify a nation as large and diverse as Sudan. At the end of the evening, Major Hassan told us he would be departing the train early the following morning when we arrived in Aweil. But he assured us we could keep our spots in the military carriage.

By the time we got back to our carriage, everyone was asleep, sprawled in the aisles and across the wooden seats. Philippa curled up in a small space beside a window. But there wasn't enough room for my larger frame. Looking around, I noticed one of the seven-foot Dinka warriors asleep on the overhead luggage rack. I thought: *What an awesome solution.* And crawled up into the rack above our own seats – for the best night's sleep I'd had in days.

Aweil came and went early the next morning and around noon the sergeant who was now in charge of the train came stomping into our carriage. I'd seen him before, back on the platform in Wau, hard to miss the H-shaped tribal scar on each cheek. He was a tall, husky Arab with dark skin and a pistol holstered on his hip and a leather strap in one hand. Not the sort of person you would mess with, no matter what the situation. The sergeant slowly worked his way down the length of our carriage, confronting each of the passengers in turn, growling at them in Arabic. Philippa translated: Scarface was threatening to toss them off the train if they didn't pay an extra 'transit fee.' In other words, a bribe.

When one of the Dinka refused, the sergeant whacked him with the leather strap. And when that had little effect, the sergeant snatched a rifle from one of his men and rapped the man across the head. Blood trickling down his skull, the man fled from the cabin. As did several other passengers who didn't want to face the sergeant's wrath. The message was obvious: Pony up or face consequences.

We had enough Sudanese currency between the five of us to cover the fees he was asking from the others. But when Scarface came to our seats, he looked us up and down disdainfully and asked for ten times as much as he was extorting from the local passengers.

'Major Hassan told us we could ride for free,' Philippa informed him.

Scarface smirked. 'I am now in charge of this train. You do as *I* say.'

Philippa argued our case as best she could, but without the protection of Major Hassan, we stood little chance of defending our ground.

'Look around you,' said Scarface. 'All of these people. How do you think they come to sit here? Do you think it's my charity? You pay what I ask ... or I throw you off.'

I looked around, out the window. We were slowly rumbling through the middle of nowhere. Nothing but uninhabited grassland as far as I could see. Getting tossed off the train here amounted to a virtual death sentence. But it never got that far. A soldier came scrambling in from another carriage, whispered something to Scarface that made his eyes bulge. There must have been a problem elsewhere in the train, because they rushed off. But not without a final warning. 'I'll be back for the money,' the sergeant snarled.

The problem was, we didn't have enough cash. Not the vast amount he was asking. And we wouldn't until we reached a bank willing to change traveler's checks. Most likely Khartoum, which was at least three days away. How were we going to fend off Scarface until then?

But we had other concerns, too. The food that we'd brought from Wau – mostly canned goods and biscuits – was almost gone. And while there was plenty for sale at whistle stops along the route, not much of it (in particular the barbecued 'bush meat') looked enticing or palatable. By the time we rolled into the big railroad junction at Babanusa, the weather had also turned mean. A habob was blowing in from the north, a combination of dust and rain storm with high winds. Outside people were dashing for cover, scrambling beneath the train or heading for the nearby mud-brick buildings. A horse was trying to buck away from its wooden cart, and in the distance I could see men on camels dashing away as fast as they could.

With no glass in the windows, the dust flew into the carriage unopposed, quickly covering our hunched-over bodies in a thick layer of grit. The heavens opened, a trickle at first but then a wind-blown deluge that poured in through the open windows, soaking everything inside the cabin. Darkness fell but the rain endured and the train just sat in Babanusa station, seemingly paralyzed by the tempest. Long after dark, a rumor came whipping through the train: There was a derailment up ahead. Our train wouldn't budge until the wreck was cleared.

We figured that must be the reason why Scarface rushed away in such a state. And why he was in no hurry to collect his bribes from us. He knew we weren't going anywhere. Not for the time being.

. . . .

By morning the storm had fled and warm rays of sun poured into the carriage. But the train was in an awful state. Puddles of water covered the floor, mixing with the rubbish and residue; the roof was leaking and a cold air blew in through the windows. What was left of the derailed train rumbled into the station around eight o'clock and our train jerked forward. After 16 hours in Babanusa we were finally on the move again, but too tired and dirty to celebrate. There was silence as the five of us ate a breakfast of grapefruit, bananas and pita bread purchased at Babanusa Station. But I knew we were all thinking the same thing: How much longer would we have to suffer this train? And when would Scarface return for his money?

With the storm gone and our bellies full for the first time in days, we discussed how to deal with Scarface. A number of ideas were kicked around. But the one we settled on was this: We'd be honest. Tell him we didn't have enough cash to pay him until we reached Khartoum and could visit a bank. But at some point before Khartoum, we would clandestinely leave the train. Studying our guidebooks and maps, we determined there was only one obvious place to make our escape – the city of Kosti on the western bank of the Nile. From Kosti, we could take a bus to Khartoum and arrive before the train. Once we arrived in the capital, Scarface would never find us. And even if he did, we could take refuge in our respective embassies.

Later that day, Scarface began summoning the passengers from our carriage into his private compartment to pay their 'special fee' for the privilege of riding in the military car.

When it was our turn, Philippa walked into his cabin with a handful of traveler's checks. 'How much did you say?' she asked casually, peeling off a couple of checks.

Scarface eyed the checks. 'I want *real* money.'

'This is real money,' Philippa retorted.

'Do I look like a bank?'

'It's all we have!'

Scarface yelled through the open door for one of his men. A corporal appeared in the doorway. 'Tell them to stop the train.'

'Wait!' said Philippa. 'We can make a deal.'

Scarface motioned for the corporal to stop. 'I'm listening.'

And that's when Philippa put our plan in motion. She hooked him right away, played on his greed with an offer to pay him even more than his original asking price if he would just wait until we reached Khartoum and could change our traveler's checks at a bank. In his felonious mind it must have seemed a slam dunk, because he eagerly agreed. What Scarface didn't count on was us having the balls to bail out early.

. . . .

It was half past one in the morning when the train rumbled into Kosti, creeping and creaking into a station beside the Nile. Insects buzzed around the platform lights and a naked bulb illuminating the inside of the all-night teahouse beside the station. I scoped up and down the tracks. The coast was clear. No sign of Scarface or his minions. We scrambled into action, tossing our backpacks and duffel bags out the carriage windows. Stumbling over chickens and sleeping passengers on our way to the exit, we hopped down onto the platform, retrieved our stuff and turned towards the station thinking we had made a clean escape.

But coming out of the teahouse was the young corporal from the train platoon, ripping open a new packet of cigarettes with his teeth. 'This isn't Khartoum,' he said in Arabic, figuring that we'd made an innocent mistake.

But Philippa quickly set him straight. 'We know. We're getting off here.'

'You can't! You haven't paid the sergeant!' he screeched.

'Tell him to go to hell,' I blurted in English, the tone of my voice enough to get the message across.

The corporal tried to block our path. But he'd made a rookie mistake. In his rush to buy smokes, he'd left his gun on the train. Unarmed, there was no way he could stop even one of us, let alone five people determined to flee.

But he still had his voice. 'Sergeant! Sergeant!' he screamed down the platform.

I looked around long enough to see Scarface charging from the back of the train, followed closely by his well-armed posse.

Clearing the station, we broke into a sprint, running down the middle of a street that was supposed to lead to the bus station – and hopefully a coach leaving at any moment now. Twenty minutes later, out of breath and options, we were crouched behind the upturned tables in the outdoor café. Scarface and his thugs were spreading out to search the area, one of them slowly moving our way.

That's when fate intervened. From a distance came a whistle, a signal that the train was about to depart. Scarface and the soldiers gathered in the middle of the street for a hectic confab. I didn't need a translator to tell me they were discussing whether to return to the train or continue their pursuit. But in the end, the prospect of missing their ride to Khartoum overruled their greed. They turned up the street, jogging back towards the river and the train station. At daybreak we boarded a bus for Khartoum. We never saw Scarface again.

Suzanne Joinson's debut novel, *A Lady Cyclist's Guide to Kashgar*, was published by Bloomsbury in 2012. She works part-time in the literature department of the British Council, and travels regularly to the Middle East, China and Europe. In 2007 she won the New Writing Ventures award for her short story 'Laila Ahmed'. She is working on a PhD in Creative Writing at Goldsmiths College, University of London.

Chasing Missionaries

BY SUZANNE JOINSON

Urumqi airport is awash with soldiers sitting on the tarmac in the full blaze of the sun. They scratch heads and smoke as yet more emerge from military-style aeroplanes. There isn't a single other European-looking person on the concourse and suddenly I feel rather hot.

I'm partway through a 28-hour journey: London–Beijing–Urumqi–Kashgar, with the added frisson that it's the first time I have left my baby. Not that he's even a baby. He's a cheerful one-year-old protected by doting relatives, but leaving him feels like I've dug out a kidney, balanced it on an unsafe window ledge in the cold night air and beckoned several hungry dogs to pace the street below.

Thanks to a prestigious grant for a research trip, I'm on the trail of English missionary Mildred Cable and her two companions. I am also deep into writing a novel about them and ruminating on the foolishness of my choice of Kashgar as the setting for most of the story. Kashgar: possibly as distant and remote from London as it's possible to get.

My missionary ladies were restless adventurers and their reasons for travelling (1900–1940) were so much more complicated than straightforward religious zeal. They hoped to carve a freedom for themselves in the Takla Makan desert. Refugees from dreary England, they were avoiding the marriage plot, and I can certainly relate to that. I've always been a committed leaver – of houses, cities, countries, husbands – but now, for the first time, leaving means leaving someone behind. My recently acquired new persona of 'mother' is still a fragile identity. If I carelessly lose it, I'm not sure what is left underneath.

Crowds of Chinese passengers photograph the soldiers through the windows and this leads me to believe that something unusual is happening. I've looked: There isn't a ticket desk in sight, even if I did want to turn round and go home now.

I sip my green tea.

. . . .

In no mood for slumming, I've opted for Kashgar's upmarket hotel, and so it is a shock to be greeted, after arriving at midnight, by an empty mini-bar. No room service. No food or bottled water. The young man on the reception is telling me something. I am telling him something. We both talk louder and shake our heads sadly but we can't understand. Finally, he gives me an English-language newspaper from the previous day:

Several hundred people rioted in Urumqi's People's Square, and then moved southward into Uighur areas, including the Grand Bazaar. Police opened fire; random people were clubbed and stoned to death. There are fears that similar outbursts will occur in Kashgar. The Chinese Government has responded to what they called 'terrorist activity' by

closing down the internet and international phone lines
between Xinjiang Province and the rest of the world.

Hotel rooms have often been my undoing, but this one is
particularly difficult. The blinds are thick, the pillow hard
and the rumbling of the AC erratic and curmudgeonly. My
useless mobile lies on the bed; its international dialling tone
is dead. I sit up all night until I deem it the beginning of
office hours and telephone through to the British Consulate
in Beijing.

'I am safe; can you let my husband know? I can't call out
from here but I guess he might be able to call me?'

The lady at the consulate calls me back: 'We recommend
that all foreign nationals leave Xinjiang Province. You need
to go as soon as possible.'

Fifteen minutes later she calls again: 'Correction, the
government has issued an order that all foreigners must
leave the province immediately. They will assume you are a
journalist and are trying to stay to cover the riots that are
expected outside the mosque on Friday.'

After breakfast, of which I eat very little, the person in
the travel bureau in the corner of the hotel foyer tells me
that there is no flight out of Kashgar for another four days.

'But the authorities have ordered me to leave.' He shrugs.
The next flight is Saturday morning. I pay $700 that has not
been budgeted for.

. . . .

In the main square Mao Zedong points away from Kashgar's
Old Town. A police van cruises, its loudspeakers
pronouncing instructions that I can't understand. The
streets are very quiet.

I stand in front of the hotel and blink into the sun. I would lose my mind if I stayed in that room and so there is nothing for it but to go out. I have straw hat, camera and notebook: the full regalia of a hapless, idiotic Western tourist.

Immediately a couple of taxi drivers approach me and I present them with my prepared piece of paper. It has the names of things I want to see neatly typed out in Mandarin and English. They can't read it, though, because of course they are Uighur. Another man comes; he is Uighur too. The discussion grows louder as they snatch the paper back and forth between them. It appears to have become an argument.

As an English, female, red-haired and fair-skinned traveller, on the (surprisingly many) occasions when men stand in a group around me arguing, I have discovered that the best thing to do is to say nothing. To wait. Or, as Mildred Cable wrote, *in situations like these remain as indifferent as the Buddha himself.* It works. Another man is coming towards us, younger, smarter, Uighur-looking and thankfully he has some English.

'Where do you want to go?'

I tell him: I need to go to the old part of town, to the souq, and to see how the Chinese town intersects with Kashgar Old Town.

He gestures me towards his car, and I follow him. Once I am settled in the back seat, he speaks: 'It is not safe for you here. Why are you here?'

'Research. I am from England, a writer.'

He lights a cigarette, looks crossly at me in the mirror. I find his crossness reassuring and decide to interpret it as a sign that he is not going to kill or kidnap me. As I think this I blush, horrified to realise that, in my mind, I am as orientalist as my missionaries.

'Can we at least drive around so I can see the town? I've come such a long way.'

We move off and I want to ask his name but feel shy about it. The adobe walls of old Kashgar rise up, pink-dusted and ancient, with the Chinese town on one side, Uighur on the other. We are driving slowly along the road that divides them.

'What's happening?'

'Han men got into a fight with Uighurs in a restaurant, now there is a lot of trouble. They have been killing. Uighurs are very angry, the Han police are very, very bad.'

'Will there be more trouble?'

'Yes.'

Before coming I had read that Beijing officials are in the process of demolishing Kashgar's Old Town. Historic blacksmith stalls, copper shops, ancient butchers, tailors and pot-makers have been destroyed and many families relocated against their will. Beijing declares the winding streets dangerous and unhygienic. Uighur leaders think the policy has more to do with ethnic control and fear that the Sunni Muslim Uighurs might behave in ways similar to comrades over the borders in Pakistan, Afghanistan, or Tibet.

We drive in silence. I stare out at the streets, watching the stalls and mopeds, bicycles and groups of men blur past. I appreciate that it is brave of him to tell me anything at all. From the tantalising glimpses of labyrinthine roads I realise that there is only so much I can see from the car.

'I need to walk into the souq.'

He shakes his head. In his mid-twenties, with a neat moustache and an air of worry about him, he clearly does not approve of my plan. I know very well what the shake of his head means: that I don't belong here, don't understand and that I should go. Despite, or because of this, I ask him, 'I need to go into the desert. Can you help?'

'What?'

'Not far, just enough to get a feel, a sense, to take photographs.'

He is squinting at me in the mirror, no doubt trying to work out if I am a journalist, a spy, or just an idiot. I don't have to try hard to look like the last. I think he is going to refuse but he nods; we make arrangements for payment and to meet in the lobby in the morning. His card has no name, just the word TAXI and a number.

· · · · · · · · · · ·

My husband calls at 4am. 'What's happening?'

'Well, I'm in this hotel room alone, there are police everywhere, a driver told me that there are likely to be violent —'

The phone goes dead, a clicking noise. I have been monitored, followed and bugged in China before, when I had spent a month with a film crew travelling around six cities. I know these things happen here, but at this moment I very much want to talk to my husband. I swear.

An hour later he manages to get through again. 'I think we are being listened to,' I say. 'Don't mention anything that is happening here or we'll be cut off.'

'OK.'

'How is Woody?'

'He misses you, but we're fine. What have you seen?'

'I went to the souq during the hottest part of the day. Children with shaved heads. Racks of mutton. There are birdcages everywhere but they all seem to be empty.'

'Stay safe,' he says.

· · · · · · · · · · ·

I didn't think it could be possible to travel further from my son but the drive into the desert is an unreal slide into another life. I eat my hotel-supplied sandwich, drink warm bottled water and watch the dusty streets of Kashgar fade into an endless, brown scrubland. A nothing landscape. I see the poplar trees described by Mildred Cable and remember a section from her journal: *The land introduces one but gradually to its desert terrors. Otherwise one might not be able to bear them. You have had your first taste of the desolating wilderness.*

After driving for several hours the heat is unbearable, my water almost gone and I am grateful when the driver turns off the main road into a smaller track. We approach a village, and pull up outside a teahouse in the central square. He is welcomed by an older man who obviously knows him well and we are shown to a table and brought tea, then shortly afterwards mutton kebabs and thick noodles.

The men talk, swirl tea in their cups, then fling it mysteriously onto the floor. They are not unfriendly; I seem to be accepted, and it is pleasant to sit in the shade and watch the village world go about its business.

He is patient with me as I photograph trees, stones, doors, windows, bicycles, shop-signs and a grey-barked shrub that grows everywhere. I look up and see my son's face in the strange clouds that hang low, not like city-clouds. The sky is too wide. I click the camera again and again to ignore the ache that has come, a pull to return to my son that is stronger and brighter than the desert-light.

. . . .

Three or four men are shaking hands and talking outside a doorway. A woman, wrapped in a colourful abaya, carries a large plate of meat and disappears into the house. There is laughter. One of the men summons us over and talks to the driver, smiling at me.

'Would you like to go in? He is inviting you in.'

I am taken through the doorway into a heavily decorated room that has bright blue walls and colourful rugs and cushions on the floor. Two men stop talking to look at me. A teenage girl, hovering behind them, gestures to us and we follow her, further into the house, to a larger room that overlooks a small courtyard space. Here there are more women who also stop talking to stare at me. I am given a chair, offered a small glass of tea. The driver stands near me, accepts tea too. It is claustrophobic; they all talk at once. I guess it is a celebration of something.

The teenage girl beckons us again and we follow her, this time across the courtyard where there are rolls of carpet and sacks of rice against the wall and children playing.

We are taken into another, much darker room. Here is an elderly woman sitting on a stool. On a blanket across her knee a naked baby lies on its belly. Next to her on the floor a young woman sits cross-legged, holding a blue bowl. They both look at me momentarily and then the ancient old lady goes on with her work: rubbing the baby, massaging it, squeezing its little legs. Unlike the newborn babies I have seen and held – purple-faced and crying – it is relaxed, floppy like a doll.

I sit on a low stool to watch. A baby was not what I was expecting to see. The woman hands a blue pot to the old lady and she takes a handful of fine white powder. She then sprinkles it onto the baby's back and rubs some more.

'What is she doing?' I whisper. He is thinking of the English word, and then says: 'Salt.'

I wonder if the old lady is blind, or didn't really see me, but then she suddenly speaks. My driver translates. 'She asks who you are. Where you come from?' I tell her.

'Can you give her my congratulations for the new baby?' He does.

'Will you tell her I have a son too?' She looks up at me. She has no teeth. She is spectacularly old, like a tree that has grown forever out of this dust. I think she is going to smile at me but she does not.

'Did you salt him?' he translates.

'No. No. We don't ... I did not.'

I recall, then, a description in Mildred Cable's book of the salting of a baby, quoting the Book of Ezekiel and a terrible insult: *You were not salted at all nor were you swaddled.* Meaning: You invited trouble.

Salt keeps demons away.

The old lady picks up a long strip of fabric and proceeds to delicately wrap it around the baby, tight. The baby is completely mummified, but seems content as the younger woman takes it away, presumably back to the mother.

There is a noise in the other room, a kerfuffle. The driver is tense. I stand up and he propels me back through the rooms. The glass is taken from my hand.

In the street a police car is waiting with three Chinese policemen standing next to it. They point at me and come towards us.

'What are they saying?'

One of the policemen waves me towards his car.

'No,' I say to the driver, touching his arm. 'I don't want to go with them. Can you drive me back?'

He speaks to them, but they are angry and begin to shout, close to his face. The men of the village stand watching and women peep around doors. One of the

Chinese policemen pushes the driver roughly, and then screams at his face. It seems unnecessary and suddenly I feel fury. What are they doing? And why is this government demolishing an ancient 500-year-old city? Why not allow Uighur children to learn to read and write their own language? I want to shout at them, but when I see the driver dejected, not fighting back, I realise that I have brought him great trouble.

I try to talk to them, 'He hasn't done anything wrong.' But I'm speaking in English. They just look blankly at me, then wave me towards the car.

'Go home and be safe,' the driver says, just as he's been saying to me all along.

'I'm sorry.'

I don't know if he hears me because two of the policemen have pulled him to the side of the road and they are handcuffing him. I am steered forcefully by the other one to the police car. The door is opened and I climb in. He speaks into his radio.

The village people are staring and I know what they are thinking: that I am an unlucky visitor with my red hair and red skin. A second policeman gets into the car with us. I look back through the rectangle of the car window at my driver's lowered head and black hair, the remaining policeman talking roughly at him; I have added, immeasurably, to his difficulties.

The people watch and I know, now, that I cannot do this again. I can't go this far across the world, such a distance away from my unsalted son. That traveller who was at her happiest when leaving has dissolved, like bird bones left in the desert sun.

· · · · ● ● ● · · ·

Waiting outside my room is an unsmiling, extremely smart Chinese man with a plane ticket in his hand. My bag is packed, at his feet. He speaks excellent English. I am to leave for the airport immediately, 'For my own safety.'

'I would just like to check I've got everything.' He nods. The bed is made and the towels straightened as if no guest has stayed here and I already know that the card with TAXI and a number on it is no longer next to the bedside lamp. He makes hurrying noises.

It is business class as far as Urumqi, and then – a nice touch – I'm bumped down to economy. I text a journalist acquaintance in Beijing.

'You're where? You're *where?*' He gives me his address. 'That's fine, you must come and stay.'

Peter Matthiessen has written eight novels, including *At Play in the Fields of the Lord* (nominated for the National Book Award) and *Far Tortuga*, and also a book of short stories, *On the River Styx*. His parallel career as a naturalist and environmental activist has produced numerous acclaimed works of nonfiction, most of them serialised in the *New Yorker*; these include *The Tree Where Man Was Born* (another National Book Award nominee) and *The Snow Leopard* (a National Book Award winner). He was elected to the American Academy of Arts and Letters in 1974.

In Bear Trap Canyon

BY PETER MATTHIESSEN

The road to Ennis, crossing the Gallatin River west of Bozeman, arrives at the Madison not far below where this renowned fishing river springs free from the mountains at the bottom end of an eight-mile chute called Bear Trap Canyon. 'Once you head down into the Bear Trap, you are fatally committed,' said my fishing partner, writer-editor Stephen Byers, as its mouth came into view. 'Those canyon walls are 1500 to 2000 feet high, and even where you can climb out, it's roadless wilderness.' Byers, a husky, bearded man who lived in Ennis for some years back in the '70s and '80s and has fished most of the rivers in this watershed, described with awe the three large rapids way back up that canyon, in particular the notorious 'Kitchen Sink' – so-called, he thought, because it sucked everything down or perhaps because its erratic torrent of white leaping waves and sudden waterfalls, boiling eddies and treacherous boulders contained 'everything but' in the way of dangerous obstacles to forward progress.

Byers himself, as a young man, had tried that rapid twice, coming to grief both times on the first hazard, a gigantic boulder like a barrier that lies athwart the head of the long rapid. In a matter of moments, he had broken off both oars ('Well, only one oar on the second try,' he grinned) and been jolted overboard. 'I was terrified,' he said. 'My hard boat had no give to it, unlike these flexible canvas rafts they're using now. There's been plenty of lives lost in that canyon, I know that much, and Eric has bombed out in there a few times, too.'

Eric Shores was our very tall, loose, lanky friend, in big broad sun hat and cowl neckerchief, who with his partner, Annie, inhabited an odd studio-type house on a high treeless bluff with a fine view of Ennis Lake, which nestles like a blue glacier in its mountain basin. Backed up behind the Madison Dam near the top of Bear Trap Canyon, the shallow lake, perhaps 2.5 miles across, extends to the broad marshes to the east where the Madison enters the lake after a smooth 60-mile descent from the Yellowstone Plateau. In other years, Byers and I, separately and together, had drifted and fished the last few miles of the upper river and its channels through those marshes, and had walked the banks and waded bars and cast to rises of the big resident rainbows and browns that lurk in the labyrinths of weeds on the shallow bottom.

We would fish those places, too, said Eric, who had signed on as our guide for this trip, but this year he wanted us to try the Bear Trap, which was nearly pristine, being very little fished. Byers and I raised eyebrows, grinning – *What? Not fished? How can that be?* – and Shores grinned, too. Even the dean of local guides, their old friend Randy Brown, whose raft had overturned in the Kitchen Sink on his first time through, had never gone near the place again. ('A boat-eatin' bugger,' the rapid had been called by retired guide Johnny France, remembering the deaths of seven people in that canyon.) Not being licensed to guide clients through the Bear Trap, Eric had generously offered to give up a day in his high season as a guide and take us in there on a friendship basis and do some fishing, too.

And the Kitchen Sink? Our friend smiled vaguely: he recalled no fatalities among his passengers, not to date. Anyway, there was a portage path along the cliffside and down around that rapid, so nobody had to risk it but the boatman. And so, on a bright cold morning, we trailered Eric's 15-foot blue 'raft' from his house on the bluff along the shore to the point where the lake flees the sun and, gathering speed as the cliffs rise, is once again a river, curling down past its 35-foot dam into the cold shade of the gorge at over 2000 cubic feet per second, in a torrent strong enough to roll big boulders.

We launched the raft in the first eddy below the powerhouse. For the next hour, perhaps two, we all caught and released fish in the beautiful long pools below the cliffs, casting behind the immense boulders where trout shelter from the current. Steve's wife, Heather Kilpatrick, a retired attorney who does not fish but enjoys the quiet under the river roar in this majestic gorge, sat straight upright on a narrow board all morning with no backrest, mostly silent and entirely uncomplaining. She maintained this composure even when, perhaps two miles downstream from the put-in, we sailed into the Whitehorse, the first of three challenging passages in this four-mile stretch of canyon, where our husky canvas craft with its long oars, precisely maneuvered, banked, and spun by broad-shouldered, long-armed Eric, negotiated the waves, boils, swirls, and bangs of this Class III rapid without bad scares or undue technical difficulty.

Not much more than a mile down, where the great canyon narrows, we approached the Kitchen Sink, rated Class IV-plus in degree of difficulty. Though approximately the same length as the Whitehorse, its two hundred yards of eccentric waves, treacherous rocks, and deeper boils make it technically so much more challenging that in seasons of high water, when the flow may exceed 3000 cubic feet per second, it is rated a dangerous Class V. (Class VI rapids are generally considered 'unfloatable' by rafters, though 'extreme' kayakers, exceptionally skilled in those light, quick craft, are starting to challenge them.)

At the last large pool above this second rapid, Eric pulled over to the bank. Because the morning had been chilly in the deep shadows of the canyon, we were happy to disembark and stretch our backs a little in the sun. Here Eric pointed out the path that climbs the steep north slope to a point high above the torrent and descends again to the first pool, beyond where he would pick us up.

No doubt intoxicated by the mountain air or over-excited by the roar of the white water, perhaps still celebrating the 23-inch rainbow – my largest ever – caught the day before in the Fletcher Channel on the far side of the lake, or perhaps – well, *what*? It doesn't really matter. With incredulity, I heard my voice tell Eric that if it was okay with him, I'd like to go. He looked at me a bit quizzically. I nodded. It's true, man; I'd like to run this rapid. And he nodded, too, as if considering the idea. Doubtless he would have much preferred to skid his lightened raft up waves and down around the pouring boulders, free of all responsibility for others, not to mention liability in case of accident for passengers who were only cargo with no way to help, a hindrance at best and at worst – should they panic or be thrown overboard – a damned nuisance, endangering everybody.

My friends stood watching, as if expecting me to change my mind. Heather, who had not been well, had no wish to risk the Kitchen Sink, nor could she be left behind to manage that precipitous path; she would need her husband. And though he might have wished to go, Steve felt he had no choice but to stay with her. I sympathized with what I supposed must be his conflicting feelings. On the east coast, Byers and I are saltwater fly-fishing partners who have great fun with the hyperbole and hard teasing that go with that; he could not be entirely happy, I suspected, that after all that talk about the perils of the Kitchen Sink, his antiquated fishing buddy (aged 82), an Eastern greenhorn on this brawling Western river of his youth, wanted to run this rapid out of pure foolishness, leaving his mentor on the bank.

In any case, he had much too much pride to bitch about it, and after all, what was there to be said? And so he teased me, saying something wry about the great loss to American literature we were about to witness. And to help ease a certain tension in the group, get everyone to lighten up, not waste such a fine day, I said half-seriously, 'It's all right, you guys, don't worry. My best work is behind me.'

We laughed, of course, but there was truth in this. I was having great trouble finding the right voice for a difficult novel-in-progress, and also with a second one I sometimes fiddled with when frustration with the first became intolerable. This was my own fault, of course: I had obstinately failed to abide by my own conviction (based on the late work of almost all American novelists I truly admire) that most writers with too much wear lose elasticity and lyric energy and perhaps the ability to startle and astonish and might be better advised to leave well enough alone.

Much more to the point was the fact that in that Whitehorse Rapid, and at other times as well, I had admired Shores' quick skill and power on those oars with the unsentimental eye of a former oarsman on an ocean haul-seine crew on the Atlantic coast, who for three years had rowed in a heavy dory through the surf. I trusted this guy and I wanted this adventure – *needed* it, in fact, before I shriveled like a grape on the autumn vine.

Eric neither encouraged nor discouraged me, suggesting instead that we all climb to that point on the path from where the would-be voyager could take a hard look down into the Kitchen Sink before deciding how best to proceed.

Through these narrows between cliffs, the river's descent is very steep and swift. Seen from high above, the Sink was a seething chute of waterfalls and big black rocks and white waves that collide and explode from bank to bank or rather wall to wall. There is virtually no shore and, as someone had observed about this rapid, 'It looks like there's no way through.' Perhaps Shores supposed that having been provided with a cautionary look, we would approve his preference to take his boat down through that chaos unladen with hapless people who might be trapped beneath or drowned were his raft to 'flip.' No, he had never lost a passenger, but he freely admits that he came too close to losing his hardy Annie in this rapid a few years ago while training her as a guide.

'I guess I could take one passenger,' he said finally, 'if someone really wants to go.' When I said, 'I meant it. I really want to go,' Shores glanced over at his old friend Byers as if to say, Well, Bud? What's to be done with this old coot? You planning to intervene or what? (And I confess I kind of hoped that Byers, a generous fishing partner who keeps a close eye on me on the saltwater, would step forth now and do his bounden duty – *do the only decent thing, for Chrissakes, Steve!* – and try to save his old buddy's ass from his own stupidhood.)

'I thought about it, all right,' he told me later, 'and I felt guilty. Maybe I should have. But who was I to try to stop you? You're a grown man and I could see you meant it.' I did mean it, that's true, but it was also true that my lungs were filling with slow dread. In the ocean surf earlier that summer, I had learned the hard way that in recent years I'd lost the strength and the endurance I might need to survive the turbulence I saw below, with those black boulders knocking sense into my head all the way downriver. On the other hand, I lacked the courage to stay behind. To refuse out of mere flimsiness and old-timer timidity what might well be my last shot at a real adventure was to face the fact that a man I used to know was gone for good.

Mustering a jaunty grin, I left my friends and followed Eric back upriver to the raft. At the torrent's edge, the boatman who turned to thrust a life vest at my chest and shout last instructions through the roar of stone and water was a grim-faced professional, suddenly all business. When he waved me forward to the bow and I hollered out that I'd rather ride behind him where his body might shield mine from the cold spray – and from where I might throw my arms around his neck in case of trouble – he barely smiled. 'Your one responsibility,' he called sternly, indicating the spare oar lightly lashed to the gunwale at my right hand, 'is to free that oar and pass it to me quick if I break one of mine. And I mean *quick*.' The broken oar is the most common mishap in an eight-knot current that may pin the boat broadside against one of those big river-twisting boulders.

I nodded and climbed in and faced forward, stowing my shades in my rain parka and groping for something to hang onto (no safety belts are worn since in case of a flip, the passenger's chances are much better when thrown free than when trapped under the boat), while reminding myself that in case of accident, thrown from the raft into the torrent and on my merry way downriver through the falls and whirlpools, theoretically upright in this life vest and coming along nicely as I shrug off the heavy blows of rocks, I must not neglect to yank my knees up to my chest. In such a strong current, a dangling foot caught in deadwood or rock fissure can neither be freed nor snapped off like an oar and in all likelihood will drown you.

'Just one more thing,' warned Eric, pushing off. 'There's a big rock down here at the bottom of a fall that we are going to hit head on. There's no way to avoid it, and it's going to fold the boat – actually fold the bow up and back toward your face, I mean – so just hang in there.'

Oddly, the dread had already subsided. I felt calm – a bit dull, perhaps, or numb, but very calm. *Okay, let's do it*, I was thinking, and right then, we did it. In the first few feet, we were seized up by the current and swept over a small waterfall, and Shores banked skillfully off that big barrier rock and around and down, and after that it was all rush and thunder of white water, with hard loud *bangs* and jolts that came too close to catapulting the unbelted passenger right overboard, and sudden falls that seemed to plunge six feet into their caldrons, and wild way-out careenings at bad angles on the wave face – *Christ!* I was amazed by the sheer *oar strength* demanded to maintain any sensible sort of course with so many perilous passages and hairbreadth escapes evolving all but simultaneously, one hard upon another, all of them controlled by the tall pale river guru on his throne somewhere up behind, for here I was, amidst surging walls of water at near arm's lengths, sometimes cresting overhead, and not one errant wave did I receive full in the face in all that very long two hundred yards ...

At the bottom, in the smooth flow again, the river silenced, in the stark beauty of the canyon, I could not stop grinning. 'Great job,' I said, utterly contented. 'Thank you very, very much.' Exhausted but relieved and happy, too, Shores eased over to the bank to await the others. Knowing they might be a while, making their way down the steep slope, he climbed out and eased his body down and back against a rock, on his face the broad sleepy smile of affable old Eric. I sighed after a while, 'I never would have done that if I hadn't trusted you.' And he nodded, saying quietly, 'Oh man. I had to trust you, too, you know. Like, taking a guy as old as you through that? I don't think so.' And we laughed some more.

All that evening, I was on a high – not only exhilarated but somehow *cleansed*, as if that passage had scoured off a rust of bad old stuff and perhaps the first dust of oncoming decrepitude. I felt full of myself in the best sense, years younger, all set to raise hell. But pride, as they say, goeth before a fall, and I got my fall that very evening when I sullied the purity of the crystal gin martinis concocted by our host in Bozeman by vaunting my great whitewater adventure, only to learn too late from Byers that some years earlier, this modest man (our pal, the writer David Quammen) had not only run the Bear Trap in a kayak but had flipped it in the Kitchen Sink. Unable to right himself, he had passed through the worst of that 'boat-eatin' bugger' upside down.

Keri Hulme's novels, short stories and poems are widely published. Her novel, *the bone people*, gained global recognition when it won the New Zealand Book Award for Fiction in 1984, and the Booker Prize in 1985. In homage to her mixed heritage, her writing interweaves diverse mythologies - Maori, Celtic, Norse - with the everyday. Hulme has published short stories and poems in several book-length collections, as well as journals and anthologies. Her long story 'Te Kaihau/The Windeater' appears in *Nine New Zealand Novellas*. She lives in the South Island of Aotearoa-New Zealand, in a region famed for reef herons and whitebait.

A Tohunga with a Promise to Keep

BY KERI HULME

It is July, 1985, and our group, Te Whanau o Aotearoa, is flying to Tahiti. We are a varied lot – *kapahaka* performers in the main, but there are other artists in paint or sculpture or words, plus three or four bureaucrats from Maori arts organisations, and our own diplomat (who is fluent in Maori and French as well as English). We are headed for the Fourth South Pacific Arts Festival and we are fairly excited. Some of us think of tropical fruit and raw fish salads, of *hangi'd* pork & chicken. Exotic new foods, like breadfruit. 'And they'll have good French wine! Cheap!' Some of us think of the free and easy sex-life of Tahitians, others of marvellous islands and beaches and lagoons. 'Bali Hai was a Tahitian island!' And most of us are thinking we are so lucky, headed for a Polynesian arts festival, where we will see the performance gamut of all the islands of Polynesia, including participants from places in Melanesia. *Waua!*

There are two forlorn protesters standing by the departure lounge doorway as we go to board the plane. We know them – they are esteemed Maori artists – and they know many of us. They try to persuade us, individually, not to go to Tahiti – but we thank them, and go on our way....

Their protest is entirely understood: Aotearoa-New Zealand and France are not friends. France has been testing atomic devices on Mururoa atoll, and Aotearoa has sent a protest fleet to the area – and two navy frigates, complete with a Cabinet minister to make it official. Meanwhile the French military rams and boards protest boats, infiltrates protest movements. Little do we know that they are also planning direct action in Aotearoa itself.

The flight to Tahiti is uneventful, and we land at dawn at Papeete. The welcome as we get off the plane is by a small party but we appreciate it very much: the man does the calling (which is a kind of mild shock), and there is a short song from the four women, but there are careful stacks of fruit, and a young pig with pale eyelashes is tied by its feet to a bamboo pole.

'Bodes well, eh?' says my seat-mate.

The transport doesn't bode well. They are weird wee diesel vehicles, with bench seats, open to the air along each side of the passenger back deck (thank heavens!) but with an airflow problem that means the diesel emissions are channelled back into the passenger compartment.

'Geez! Travelling gas chambers!' says someone.

We arrive at our accommodation. It is a secondary school, emptied for the holidays. In the dining room there are set out, for exactly the number of people who are expected, a bowl, white bread rolls, made-up milk, and canisters of black coffee. O, and sugar bowls.

'Fuck o dear,' says someone, 'this is it?'

It was.

A person guided us to the student dormitory we were to sleep in.

The aunties sent out all the able-bodied men immediately to buy cleaning materials and extra sarongs. That's when we discovered Tahiti was an *extremely* expensive place to live.

Maori generally travel with their own pillows and blankets. At home, when you arrive to stay at another community's *marae*, you know you'll find a supply of good mattresses and sheets. You know the place will be clean, hospitable, and able to cope with anything. Most of us had brought our pillows and a blanket, but these mattresses – and all the amenities – were something else.

Much later that day, someone said, 'Shit. We shoulda listened to those fellas at Auckland.'

It didn't bode well.

. . . .

The festival itself was genuine, engrossing, wonderful. Some very small islands had spent the last year preparing materials for their costumes and accoutrements and instruments, and their performances – well, pretty well every island's performances – were riveting, spine-tingling, brain-enhancing. I didn't have a camera then but I can still review what I saw in my head ... What will never be seen again.

I was wearily astonished that there weren't a lot of Pakeha people in the audiences.

But then, the amazing trip happened....

. . . .

Before we'd left home, it had been canvassed among Te Whanau of Aotearoa that since we would be so close to the most sacred space in all of Polynesia, would any of us like to go there?

'Yes!' said twenty of us, and so we had prepaid the necessary extra ferry fees and beachside motel accommodation and transport costs. However *after* Tahiti-nui, a lot of us were having second thoughts....

Three good things had happened in Tahiti-nui. We had seen the small but wonderful group of performers from Easter Island/Te Pito o te Ao: 'Goodness!' I'd thought as they'd come out –male with topknot, females calling, loincloth and thatchy cloaks – 'That's my lot from the far south, 200 years ago.' (And I could understand quite a bit of their dialect.)

And the Fijian contingent had invited us all for a *kai*. Their quarters were even more spartan than ours. But the meal was corned beef and coconut cream, rice and greenery, and they must've paid heaps for it. It was so warm-hearted, so spontaneous, so very Polynesian/ Melanesian-peoples proud of being able to be hospitable, that I nearly cried.

And we had, as a group, been invited to the home of people who lived a traditional lifestyle. The man came out and *haeremai'd* us, waving greenery while in the background his wife *tangi'd* (again, not unfamiliar to Maori). We were then welcomed into their home, *hongi* and hug, take your footwear off, and go into a traditionally-built house.... There was an in-built *hangi*-pit, and there was breadfruit cooking. There were also fish, fruits I had never tasted (and loved!), green coconut juice and coconut milk.

Around the eating area, altogether seated on the ground, was a man I'd never noticed before. He wore our group's 'Whanau o Aotearoa' tag but seemed withdrawn, otherwise absorbed. I figured he was one of the bureaucrats, staying in Papeete motels. I said to my mate, the other Keri, 'Big fucking bureauwig, eh?'

'Nah,' she answered. 'That's a *tohunga* who nearly died last year. He made a promise to *nga atua tawhito* to bring a tribal treasure to Taputapuatea and leave it there in thanksgiving.'

It was sitting there inside that *whare*, listening to that man and others speak, that I learnt more of our shining-cuckoo lore and that my great-grandfather on the wahine-Maori-side, a whale-ship captain, was almost certainly half/Tahitian. You get a *tohunga* and foreign locals speaking together...oh, it should happen so much more!

So, in late-ish July, we boarded the overnight ferry from Tahiti-nui to Raiatea. It was a large-enough vessel to feel comfortable on – about half the size of the old Cook Strait ferries. We were deck passengers – the old blanket and pillow-carrying habit worked fine – and the few stops at smaller intervening islands didn't really make much impression (the smell of kerosene lamps and diesel generators were childhood memories, and the evocative scent of fried meats meant buggerall to a fish-eating vegetarian). But the arrival in Raiatea did....

Firstly, there had been the extraordinary double rainbow round the ferry as we approached the island. And that it had an entirely different atmosphere from Tahiti-nui. There were excited people at the wharf. They used cars and a tractor-with-trailer to transport us to our motels. They gave us real *lei*, made of flower and shell, *hongi'd* properly, and presented spontaneous gifts. And the motels were a revelation: they literally were built over the sea, and you could see fish and other marine creatures under your veranda; they were clean and more than adequate. We all had a celebratory drink – of non-French wine (the wine had turned out to be so bad in Tahiti that we joked it was dried Algerian plonk, revivified). *This* wine was good. And in the morrow – Taputapuatea....

Breakfast was substantial, the first good one we'd had for a fortnight. Lot of fruit, omelettes, really good croissants, excellent coffee (did I mention the coffee in Tahitinui was shit-awful?). And now, we were all *really* excited.

I hadn't seen the old *tohunga* on the voyage to Raiatea, but he was there when our party's two *waka* arrived. The *waka* were motorised single-outrigger jobs, perfect for travelling by sea round the island. It didn't take long to get to the hallowed place.

Let me briefly explain what Raiatea, and especially Taputapuatea, mean to Aotearoa Maori: we know where we come from, and we know where the sacred spaces were and are. The *tohunga* knew the names of the mountains, the islands, into Raiatea – he chanted them as we came past them, that next day. He'd never been there. He didn't have a savoury past – but he was trusted because, since early childhood, he'd been taught and entrusted with deep knowledge.

Taputapuatea, the Sacred/Sacred Open Gathering Space, is part of that deep and ancient learning – it is the centre of Polynesian being.

When I woke that morning, my mate said, 'Ooo, look! Your friend has followed you!'

Outside her window was a reef heron – which also lives in my area of the world especially.

A good omen, eh? I trust my birds.

The *waka* were driven by skilled boatmen. As soon as we got into open water, a pair of *Tursiops truncatus* surfaced, and accompanied us for many kilometres. Now, I love bottlenose dolphins, know their colouration at home in Aotearoa very well. These ones were a kind of greenish colour I wasn't familiar with – anyway, they took us to the entry to the bay before Taputapuatea....

. . . .

What did I expect, especially with all the good omens?

A place where, for once, I would feel unadulterated holiness?

Yeah.

Something like that.

. . . .

I've been partially trained in a Japanese fighting art (*aikido*): this training means you have some ingrained, almost automatic responses. When I arrived on the grotty rubbish-bestricken beach at Taputapuatea – there were stray jandals and plastic water bottles and worse floating in the water – I found myself adopting a fighting stance. And I kept it, as the strong *karanga* group of women led us on to the *marae*.

Taputapuatea is not physically impressive. It is a black coral wall, and side walls, not all that high, with some old trees (but the *tohunga* knew their names – those trees, those walls... they'd been around for a while). He chanted, and then stooped, and *crawled* towards the wall (everybody averted their eyes – but I can't, I am an observer, a note-taker) and poked the tribal treasure into a crevice in the wall.

And then backed away, still crawling, until he reached an unseen boundary whereupon he stood up. The aunties burst into song and the atmosphere immediately became much lighter.

. . . .

The only time I asked a question of the *tohunga* was as we were leaving. It was, 'Given the *tohu* before I came to Taputapuatea, why did I adopt a fighting stance?'

He explained that it was in my blood: 'One of your *tipuna* was killed there.'

Well – who knows?

. . . .

We went back to Tahiti. Gauguin paintings in a church didn't make the place any more welcoming.

The day before we left, I had a dish of raw fish that tasted mainly of garlic (and left me with diarrhoea and complications for the next two months).

And, halfway through the flight home (the *tohunga* huddled with his guard of aunties), the captain of the plane announced, 'We have just learned that the *Rainbow Warrior* has been blown up and one person is dead.'

Peter Ho Davies is the author of a novel, *The Welsh Girl*, longlisted for the Man Booker Prize, and two story collections, *The Ugliest House in the World* and *Equal Love*. One of *Granta*'s 'Best of Young British Novelists', he currently teaches in the Creative Writing Program at the University of Michigan.

Death Trip

BY PETER HO DAVIES

The first time my wife and I moved across the US – from Atlanta to Eugene, Oregon – was in the late summer of 1997. I was changing jobs, swapping one university for another, and although my new position came with relocation expenses, we opted against putting our car on a truck and flying out, and instead decided to take a week and drive west.

We were young(ish) and indulging in the romance of the great American road trip, as popularized in books and movies and, in a sense, reaching back to before there even were roads to take such trips on. We crossed the Mississippi in the shadow of the St Louis Arch, monument to the city's role as gateway to the West, stopped outside Salt Lake City at Promontory Summit where the tracks of the first transcontinental railroad were joined, and paused near journey's end at an Oregon Trail museum, where the original wagon ruts of the pioneers could still be seen worn deep into the rocky ground. This wasn't my history – I'm an expat Brit – but I was at least as thrilled as my American wife to see these famous sights (and several lesser ones). To see them and, of course, be seen with them in the obligatory photos, since secure in the knowledge that our trip was purposeful, necessary, we could while away the miles – guiltlessly – as gawking tourists.

We got to Oregon, to a friend's house in Portland, on my 31st birthday, and after celebrating late into the evening, woke the next morning to the news that Princess Diana had been killed in a car crash in Paris.

It felt like news from another planet. Not just for its abruptness – we'd barely looked at a newspaper in days – but because after a week of travel, all of it westward, England and France felt impossibly remote. And then, in the days that followed, came the unreality of the mourning, watching the funeral in the small hours of the morning on a borrowed TV in our otherwise empty house in Eugene (our furniture wouldn't arrive on the delayed moving truck for two more weeks, adding to the dislocating sense of limbo). Britain seemed distant geographically, but also suddenly culturally and emotionally, to judge from the unprecedented scenes of mass public grief. Diana's death dismayed me, as that of any young person would, but never having paid much attention to the Royal Family, I didn't feel the loss with the personal intensity of those crowds on TV. To make matters stranger, as the new Brit in town, I was constantly being asked about her death, and even having people offer me their condolences. Britain seemed at once farther away and yet more American than I'd ever imagined.

. . . .

The second time my wife and I moved across the US – this time heading east – was two years later, for another job. We'd enjoyed the cross-country drive so much we decided to do it again in reverse, this time via a more northern route that took in Yellowstone Park and Old Faithful, Little Big Horn, Mount Rushmore, Niagara Falls. Along the way, we pitched up late one night in Cody, Wyoming, to find it was the weekend of the Buffalo Bill Stampede Rodeo, and the only room to be had was in a particularly seedy motel. The shag carpeting in the room was so long and unkempt it looked like it could hide cigarette butts and hypodermic needles. On the inside of the door my wife counted the screw-hole stigmata of three previous locks. We slept with a chair propped against the current one, and woke the next morning to the cable news that John F. Kennedy Jr's plane was missing, presumed lost, in Nantucket Sound en route to Martha's Vineyard.

Later that day, back in the car, tracking the search on the radio, but already knowing the worst, my wife joked bleakly that we'd better not take any more cross-country drives, but I could tell she was affected. She felt she knew 'John-John,' his family, the way others felt they had known Princess Diana. We can't know such distant figures personally, of course, she seemed to be saying, but we can know what they mean to us. Our mourning is for them, but also for some part of ourselves.

. . . .

You have a lot of time to think on a three-thousand-mile drive: of where you're leaving, where you're going, but mostly, in my case, of how long it's taking. As I had moved to the US only a few years earlier, the sheer scale of the country was still being revealed to me on those trips. I understood it intellectually, from maps, but I'd never *felt* it before – felt it in my aching back after sitting in a car for ten hours a day, felt it in my desperation to stop and get out of the car and see … well, almost anything (including the world's largest ketchup bottle on one occasion).

The very words *country* or *nation*, in a Western European context at least, seem to mean something different, something smaller, more cohesive and *graspable*. Consider that casually naive question from friends and family at home after I first arrived in the US, 'What's America like?' – a question I could answer tentatively about New England where I first lived, but which I couldn't begin to address in regard to the West, or the Midwest, the Gulf Coast, or the Mountain States. The British, myself included, are occasionally amused (and/or exasperated) by the American error that on such a small island we must all know each other, but the analogous error is our assuming one can know America based on the experience of one region. Even the British habit of referring to *America*, rather than *the United States*, makes a subtle assumption of wholeness. To put it another way, I knew about as much of San Francisco from my time in Boston as your average Londoner might know of Moscow.

Projected on to the scale of a continent, familiar concepts like *country* and *nation* began to seem less certain, less descriptive than *aspirational*. Somewhere on those long drives, it came to me that a vast and relatively young nation like the US – for all its vaunted self-confidence – is still trying desperately to reassure itself of its very nationhood. This is a country, after all, that still vividly recalls its own divisive civil war, not to mention the divisive struggles a hundred years later for civil rights. The prevalence of US flags, fluttering from post offices and town halls, from schools and houses, so easily mistaken for rampant jingoism by a European, serve, in fact, as a reminder, a fluttering hope, of something shared by people spread out over thousands of square miles. Even the stultifying sameness of those widely bemoaned aspects of

American culture – chain stores, strip malls, ubiquitous fast-food restaurants – speaks to an effort to tame the nation's scale, to offer the comfort of familiarity across the vastness (a descendant of the pioneering tendency to name the new after the old: New York, New England, New Orleans), to *unite*, in a word.

But, of course, the deaths of Diana and John Kennedy during those trips also put me in mind of that other great American obsession (now exported globally) – *fame* – and made me think of it, too, as a response to scale. An obsession with mass media, with popular culture, with all the celebrity faces glowing on screens and glossy pages, seemed like yet another attempt to clutch at something shared.

· · · · · ● ● ● · · ·

Even before those deaths and their blanket media coverage, though, my wife and I were being reminded of another brand of fame on those road trips, for surely famous sights and landmarks count as celebrities of sorts, too, immortalized as they are in photographs, on television, in books and movies. Landmarks, indeed, might qualify as our oldest celebrities – think of the pyramids, or the Coliseum, the Parthenon or the Great Wall – global images, like those of more recent 'stars' such as the Eiffel Tower, or Big Ben, or the Empire State Building, that we grow up with and encounter countless times in our lives.

But if the famous – whether people or sights – give us something to share, there are obvious differences between them, too. It's easier to visit the latter, for one thing, though when we do, we experience in part the same odd shock of recognition that we feel when we spot a famous person on the street. We sense at once that we know them intimately, have always known them, even if we've never met them before, never set foot in this place before.

I used to think that we visited such places to assure ourselves – to confirm that such sights, previously only glimpsed in two dimensions, really exist – but I suspect that what also thrills us in such encounters is a momentary, vertiginous sense of our own *un*reality. These places are iconic, and by approaching them we become briefly iconic too, just as we might glancingly enter the aura of a famous person we're photographed with. Consider how swiftly we rush to put ourselves *in* the picture, literally, how intent we are on rendering the three-dimensional reality before us two-dimensional again via photography – the key difference being that once that image is printed or displayed, we'll now be in the scene ourselves. I'm reminded here of the Leaning Tower of Pisa, which I saw years earlier as a teenager on a brief stop-over in that city, and the iconic/ ironic photo opportunity we all succumb to there, posing, hands out, as if propping up the toppling tower, an illusion – of interaction, of proximity – only possible in two dimensions.

The other distinction between famous people and famous places, of course, is that the former will inevitably die. When they do we mourn them, but perhaps we also mourn the very fact that they *can* die. The ultimate allure of fame, after all, is the illusion of immortality. It's the nearest many of us can get to imagining an afterlife.

. . . . . • . . . . .

One last US trip, alone this time, and not by car. I was in Washington, DC, on the morning of 9/11, serving as a judge for the National Endowment for the Arts' fellowships, one of a group of writers gathered in an upper-floor conference room in the Old Post Office building at 1100 Pennsylvania Avenue (about halfway between the White House and the Capitol building). From its windows we could glimpse the smoke from the Pentagon as a smudge on the horizon before we were evacuated back to our hotel seven blocks north. There, on TV, I watched the towers of the World Trade Center come down. And while the loss of life was appalling, it was the image of those landmarks collapsing that staggered me most. I didn't know those poor people (though reading their obituaries in the weeks to come was heartbreaking), but I knew those buildings, had been in them myself.

Reality itself seemed to shudder in those moments. And the terrorists surely knew that it would. They were tourists, too, after all. They passed their free time at Sea World and the San Diego Zoo; they met up in Las Vegas, large-scale models of all the famous world sights craning over their shoulders as they plotted; they bought their tickets on expedia.com. Mohammed Atta signed up for American Airlines' frequent flyer program on August 25th, 2001. And the sights we see today – the Golden Gate Bridge, the Sears Tower, the Washington Monument, the Statue of Liberty, and farther afield, St Peter's, the Taj Mahal, the Sydney Opera House – are all altered since, each overlaid with a ghostly pair of cross-hairs.

Those terrorists killed three thousand people, destroyed buildings, put a stop to air travel for several days, and altered it for all of us for years to come. I and my fellow writers, for want of anything else to do, went back to our deliberations, and then when we were allowed and able left town as best we could. One colleague bought a car – none could be rented – to drive home cross-country (to the Pacific

Northwest as it happened). I caught the train north to Boston, where I (and the terrorists) had earlier flown from, passing through New York on the way, seeing the smoke and the absence over lower Manhattan – that iconic, altered skyline – from a slowly moving train car.

But on the night of 9/11, I'd walked out of my hotel into the quiet streets of the capital. I'd been able to get through to my wife by phone and she'd begged me to keep safe, stay indoors, and I'd promised I would. But I lied. I wanted to see the White House, felt drawn to it, and so I walked the half-dozen or so blocks towards the flood-lit glow of it. There were police cruisers blocking Pennsylvania Avenue in front, but it was *there*, and so were we – myself, and others like me who'd come to see it. We were staring at it, drinking it in, imprinting it, as if we'd never seen it before – which in a way we hadn't, not like this, small and brittle looking, pale as bone against the night sky. And no one was taking photos. In retrospect it feels as if it would have been inappropriate somehow, disrespectful even, but perhaps it was simply because we didn't need to. The building had never been more real.

Postscript

No one may have been taking photos outside the White House that night, but a couple of weeks later a briefly famous photo appeared on the internet. It shows a man, nondescript but clearly a tourist by the tense casualness of his pose, on the observation deck of one of the Twin Towers. It's a bright sunny day, the sky is blue, and below him, looming hugely over his shoulder as he smiles at the camera (you want to shout, as if at a pantomime, *Behind you!*) is a plane. A stunning image, the photo was supposedly found in a camera in the ruins at Ground Zero.

Only it wasn't. It's a fake, created by a Hungarian man called Peter, sometimes known as the 'tourist of death' (his face and figure have subsequently been photoshopped into dozens of other disaster scenes – floods, earthquakes – giving him a macabre ubiquity somewhere between Waldo and the Grim Reaper).

If this seems appalling, it is. But if it also seems on reflection queasily beguiling, it's that too, I think. This image of the frozen *before* renders the disaster at once more and less real. We stare the horror in the face, even as – once we know the photo is faked – we feel a kind of giddy relief that this one 'victim' has been spared. What really fascinates though is the motive to make such an image, to put oneself *in* the picture. It feels both empathic – a reaching out – and a denial, not of the dead, but of death itself. The photo might be a cheat – one reason we decry it – but perhaps it's not meant to cheat *us*.

After all, much as it shocks us when Diana, or a Kennedy, Marilyn, Elvis, James Dean or Buddy Holly (two more travel fatalities) dies, what stirs us too is the way their fame lives on, undiminished (even enhanced). Their very ends become famous, their deaths immortal. And then we visit their remains – their homes, their statues, their graves – and all the other monuments to the dead (Mount Rushmore and Little Big Horn among them, but really what monument isn't a mausoleum to someone who built it, or lived in it, or even visited it). And we take our pictures with them.

In some sense we are, all of us, in the end, tourists of death.

Joyce Carol Oates is a recipient of the National Humanities Medal, the National Book Critics Circle Ivan Sandrof Lifetime Achievement Award, the National Book Award and the PEN/Malamud Award for Excellence in Short Fiction. Author of the national bestsellers *A Widow's Story, We Were the Mulvaneys, Blonde* and *The Falls*, she is the Roger S. Berlind Distinguished Professor of the Humanities at Princeton University and has been a member of the American Academy of Arts and Letters since 1978. Her most recent books are the novel *Mudwoman* and the story collection *The Corn Maiden*. In the spring of 2011, she co-taught a course in creative writing at San Quentin.

A Visit to San Quentin

BY JOYCE CAROL OATES

We came to San Quentin on a chill sunny morning in April 2011.

The visitor to San Quentin is surprised that, from a little distance, the prison buildings are very distinctive. The main building is likely to be warmly glowing in sunshine and more resembles a historic architectural landmark, or a resort hotel, than one of the most notorious prisons in North America. Beyond the prison compound, to the south, are hills as denuded of trees as the rolling, dreamlike hills in a Grant Wood painting; to the north are blue-sparkling San Francisco Bay and beyond it the glittering high-rise buildings of the fabled city of San Francisco several miles away.

San Quentin Point is one of the most valuable real estate parcels in the United States, so it's ironic that the prison, first built in 1852, the oldest prison in California, takes up 275 acres of this waterside property. You would almost think that some of the inmates must have spectacular views from their cell windows – except you will learn that San Quentin's cells, arranged in densely populated 'cell blocks' in the interiors of the buildings, like rabbit warrens, don't have windows.

On the morning we drove to San Quentin from
Berkeley, the sky was vivid-blue and the air in continual
 gusts. The hills beyond the prison were vivid-green
from an unusually wet and protracted Northern
California winter.

Is that the *prison?* – a first-time visitor is likely to exclaim.
But this is from a distance.

I had visited a maximum-security prison once before, in
Trenton, New Jersey, in the 1980s. It had not been a
pleasant experience nor one I had ever anticipated
repeating – and yet, on this day, I was scheduled to be
taken on a guided tour through San Quentin with
approximately fifteen other individuals of whom the great
majority were young women graduate students and their
female professor from a criminology course at a university
in San Francisco.

Waiting in line for the guided-tour leader to arrive, the
young women – you would have to call them girls in their
behavior, appearance, mannerisms – talked loudly and
vivaciously together as if oblivious of their surroundings;
once the tour began, they were to fall silent; and when the
tour led us into the very interior of the prison, where the
fact of what a prison *is* becomes viscerally evident, they
were very silent, abashed and intimidated. That is always
the way with the guided tour into a maximum security
prison: You are not being taken on a mere tour but 'taught a
lesson.' And you are not quite the person emerging whom
you'd believed yourself to be, entering.

In the parking lot, in the trunk of our car, we'd had to
leave behind all electronic devices, as well as our wallets,
from which we'd taken our IDs. In San Quentin you are
forbidden to bring many things designated as 'contraband'
and you are forbidden to wear certain colors – primarily

blue, the prisoners' color. Even men must not wear 'open' shoes, i.e. sandals. Your arms must be covered, and clothing 'appropriate.'

Despite the warning beforehand, one of our group, a man, was discovered to be wearing sandals; he had to acquire proper footwear from one of the guards before he was allowed into the facility.

Our tour guide was late. From remarks told to us, the man's 'lateness' was a matter of his own discretion: He was not often 'on time.' There was the sense, communicated to us subtly by guards, that civilians were not particularly welcome in the facility; it was a 'favor' to the public that guided tours were arranged from time to time. And so we were made to wait in the sunny, gusty air outside the first checkpoint, which was both a vehicular and a pedestrian checkpoint manned by a number of guards.

In the imagination a prison is a remote and lonely place, but in reality, a prison is a place of business: a busy place. Delivery vehicles constantly arrived to move through the checkpoint. Corrections officers and other employees arrived. When at last our tour leader arrived, a lieutenant corrections officer, we were led singly through the pedestrian checkpoint and along a hilly pavement in the direction of the prison, some distance away – to our left, beautiful San Francisco Bay reflecting the sun; to our right, the rolling hills of a pastoral landscape. The visitor is tempted to think, *This is a magical place. This is not an ugly place.*

We proceeded through the second checkpoint where we signed into a log and where, when we left, we would have to sign out: Otherwise, the prison would go into 'lockdown' – the assumption being that a visitor was unaccounted-for inside the facility.

Our wrists were stamped with invisible ink. Grimly we were told that if we forgot and washed our hands, and washed away the ink, we would precipitate another 'lockdown' – the assumption being that there was a visitor unaccounted-for inside the facility.

COs were passing through the checkpoint as we prepared to go through. It was prison protocol to allow them to go first. The guards were both female and male – the females as sturdy-bodied as the males, sexless in their dun-colored uniforms. They did not greet us, smile at us, acknowledge us at all.

The lieutenant led us into a spacious sun-filled courtyard. Here were extensive flowerbeds, planted by prisoners. There was not a prisoner in sight.

'The flag always flies at half-mast here.'

We stared at a memorial stone as the lieutenant spoke of COs who'd 'died in the line of duty' at San Quentin, a double column of names dating back to the nineteenth century. The lieutenant recounted for us how as a young CO he'd been on duty during the 'most violent ten minutes' in the prison's history, in 1969: A Black Panther defense attorney had smuggled a firearm into the prison to give to his client who hid it inside his clothing until, as he was being escorted back to his cell block, he suddenly began shooting, killing several COs and fellow prisoners before tower-guards shot him dead.

We were aware now of tower-guards. We were aware of high stone walls strung with razor wire like a deranged sort of tinsel. We were told that if a siren sounded, if the commandment *All down! All down!* was broadcast, we were to throw ourselves down to the ground without question. If we remained standing, we would be in danger of being shot down by guards in the towers. They would be training their rifles on us, invisibly.

Did we understand?

My old unease, that had begun at the first checkpoint, quickened now. For always you think, too late – *I have made a mistake coming here. Why did I come to this terrible place!*

The answers are idealist: To learn. To learn more about the world. To be less sheltered. To be less naïve. To *know*.

Americans imprison – and execute – so many more individuals in proportion to our population than any other country in the world except China, one is compelled to *know*.

The lieutenant was saying that a CO's family doesn't know if he or she will be returning home from the prison. Inside, anything can happen, and it is likely to happen suddenly and unexpectedly and irrevocably.

'Irrevocably' was not the lieutenant's exact word. But this was his meaning.

He led us across the square and into the prison chapel, which was non-denominational. At the front of the room, which had seats for perhaps one hundred and fifty people, was, not a crucifix, but a large cross in the shape of a T.

At a pulpit stood an inmate in blue prison attire, to address the tour group. He was in his thirties perhaps, with Hispanic features. Like one who has given a presentation many times before, he told us with disarming frankness about his life: how he'd belonged to a gang, how he'd killed his own sister in a moment of panicked confusion, how he'd been sentenced to thirty-years-to-life – meaning that he was a 'lifer,' who might be granted parole sometime, if he didn't jeopardize his chances inside the prison.

The inmate wore blue: blue shirt, blue sweatpants, loose clothing. Down the sides of the trouser legs were letters in vivid white:

P
R
I
S
O
N
E
R

The inmate prayed, he said. Every day of his life he prayed for his sister, his mother, his family, himself. His manner was eager, earnest. He was due to meet with the parole board that very afternoon, he said. (He'd been turned down for parole at least once; inmates are typically turned down many times before being granted parole, if ever.) You could see that this was a San Quentin inmate who had accrued the approval of the prison authority, and would not ever risk losing it: Once a gang member, now he was one of *theirs*.

One of *ours*. Someone like *ourselves*.

Obviously he'd been 'rehabilitated' in prison. And this was the goal of the enlightened prison – of course.

Abruptly then the session ended. The inmate was escorted from the pulpit by guards and the tour group was led out of the chapel by the lieutenant.

Now we were being led into the interior of the prison – the 'real' prison. We were led from the picturesque courtyard along a hilly paved walk, in a chilly wind. Around a corner, and into the 'Yard.'

That is, we stepped onto the edge of the 'Yard.' Here was a vast windswept space, part pavement and part scrubby grassland. We stared. Hundreds – could it really be

hundreds? – of inmates were in the Yard under the
supervision of what appeared to be, to the casual eye, a
dismayingly few guards.

Of course, there were the guard-towers: the armed guards.

The prison population was somewhere beyond 5000
inmates though the 'design capacity' was for 3082. Clearly
just a fraction of these inmates were in the Yard at this time
but their numbers seemed daunting.

We were led relentlessly forward, skirting the edge of the
Yard. We were surprised to see a number of older inmates,
several with long white beards, like comic representations
of elderly men; they walked with canes, on the dirt track,
while younger inmates jogged past them or, elsewhere in
the Yard, tossed basket balls at netless rims, lifted weights
and did exercises, or stood together talking, pacing about.
You had the impression of rippling, seething, pulsing energy
and restlessness, and you had the impression that the
nearer of the inmates were watching us covertly, intensely.
Everyone in the guided tour was very quiet now. The young
women visitors were quiet. The fact of the prison and what
it contained was beginning to become real to us, not merely
an idea. For there were no fences between the inmates and
us, only just open space.

The lieutenant advised us not to look at the inmates. Not
to stare.

'No "eye-contact." No "fraternizing" with inmates.'

The lieutenant explained how the prison population was
divided into gangs, primarily; and these gangs – African-
Americans, Hispanics, Mexicans (northern California,
southern California), 'whites,' and 'Chinese' (Asian) – had
territorial possession of particular parts of the Yard that
were off-limits to non-gang-members. There were desirable
areas of the Yard dominated by Hispanics and 'whites'

(Aryan Brotherhood) and less desirable areas, near the urinals, where African-Americans gathered. (Why? Because California African-Americans are so divided into warring gangs, they can't make up their differences in prison.)

We were shocked to see, not many yards away, open urinals in a row, against a wall. We were warned – *If anybody is using a urinal, don't look.*

It was a protocol of the Yard: *Don't look, don't stare. A man using one of the open-air urinals is invisible and to cause him to feel visible is to invite trouble.*

The lieutenant led us past the single-story wooden structure that held classrooms. He led us into a dining hall – a vast, double dining hall – with rows of tables empty at this time of day. You could not imagine this enormous dining hall filled with men: the noise, the restlessness; the food-smells, the smells of men's bodies. The lieutenant spoke of the murals on the walls, that had been painted by an inmate named Alfredo Santos in the 1950s: striking, bizarre, a collage of renderings of newspaper photos and more ordinary individuals including a heroin addict (Santos himself). They called to mind the slickly illustrative work of Thomas Hart Benton but also the matter-of-fact distortions of Hieronymus Bosch.

The lieutenant meant to entertain us by summoning a food-worker, to provide us with food-samples from the kitchen – 'Any volunteers?'

Two members of the tour volunteered, a man and one of the young criminology women. They took bites of what resembled chicken nuggets, burritos, French fries, and something that resembled cornmeal, and pronounced them 'Good.'

The lieutenant told of the feat of feeding thousands of men three times a day. The lieutenant spoke proudly

of the fact that the prison was mostly inmate-staffed –
'Otherwise, there couldn't be a prison.'

The original San Quentin had been built by prisoners, in fact.
It had housed only sixty-eight inmates. Prior to that, California's
first prison had been a 268-ton wooden ship anchored in San
Francisco Bay and equipped to hold thirty prisoners.

Now, the prison facility was badly overcrowded, like all
prison facilities in the economically stressed state of
California. Where there is overcrowding, three men to a cell,
men quartered in places meant for other purposes, like a
gym, there is likely to be more trouble.

The lieutenant told of uprisings in the dining hall,
sudden riots, gang-killings. At any meal there is the
possibility of violence, so many men crammed into so
relatively small a space. The lieutenant showed us a cache
of home-made weapons: a toothbrush sharpened to a deadly
point, a razor blade attached to a papier-mâché handle, a
metal hook fashioned out of paper clips, a spike, a nail, a
pencil … In the Yard, buried in the ground in certain places,
were similar weapons, which gangs controlled; as soon as
guards discovered the weapons and confiscated them, more
weapons appeared and were buried in the ground.

During our visit in the dining hall, sirens erupted. Bells
clanged. For a terrible few seconds it seemed to us that the
prison was after all going to go into 'lockdown' (whatever
precisely that meant: we had a vague, ominous sense of its
meaning), but fortunately, the sirens turned out to be a
false alarm.

Maybe it was a suicide attempt, the lieutenant said. Or
a suicide.

The lieutenant next led us to another grim building, and
another time, we went through a checkpoint. The invisible
ink on our wrists was examined in ultra-violet light.

I was trying to imagine a plausible scenario in which an individual who had not been officially admitted to San Quentin was now discovered in the very interior of the prison and would be identified as an impostor or an intruder through this scrutiny, but I could not imagine this scenario.

He was taking us to Cell-Block C, the lieutenant said. Into the very bowels of the prison, he might have said.

Until now, the visit to San Quentin had been bearable. It had not provoked anxiety or even much unease, I think. If there was unease, I had resolved not to think about it, at least not yet. I had come here to be educated and illuminated and not entertained. And the others in our group must have felt more or less the same. For nothing threatening had happened to us, except the temporary alarms in the dining room. Our only first-hand experience of an inmate had been the speaker in the chapel who had seemed to want to please us, like an earnest student. In the Yard, we'd seen men at a distance – it had seemed a safe distance.

But now in Cell-Block C there was a very different atmosphere. The air was tense as the air before an electrical storm. There was a powerful smell of men's bodies. And a high din as of the thrum of a hive – if you brought your ear close to the hive, you would be shocked at the myriad angry-sounding vibrations, that never sleep. We would see now the typical inmates of San Quentin, in their own habitat.

These were 'new recruits' in Cell-Block C. Their gang identifications had not yet been determined. They were younger than the typical San Quentin inmate, and more 'restless.' This was the population that was most susceptible to suicides, the lieutenant said, as well as 'other kinds of violence.'

The lieutenant introduced us to cell-block guards, who barely nodded at us. We were of no interest to them and if they felt anything for us, it was likely to be contempt. What the criminology students were thinking by this time, I could only guess. I knew, from my experience at the Trenton prison, that any close confrontation with prison inmates, though there are bars between you and them, is not going to be a pleasant experience and still less so for women.

As the lieutenant was telling us about the history of the cellblocks – and of their present-day overcrowding – a movement overhead attracted my attention and I looked up to see, on a catwalk about five feet above the lieutenant's head, a uniformed guard with a rifle resting in the crook of his arm. The guard did not so much as glance down at me. He was as indifferent to the guided tour as to the recited words of the tour guide. The barrel of his rifle did not seem quite aimed at anyone in the cell block but it was clearly in readiness of being aimed. On a wall nearby was the ominous sign NO WARNING SHOTS.

Three inmates had been taken from their cells and were standing in the narrow passageway, not far from us. We could not help but stare – as they stared at us, in turn – for these were prison-inmates of a kind you would find in a Hollywood action film: two Hispanics and a 'white' man, husky, muscled, beefy, deep-chested, with thick necks. The white man had a shaved head and was covered in tattoos of a lurid sort, Nazi swastikas primarily. I had never seen anyone with a scalp tattooed in Nazi tattoos. The man had to be a member of the notorious Aryan Brotherhood, a prison gang. Yet this man had been taken from his cell, he stood quietly in the aisle among guards as if in an easy sort of fraternization; apparently he was no threat to the guards or to us. As it turned out, he and the other two inmates had been paroled and would now be escorted out of the prison.

I thought, *But who would hire a man covered in Nazi tattoos?*

The answer could only be, *Another man covered in Nazi tattoos.*

The lieutenant now said, as I'd been hoping he would not, that it was time for a 'walk around the block.'

In Trenton, something of the same phraseology had been used. But the inmates we'd seen had not been confined to a cell block, but to a large grim windowless space like an animal pen. They'd been loose, milling and pacing about, restless, edgy, staring in our direction as we'd looked down at them from a raised platform, at a height of about five feet.

The situation was different here, I thought. Yet I felt a stab of panic, for perhaps the situation would come to the same thing. It had been a nightmare I'd more or less managed to forget, or had pushed out of my mind. I told myself, *It won't be the same thing again. I am prepared this time.*

I was safer here in the cell block because of the abundance of other, younger women in the group. To the inmates, some of whom had already glimpsed them, the criminology students must have looked like high school girls. Their presence in this grim place was a kind of outrage, a provocation; it would arouse excitement, frustration, incredulity, wrath. Adroitly I'd maneuvered myself to the front of the line, just behind the lieutenant. I would walk just behind him 'around the block' – I would not make the mistake of holding back and coming late in the line. For at the start of the walk, the inmates whose cells we passed wouldn't quite grasp the situation as we walked quickly by; but by the time the fourth or fifth visitor passed a cell, all the prisoners would have been alerted by shouts and whistles. There would be a nightmare, but it would be a contained nightmare and it would not be mine this time.

The lieutenant warned: 'Walk fast – move along. Don't stare into the cells. Don't get too close to the cells. Walk as far to the left as you can. If they can reach you, if they grab you, you might be seriously hurt. And the prison might go into lockdown.'

Several of the criminology students were asking if they could stay behind, if they could just wait and rejoin the group after the walk-around-the-block. Their voices were plaintive and pleading but the lieutenant explained that this was not possible.

'The tour takes us through Cell-Block C. We are all going to "walk around the block" together.'

Quietly enough the walk began along a walkway that spanned the full length of the first tier of cells. I was close behind the lieutenant and I was not going to look into the cells for I did not want to make 'eye-contact' with an inmate whose desire at that moment might be to reach grunting through the bars and grab me and not let go until guards swarmed to his cell. I did not have that sort of curiosity – I was determined to walk fast, and to keep in motion. And so, as I passed the cells, one after another after another, the men inside had but a blurred awareness of me, as, at the periphery of my vision, they were but a blurred presence to me, though I glimpsed enough to be aware of the cramped living conditions: bunk beds so close to the wall that inmates would have to pass sideways between the bunks and the walls, and a cell size of about nine by twelve feet. I was very nervous, and I was perspiring; I could hear, behind us, the uplifted voices of men, shouts, whistles, whooping noises of elation, derision. I would have liked to press my hands over my ears. I did not glance back, at the terrified young women, forced to walk this gauntlet as close as possible to the wall, away from the prison bars. I knew what they were feeling, as I'd had to run a gauntlet of a kind in Trenton.

But I'd been alone in my misery, in Trenton. For there, by chance, I'd been the single female in the guided tour, a much smaller group than that at San Quentin, only about five or six people. The Trenton prison had not seemed so 'secure' as San Quentin and the tour guide not so experienced, but that might have been a misconception.

In a haze of discomfort, I followed the lieutenant in the 'walk-around-the-block.' I did not inflame any inmate by passing too near his cell, or looking overtly into it; but I was aware of the rippling, rising excitement in my wake, as the young women were forced to march past the cells, one by one by one. The slumberous hive was being roused, shaken; the buzzing hum rose to crude shouts, whistles, whoops. *But I am spared, this time.*

When we left the cell block, to return to the outside air, the tour group was abashed, shaken. What a relief to get outside, to *breathe!* Especially the young women had been made to realize how little their *femininity* was valued, in such a place; to be *pretty* here, to suggest *sexual empowerment* here, was to invite the most primitive and pitiless violence, as in an atavistic revenge of the male against the female. Civilization protects the female against the male, essentially: This is a hard, crude truth to ponder.

The meaning of the walk-around-the-block is to make a woman understand this simple biological fact. Yet there are political overtones.

The meaning of the walk-around-the-block is to make both men and women understand: You must be protected from your fellow man, by rifles. And if you don't think so, you are very naïve, or a fool

Or, you're dead.

. . . . . • . • . . . .

We were exhausted by the cell block gauntlet and we were eager for the tour to end, but there was a final destination awaiting.

Not Death Row: 'We don't take visitors to Death Row.'

But we were led past a tall ugly building – the 'Condemned Unit' – which housed over seven hundred men awaiting execution. (Condemned women, of whom there are far fewer, are housed at the Central California Women's Facility in Chowchilla.) The lieutenant spoke to us with a sort of grim boastfulness of the famous inmates who'd been executed at San Quentin: Caryl Chessman, William Bonin (the 'Freeway Killer'), Clarence Ray Allen (at seventy-six, the 'oldest person ever executed in California,' in 2006) among many others. And there were those awaiting execution: pregnant-wife-killer Scott Peterson, serial killer-sadist Charles Ng, Richard Ramirez, the 'Night Stalker' of the 1980s. In a perverse way, the San Quentin authority was proud of its list of executed and condemned prisoners and proud of its distinction as the sole Death Row for men in the state of California.

When I'd asked the lieutenant which part of the prison he had most liked to work in, without hesitation he'd said Death Row.

This was a surprise to me. I asked him why and he said that the Death Row inmate was 'more settled.'

The Death Row inmate had 'come to accept' that he was going to die and some of them had acquired 'wisdom.'

Of course, some of them were hoping for reprieves. Many were involved with Legal Defense lawyers and anti-capital punishment volunteers working to get their death-sentences commuted. But the ones the lieutenant had liked to work with, he said, were the older men, that were 'settled' in their minds.

The lieutenant had not talked so much to any one of us, or so warmly.

He led us now to a nondescript building that housed the 'execution chamber.' With a key he unlocked the door that led directly into the chamber and so we did not have to pass through another checkpoint. We were not very enthusiastic about entering the 'execution chamber' but there was no escape.

'When the Death Warrant is signed, the clock starts ticking for the condemned man. When it's time, the Death Team comes for him and brings him here.'

The room was not large, windowless and dimly lighted. There was a feeling here of *underground*. Plain straight-back wooden chairs arranged in a semicircle in an incongruously ordinary space except that, at the front of the room, was a bathosphere.

A bathosphere! Painted robin's-egg blue.

The lieutenant explained that the prison had purchased a 'deep-sea diving bell' from a marine carnival some years ago, when execution was by cyanide gas. The diving bell was airproof, and efficient.

Slowly we shuffled inside. There was a bad odor here. The lieutenant was trying to seat us in 'witness's chairs' at the front of the room, that provided an intimate look through the slotted windows of the diving bell into the interior where what appeared to be a hospital gurney, outfitted with straps, was prominent.

'In the days when there was gas, it was practical to execute two at a time. Now, with lethal injection, they don't do that. And when we had an electric chair, they had just the one chair, not two.'

'Two men executed at once?'

'Yes, sir. When there was gas.'

But now, the lieutenant explained, gas had been declared *cruel and unusual punishment.* So there was just lethal injection – 'People think it's some easy way to die. But it ain't.'

A few of the young women students were sitting, weakly. But not at the front of the room; no one wanted to sit in these chairs which brought witnesses within mere inches of the diving-bell windows. (The chairs were so bizarrely close; a witness's knees would be pressed against the exterior of the diving-bell.) Most of us did not want to sit down at all, as if to remain standing might be to accelerate the visit, and our escape.

The plain wooden chairs so arranged suggested amateur theatrics – very amateur, as in a middle school. The (somewhat dingy) robin's-egg blue diving bell suggested sport, recreation, carny fun. But inside the bell, the death-apparatus with its sinister black straps suggested a makeshift operation room, as in a cheap horror film.

The lieutenant was indicating those front-row chairs reserved for 'family members of the victim.' Beside these were chairs for the warden and other prison officials and law enforcement officers who'd apprehended the inmate; in the second row were chairs for other professionals and interested parties; in the back row, chairs for the 'press.'

Someone asked if executions were televised or recorded. The lieutenant shook his head with a frown – 'No.'

I was wondering how the family of the victim could bear to sit so close to the diving bell, to peer through the narrow windows at the writhings of a dying man only inches away. Was this a way of assuaging grief, horror? Was this a way of providing 'closure'? I thought rather it must be another element of nightmare, a stark and irremediable image to set beside other, horrific images of loss and degradation. Yet it seemed to be an honored custom that the family of a murderer's victim was invited to the execution. Perhaps in older, less civilized societies the murderer's heart was also given to the victim's family, to do with it what they would.

But maybe it isn't given to us to understand, who have not suffered such losses, who cannot comprehend the appetite for blood, for revenge, for a settling of 'injustice' that so fueled ancient Greek tragedies, as the great revenge tragedies of the Renaissance amid which Shakespeare's *Hamlet* is the surpassing model.

Yet, I don't think I would want to 'witness.' Probably, I could not forgive, and I could not forget – but I would not want to 'witness' another's death, even for the sake of revenge.

The lieutenant was telling us that no one had been executed at San Quentin since 2006 – 'There's some court case pending.' But, he said, in a neutral voice that nonetheless suggested optimism, that was going to change soon – 'In another year or two, executions will be resumed.'

In the meantime, the numbers of the condemned were increasing in the 'Condemned Unit.'

'Now ladies, gentlemen – how would *you* choose to die?'

It was a jaunty, friendly question posed to us by the tour guide. Of course, it was a ritual question: You could assume that the lieutenant had asked it many times before.

'Gas, or lethal injection? Or – electrocution, hanging, firing squad? All were approved methods at one time.'

At first no one spoke. It was a disconcerting question and there seemed no good answer.

More fancifully the lieutenant said: 'Or maybe – hit by a truck? Jump off Golden Gate Bridge?'

Then, there were hesitant answers. The criminology students and their female professor volunteered: 'Lethal injection.'

The newest way of execution must always seem the most humane, I supposed. At one time, hanging. Or firing squad. Then, electrocution. Then gas. And now, with its suggestion of hospital care gone just slightly wrong – 'lethal injection.'

I said, I would start with one way of being executed and if I didn't like it, I'd switch to another.

It was an awkward sort of joke. It was the sort of joke a bright, brash ninth-grade boy might make to startle and impress his teacher. Why I said this, when I was feeling in no way like joking, I have no idea.

Except I resented the tour-guide quizzing us in this way. I resented the tour-guide punishing us, in his not so subtle prison-authority contempt for civilians.

No one laughed at my joke. The lieutenant frowned at me. 'But you have to choose,' he said. 'Gas, electrocution, lethal injection, hanging —'

I could not seem to reply. My awkward joke had been a surprise to me. Another party said, as I should have said, that he wouldn't choose – he would not participate in his own death. The lieutenant objected: If you don't choose, the warden will choose for you. But the man persisted: He would not participate in his own death.

This was a good answer, I thought. But really there was no good answer to the lieutenant's question.

It is said that, if you are resolutely against capital punishment, you should not educate yourself in the sorts of crimes for which the 'condemned' are executed. 'An eye for an eye, a tooth for a tooth' – originally, this was a liberal principle, to discourage disproportionate punishments, and punishments against relatives of the alleged criminal. It was not considered harsh but rather a reasonable and equitable punishment.

By this time I'd begun to feel very strange. My sense of myself was shrinking like a light made dim, dimmer – about to be extinguished. In a panic I thought, *Not here! I can't faint here.*

Somehow I made my way outside, into fresh air. Or maybe the tour was ending now. I was careful not to trip and fall, lose my balance and fall, for I did not want to attract attention, and I did not want to be 'weak.' It was my impression that the women in the group did not want to appear 'weak.' We had managed to get through the tour, and we were all still standing, though exhausted, and light-headed. A prison facility will suck the oxygen from your brain: You are left dazed and depleted and depressed and the depression will not lighten but in fact increase for several days as you think back over the experience; then, the depression will begin to fade, as even the worst memories will fade.

The execution chamber was the last stop at San Quentin. The lieutenant led us around a maze of buildings to the inner checkpoint and through the courtyard where the American flag flew at perpetual half-mast and so to the first, outer checkpoint and to freedom outside the gates. We dispersed, we were eager to be free of one another, hurrying in the parking lot to our vehicles, wind whipping our hair.

I felt the surge of relief and joy I'd felt in Trenton, exiting the prison there after what had seemed several hours of misery, but had been only a little more than a single hour. Never again!

On San Francisco Bay, sun glittered in dazzling ripples in slate-blue water.

Lloyd Jones is a writer based in Wellington, New Zealand. Among his published works are *The Book of Fame*, *Mister Pip* and *Hand Me Down World*. He studied politics at Victoria University, Wellington, from where he received an Honorary Doctorate in Literature in 2010. He has travelled extensively, particularly in Europe, the USA and the Pacific.

On My Way Home

BY LLOYD JONES

I sat in the bus, face pressed to the window, and her face in the very pink of youth gazed up at me; then the bus began to move and her face slid from one side of the window to the other.

For weeks, months actually, my expired visa had hung over our happy life in San Francisco. We lived in a walk-up apartment on McAllister, opposite a black Baptist church and above a black barber who never knew what to do with my straight licks, and so circled the problem with his clippers and yakked about a time during the war when he had visited Sydney, Australia. Sydney, Australia, he said, and it sounded odd and quite cool to hear it qualified in this way – *Sydney, Australia* – to the extent that it sounded like it might be a different place from the Sydney I knew, and undoubtedly was, because the barber had visited it before I was born.

Anyway, above the barbers and across from the Baptist church where on any Sunday night crowds of the faithful glowing with goodwill and love and certainty in their redemption spilled out onto the street, we went on living in a state of stubborn denial. One day I would have to leave. We both knew it. Now it was happening, the parting we had talked about, though always as an event cloaked in

unvisited time, like Sydney, Australia. She waved up
at the bus window, and I replied with a self-conscious
crowd-pleasing wave.

The bus moved across a judder bar and eased across like a
huge slug into the seedy downtown area of San Francisco.
There came another sickening bump as the bus moved onto
the freeway.

I should have gotten off that Greyhound bus, I should
have, and in my regret I had a moment of clarity about the
kind of fatal mistake that had led to any one of those
flopped-out lives on the street I used to marvel at, seeing as
how they appeared to have been flung so far from the
epicentre of another life, which I imagine at some point had
included a mother, a classroom, playing fields, and the
bright promise of a future.

Between San Francisco and LA I lost my hearing. I
wondered if medication for a head cold was responsible.
But this deafness wasn't the muffled hearing that comes with
a head cold. I was stone deaf. I couldn't hear a thing. The
couple in the next seat were chipping away at one another
but I couldn't hear any of it. I just watched their fish
mouths twitching.

The silence spread to LA. In and around the Greyhound
station downtown cars pushed and shoved into silent lanes,
the sidewalks were packed, but all silent, under silent skies.
Cars slipped out of shadows. Hispanic faces lit up with
laughter. I didn't hear any of it.

The neighbourhood felt familiar. In those days, and those
days need to be qualified – this was more than thirty years
ago, a different world in so many ways – my line into the
world was wholly and solely literature. I couldn't get enough
of the Black Sparrow Press writers, John Fante and in
particular Charles Bukowski, whose novels *Post Office* and

Factotum mapped the desperate kind of neighbourhood I now found myself in and suddenly had no appetite for.

So I hurried back to the station and caught a bus to San Diego. It would be just as easy as spending a night in LA. In the morning I would catch the bus back up there for my flight back home. And that's how it turned out; the next day I whizzed back up on the Greyhound and caught the night flight across the Pacific.

I need to say something about that night in San Diego. Because all misery aside, heartbreak and deafness, San Diego provided a moment that has outlasted the heartache of leaving everything behind.

It was dark by the time the bus rolled in. I couldn't be bothered with hunting down a budget hotel; not that where I stayed was any great shakes, but it did have a doorman and air conditioning. I changed out of my bus clothes and showered. I didn't have my hearing back but I felt more solid, more my old self.

I sat down by the window overlooking the street and that's when I saw the women. At first I didn't think of them as a discrete group. Nearby was a bus stop, but the women didn't strike me as a bus stop crowd. Some appeared to know one another; at least they were chatting away. They spread along the road, too many to be hookers, and in any case barely a car passed down that street while I stood at the window. As well, some of the women looked to be a bit long in the tooth to be plying that trade.

The building across the way from the hotel was nondescript, no windows, I thought maybe a warehouse of some kind; and that's where the women directed their attention. They gazed up to a place that I couldn't see because the curtain rod was in the way and I couldn't press my face to the window any harder. I gave up and switched my attention to the street below.

This time a woman wandered out to the road and craned her head. I shoved my face back against the window and managed to see a strip of blue lights come on in the top floor of the building. Down on the street the women were eleven; I thought to count them just in case it was information later required by the police because it had crossed my mind I might be witnessing the kind of event that leads to something else.

When I next looked, the women were reaching up with their arms and hands to catch bits of paper fluttering down the side of the building.

The papers have the same drifty floaty feel as snow, they shine as they enter the lit side of the building, and the women leap to catch them.

One of them, much younger than the others, is like a cat with a morsel. She carries a note away from the others to read under a streetlamp. I would like to know what is written on that note; I'd really love to know. The pain of separation is not much of a secret, but the thrill of that secret correspondence is.

While I have my face at the window she begins whooping and carrying on. The other women hurry over. She holds up the paper for them to read. Now they are all laughing and clapping. One woman jumps clean out of her shoes.

I try the window but it is sealed – not that it would do me any good anyhow, I am still stone deaf.

Next morning I crossed the road to search the pavement, but all the paper was gone. When I looked up, the brick side of the building reared away from me. It was impossible to tell at a glance what kind of a building it was, so I started to walk around in search of a way in, a door or a sign. But oddly, as I came around one corner I kept finding another corner, and so on it went, corner after corner, until I gave up and backtracked to where I had started.

I began to doubt what I had seen the night before. I counted up the floors in the hotel and found my window. No. I was not in doubt at all, but still it was mystifying.

I picked up my bag and re-crossed the road to the hotel. As I came through the doors, the receptionist looked up, not quite as pleased to see me as when I had checked in.

I described to him what I had seen from my window the night before, the women, the drifts of paper. Nothing I said seemed to come as a surprise. He heard me out, rammed his glasses back on, and taking my notebook because I was still stone deaf, wrote down the word 'jail'. And I thought of those women parading like cats in heat, casting their thin high-heeled shadows against the walls of the jail, and above all the need for words to be put down and their urgent need to be read.

I doubt I have ever seen a more devoted audience than those women standing on tiptoes to catch a note written by an inmate. And as I left town I remembered two years earlier when I had first got to the US, sitting in the local San Diego courtroom for something to do and marvelling at the parade of men in orange overalls, like something out of television that I might have seen at home, and at the process and the regular business-done sound of the judge's gavel coming down, when I followed the crazy smile of one bearded inmate – he wouldn't have been older than myself – to the young woman in the next row down from me, a little to my right, in a denim blue top and long brown hair tied in a knot at the nape, who, as I recollect, with a Madonna-like smile had slowly unbuttoned her blouse to pull her bare breast free. The judge banged his gavel down and roared out something like, 'Now that's enough, young lady.' That judge couldn't have been more wrong.

Steven Hall's first novel, *The Raw Shark Texts*, won the Somerset Maugham Award and the Borders Original Voices Award, and has been published in over thirty languages. In 2010 he was included on the *Telegraph*'s list of the twenty best British novelists under forty. He currently lives in London.

You, Me and the Sea

BY STEVEN HALL

It's 2007 and I'm walking along the beach at the bottom of Sea Lane, in Middleton-on-Sea, West Sussex, UK – about a mile from the faded seaside town of Bognor Regis.

The tide is almost all the way out, exposing the rock pools beyond the breakwater. It's raining, late afternoon, and I'm the only person on the beach. I have miles of wet, rippled sand to myself. Blue-grey thunderclouds are piled in the big, wide sky.

I'm in the process of leaving my partner. It's slow and painful and I feel awful a lot of the time. I say I've come here to think, but I suppose, really, what I'm doing is waiting. I don't know whether this is a good or horrible thing for me to do, because, by now, my compass is completely shot from it all. How many people in the same position are really doing the same thing when they say I need to get away and think? How many are actually waiting a few days out of respect or properness – a sort of extended minute's silence – because it's such an unkind and ridiculous truth that one not-very-special moment, on one not-very-special day or night, they simply knew it was all over?

So here I am. Staying at my aunt's seaside home and spending most of my time walking on the beach, hoping the wind and bad weather will eventually blow all this out of my head – blow my brain clear of everything – and I can *just stop thinking*.

It's important to say that my first novel had been published seven months earlier. The book is an entirely fictional story about loss and grief and a man being hunted by a very strange type of shark. I should also say that everything in *this* story, the story you're now reading, actually happened. It's all completely true. It's important to remember this, because, written as fiction, what happens next would seem pretty ridiculous.

So.

I'm walking along the empty beach in the rain, feeling sick and worrying and wondering about what I'm going to do or write next and how, when something moves, something down towards the sea, at the edge of the rock pools. A sinuous, solid black something. It flips or flaps – like a muscle spasm – up off the sand, then it falls back, lying flat.

I stop walking and watch.

The thing lies completely still.

I think maybe it's washed-up rubbish – a black carrier bag, caught and flapped by the wind. Or perhaps it's just my eyes, blurred by the rain and the cold, seeing jumps and movements that aren't really there at all.

But then the *something* flips itself into the air again, and there's no mistaking it – it's alive.

Fuck, I say.

The thing has to be a fish. But that isn't what surprises me.

You know how a goldfish looks when you lift it out of its tank? A sort of round, deflated, useless creature, wriggling hopelessly? Well, this is nothing at all like that. And it isn't like the chubby trout you see on ice in a fishmonger's either.

Even from some distance, it looks – aerodynamic.

This is a dark, sleek, serious thing.

I set off down the beach towards it, thinking I *know* those proportions, but also that it can't be what I think it is. Not on a rainy beach in West Sussex, England. Not on a beach a mile from Bognor Regis, for God's sake.

But the closer I get to the thing, the more it refuses to resolve itself into anything else. The closer I get, the more I know that the thing is *exactly* what I think it is. It flips itself into the air again as I get closer and then I'm standing over it and there's no doubt left at all ...

It's a shark.

It has the full complement of stiff, triangular fins, a long, curved tail, a big round shark-eye looking up at me from the sand, and a C-shaped mouth full of teeth.

It's a small, grey/brown, perfectly formed shark.

In length, it's about the same as the distance from my fingertips to my elbow, or perhaps a bit longer. Something between a foot-and-a-half and two feet, I guess. It must've been trapped as the tide retreated over the rock pools, then left high and dry when the sea pulled back altogether.

The shark springs again, then falls back to the sand.

Of course, if the shark doesn't go back in the water, it's going to die.

And at this moment, I realise it's incredibly important to me that the shark does not die. Not just because I hate to see any animal suffer, but because there is a task to be performed here, and the task is so stripped down and obvious, and the situation so very surreal, that it takes on the unnatural, stylised air of myth or parable, despite the fact that it is also entirely real and happening in the here-and-now. It's one of the strangest sensations of my entire life, but the facts seem perfectly clear:

I'm wet and cold and alone on a beach near Bognor Regis with a dying shark, and somehow I have to get this shark into the water.

I look up and down the beach.

There's nobody at all around.

Just me and the shark.

There's also nothing around that I can use to move the shark. The part of my brain that understands stories tells me this, tells me that's how it's going to be before I even begin to look, and sure enough, it's true. I try anyway. I try with all there is – a hopelessly small piece of driftwood and seaweed as a sort of scoop, but it's never going to work.

If I want to save the shark's life, the only way to do so is to reach down, grab hold of the shark around its middle, pick it up, and physically put it back in the sea myself.

And, to my surprise, I realise this is exactly what I'm about to do.

I push my jacket sleeve up my arm and look down at the shark, full of a sort of wild, giddy disbelief.

How to do this?

The shark has teeth, so I know I'm going to need to take hold of it quickly and firmly. But how solid are sharks? How robust? I have no idea. If I grab it too hard, am I going to kill it? On the other hand, if I don't grab it firmly enough, am I risking being bitten? Looking at the thing – very probably.

I decide I'm going to lunge and grab hold of it quickly and tightly behind the dorsal fin. If it turns out that sharks are actually fragile creatures – well.

I make a grab for the shark and know at once I've made the right choice – the creature is all rough skin and solid muscle, a gymnast's bicep wrapped in medium-grain sandpaper. The moment I have hold of it, the shark arches itself into a tense C-shape, like a taut bow, trying to get its mouth around to bite me. It doesn't wriggle or thrash at all, but tries with every bit of strength it has left to get its teeth to where my fingers are. But it can't.

I lift it up and take the few steps to the water's edge, shark held out in front of me, then I carefully lower it into the sea. I release my grip and pull my hand back fast.

The shark darts away amongst the submerged rock pools. In less than a second, it's gone.

I turn away, walk back up the beach.

It feels like something has been achieved, something great, something ridiculous, something not quite part of the real world – all of these things at once.

It's not until I get right back to the top of the beach that I realise I've made a mistake. I turn to look back at the place where I released the shark, and see a familiar black shape flipping and flopping on the sand.

The tide hasn't gone out. It's still *going* out.

All I'd managed to do was put the shark into another shallow, draining rock pool, so it could beach itself all over again. To save the shark's life, I'd have needed to actually wade out into the sea with it, past the rock pools, and let it go there.

I've underestimated the task. I've achieved nothing.

I set off back down the beach.

Picking up a small shark the second time is easier. You know how it's going to feel, what it will do (arch into that angry C shape, thrash a couple of times, but not so violently that you can't hold on) and what it will try to do (bite your fingers off). Almost before I know it, I'm walking out into the sea, feeling the cold water seep into my boots and soak my jeans, with the shark held out in front of me. I have to go slowly and carefully over the submerged rocks – the absolute last thing I want to do is trip and fall, fumbling face-first into the sea while carrying a small shark. This, I am quite sure, would be bad.

Eventually, I make it out past the rocks and feel soft sand under me again. I'm almost waist-deep in very cold seawater now. Wading towards the horizon. The drag of my jeans and waterlogged boots makes it hard to move quickly.

I stop.

Of course, there's now the one, obvious problem.

I have to put this small but angry shark back into the sea, with me.

I'm holding it so that its nose points out to the horizon, and I decide that what I should probably do is put a bit of distance between the two of us by releasing it before it actually hits the water – or, in other words, launch the shark a few feet away with a gentle throw, so that when it slips into the sea it'll be travelling away from me, and will then hopefully decide to continue doing so, and not turn around and come back.

Understanding that I have no control whatsoever over what happens the moment I let go, I throw the shark forward, and it slides into the sea a few feet away with an aerodynamic plop.

I see its shape in the swell for a second – powering out to sea (out to sea!) – and then it's gone.

I wade back, struggling over and around rocks on the way back to shore, cold, wet and starting to shiver.

Dripping on the beach, I pace, I crouch, I stamp my squelching feet.

I wait at the waterside for a long time.

I have to be sure that the job is done, and done properly.

But the small shark doesn't come back.

I walk up and down the beach to be sure. Then I walk up and down again.

I'm utterly soaked from sea and rain. I'm so cold I can barely feel my feet, fingers, mouth or nose. The whole, strange episode seems utterly remarkable to me. And obvious. Utterly, impossibly obvious, and all the more bizarre because of that.

I suppose that, by now, I've been waiting by the sea for around an hour.

Yes, the shark is most definitely gone.

The task is done.

I turn away from the water, and set off home.

Born in 1982, **Stefan Merrill Block** grew up in Plano, Texas. His first book, *The Story of Forgetting*, was an international bestseller and the winner of the Best First Fiction prize at the Rome International Festival of Literature, the Merck Serono Literature Prize, the Fiction Award from the Writers' League of Texas and the OVID Festival Prize from the Writers' Union of Romania. It was also a finalist for the debut fiction awards from IndieBound, Salon du Livre and the Center for Fiction. Following the publication of his second novel, *The Storm at the Door*, Stefan was awarded the University of Texas Dobie-Paisano Fellowship and a fellowship at the Santa Maddalena Foundation in Italy. Stefan's nonfiction has appeared in the *New York Times*, *Granta*, the *Guardian*, the *Los Angeles Times*, *Corriere della Sera* and other publications. He lives in Brooklyn.

The Fairbanks Shakespeare Camp

BY STEFAN MERRILL BLOCK

It was a bright 2am when my connecting flight from Utah descended toward the tarmac, a gray slot in the tundra. I had been sure to get a window seat; I pressed my nose against the plastic oval, searching for the mountain-fanged idyll I had imagined for weeks. But the landscape of Fairbanks, Alaska, appeared to be just an infinity of stunted evergreen forest, punctuated by the boring geometry of mass-produced buildings.

Typically, when planning a trip, I spend a good part of the preceding weeks researching the place online, luxuriating before the digitized splendors of my near future. But when my roommate, Anne, invited me to Fairbanks, where she had a stint as an actor for the Fairbanks Shakespeare Theatre, I accepted immediately and deliberately avoided learning anything about the place. Fairbanks seemed impossibly far, the edge of the habitable world, a liminal place between human civilization and hostile nature. Any uploaded snapshot would have trespassed upon my imaginings. And imagine I did: I would spend the two weeks of my trip in the verdant meadows that stretched all the way to the dead mountainous north, a landscape that fit well the brutal, romantic lives of its famous pilgrims, people like Timothy Treadwell, the ill-fated activist of *Grizzly Man*, or Christopher McCandless, the ill-fated adventurer of *Into the Wild*. Only now do I realize that every famous Alaskan traveler I can think of could be described as ill-fated.

Anne, who had been working in Fairbanks for the last couple months, picked me up outside baggage claim in a diesel truck with Hefty bags for windows. She had traded in her low-cut blouses for a paint-streaked hoodie and her feet, typically propped up in black pumps, now inhabited a dirt-grayed pair of sneakers. On the drive, as we shared our stories from the last weeks, I tried not to look out the window, wanting to delay the register of my disappointment at the nothing of the horizon, still just an endlessness of scraggly pines whimpering off into the distance. This landscape seemed more Ingmar Bergman than Timothy Treadwell.

We drove north out of Fairbanks, the road signs counting our distance from places called Chicken and North Pole. We were headed for the Fairbanks Shakespeare Camp, a settlement that the theater company had carved out of a birch forest to provide its cast and crew a place to live rent-free.

The expressway thinned to a two-lane highway, which soon gave way to a dirt road, and at last unspooled into a rutted path that ribboned through an anonymous patch of forest. Looking out the window, I understood that proximity to pavement was the Alaskan metric for wealth: modern, aluminum-sided houses lined the freeway; the dusted windows of log cabins stared vacantly out at the cracked highway; sheds and shacks slouched along the dirt road. And in the slow, hiccupping movement down that rutted path I looked out at the corpse of a school bus, its roof staved in, looking remarkably similar to the place where Christopher

McCandless died, but in a far less romantic setting. Next to the bus was a rusting travel-trailer, forsaken on cinder blocks, and the mess of clothes left out front suggested current or at least recent habitation. My liberal guilt jabbed at me. I thought of the impoverished people who lived this lonesome way, powerless and without water in a moldering camper at the edge of the world. I wondered about the aspirant McCandless who might be living there now, the sort of hale and hirsute man who could bear such an existence.

And then, as if my imagination had summoned him, my Alaskan stereotype came waddling from the birch forest: a silver-bearded man, as round as tall, carrying a construction worker's stop sign on a pole, which he drove into the soft earth of the path. *STOP*, his sign commanded, and so we stopped for a long, blinking moment. From the road's opposite side, his stooped, feminine equivalent caned her way from the forest, a scroll of paper rolled under her arm. The dashboard clock read 4am. From the dusky forest came the sounds of men screaming.

. . . .

I went to the woods, like a type-A Thoreau, because I wished to work deliberately. Over the previous spring and summer in New York, I had sprinted through the first draft of a novel. Ablaze with productivity, I had powered through paragraphs at speeds clockable by radar gun. And yet, when I finally read those pages, I found little to care about, and I immediately consigned the whole thing to my graveyard of literary projects, a memory stick I keep in the top of my closet. For the following weeks, bookless and aimless, I focused on ways to make my days feel purposeful – over pricey Brooklyn microbrews, I made a boozy para-career out of complaining to other writers about the difficulty of the writing I was no longer doing. Each morning, I'd wake to palpate a liver-shaped ache and spend a morose few minutes regretting the ways I had saddened my already depressed savings account. From my bed, I could almost hear the whistle of the deep absence on my computer's hard drive.

Eliminate my distractions, I decided, and I would have no choice but to produce pages. I lived in New York City, but I was going to a theater camp in Fairbanks to become more productive. Writers play all sorts of tricks on themselves.

· · · · · • • · · · ·

The shouting grew louder, a cacophony that resolved into what sounded, to my ears, like rebel yells, blood-rich screams. The shouters were drawing closer, fleshy movement flitting between the dusky birch trees. I turned to Anne, who was hysterical, but I couldn't tell if she was weeping or laughing. Such was my panic that I had forgotten Ma and Pa Cerberus, the gatekeepers to our passage. But the hunched woman waved at me and unfurled the sign under her arm. On the paper, someone had drawn a crude rendition of a duck-crossing road sign, and – beneath it – painted the word *WELCOME*. No, not a Rebel Yell – it was something equally avid but sillier, men quacking as ducks. And, at last, the quackers were upon us. Five bearded men, doing their best duck-waddle in a row, naked but for their dirt and bruises.

What the fuck? I said.

This, Anne choked through tears, *is the welcome committee.*

We're – what? There?

Welcome to camp!

I surveyed the mess of rust-trimmed trailers and sheds in the distance. Nothing looked like it could survive a hard rain.

But, wait. Wait. Where are the cabins?

I think they picked that one out for you, Anne said, gesturing at the trailer I had just pitied.

. . . . . • . . . . .

After nine hours of travel, my frayed thoughts could focus only on a vision of a cool pillow against my face. Already, I had begun to worry about how my exhaustion would ruin the next day of writing. As I mounted a musty futon, grateful for the powerless camper's dim light that forbade a good look at the stains on the sheets, I told myself, *1000 words tomorrow, no matter what.*

It would have been a fine resolution, if in the Fairbanks Shakespeare Camp in the month of July there were such a thing as today or tomorrow.

I closed my eyes. With the swift efficiency of a toilet's flush, my mind swirled toward sleep, when the bearded men came back. They pounded at the door and did not wait for a reply to enter the crouched, tin space of my camper, where two of them informed me, with a little offense, that I was missing the welcome party they had just begun for me.

Welcome party? But it's five in the morning!

Hey, bub, it's summertime! one of the beards told me, his crisp thespian's voice incongruous, coming from the hole in the red nest of his face. *No day, no night, no bedtime!*

I sat up, gravity twice its normal pull.

So when do you sleep?

Whenever you drop!

I think I'm dropping.

No, you're not, the other beard said. *You, my friend, are drinking.*

I followed my hosts down the gravel path that led to the center of camp: a shed that housed a jury-rigged kitchen, a scattering of shacks and outhouses, and the fire pit, where a stack of wood from an old theater set burned. Scraps of old sets and props were everywhere. The plywood Verona of a long-ago production of *Romeo and Juliet* had been refashioned into a cabin. The main outhouse was a converted two-floor gallows, the wood painted the festive colors of Elizabethan England. One of the men wore a Falstaff's velvet cap.

500 words, I thought. *That will be a good enough start.*

A man cannot make him laugh, the feral-bearded Falstaff said, lobbing a can of Red Dog Lager in my direction. *But that's no marvel; he drinks no wine.*

. . . .

Was it that I welcomed these new distractions as I had the old ones in New York? Or did I just want to be an accommodating guest? With the unburdening of six or seven tall boys and a few tokes of a greasy *medicine pipe,* I stopped counting words and hours.

Those days (nights? afternoons? mornings?) are hazy. I remember participating in a tomahawk-throwing contest, digging up a suitcase of cheese the men had buried in the permafrost, helping to assemble a makeshift stage for the local band that had decided to put on an impromptu show. Is it possible that the hundreds of dreadlocked, hemp-sacked Alaskans that I remember actually came? That is how I remember it. The grease of our cooking rose into my unshaven face, already thickening my stubble into a grimy short beard.

. . . .

The Fairbanks Shakespeare Theater's main stage was a few miles away, but the real show, I saw from my boozy vantage, was here. It was a camp, but it was also a living set that the crew and actors continuously constructed and demolished, the set of an impromptu campfire cabaret. Just as day became night without any distinction, audience became performer became audience, a booze- and hallucinogen-generated theater of improvisation.

Some of these performances were camp classics: One of the beards would pick up a guitar and serenade us with wandering Dylan tunes, or worry us with tales of the people who had gone missing in the forest that was all around us. And yet, just as often, the performances were delightfully bizarre. We heated the fire poker and singed portraits of one another into the trees. Another beard, a set designer, showed us how he had recently used the same poker to brand primitive designs into his forearm. Anne and her fellow cast members recited Shakespeare's soliloquies over the fire like incantations. A guest of the camp, a comely and diffident-seeming young woman, told me she was a performance artist, and later gave us a demonstration of her work, lancing needle-tipped feathers into her skin, hanging herself from meat hooks through the nape of her neck, and swinging from the rafters. At all hours, a pack of Alaskan sled dogs penned next door bayed and whined.

Eventually, of course, my Fairbanks bedtime came, and when I woke, I woke with a hangover beyond all reckoning. My laptop still slept in my backpack. The wan light in my trailer was like my aching sobriety, grimly lighting an alternate and far less generous view of the place: My *cabin*, once again, was just a broken-down trailer in a squalid camp. I counted off bitter diagnoses: alcoholism, poverty, aimlessness. When I opened my computer at the table in the kitchen shed, I saw a still blank Word document and a date that was nearly a week after my arrival. I had come here to escape distractions, but I began plotting an escape from my escape.

While I was on hold with my airline, one of the beards came into the kitchen, dug through a cooler and tossed me another can of Red Dog. *Finish up whatever you're doing,* he told me, *we're gonna go see the play.*

Oh, right, the play. In the theater of camp life, I had nearly forgotten the actual stage. Anne and a few of the others would sometimes leave for a few hours, but always they soon returned with a few fresh 30-packs, and back at camp it could seem that their stage work was just some side errand they did while going on a beer run.

But don't worry, the beard reassured me. *First, we'll get loaded.*

Jesus, I said. *How do you ever get anything done?*

Oh, that's a winter worry. It's summertime! Get in the truck.

. . . .

The outdoor stage of the Fairbanks Shakespeare Theater was like the dressed-up version of camp: the same warped, secondhand wood, nailed and freshly painted. Like we campers who had put on our button-up shirts for a night at the theater, the set was passable but wouldn't really fool anyone. This performance of *The Taming of the Shrew,* which starred Anne in the role of Katherina, would be the last of the season. I found a folding chair and sat.

Like a tongue to a sore tooth, my thoughts returned, as ever, to my abandoned book. What had gone wrong? Should I have known sooner that I was wasting my time? I asked myself the question I'd been asking all day, and also for the last weeks: How had I let myself go as I had, drifting so far from my work?

The old stereo system bleated sickly, a worn-out recording of a Renaissance trumpet signal. I looked up, surprised to find myself in a packed theater, every seat taken, many double-occupied with children on their parents' laps, all craning their necks for a clear view of the Fairbanks Shakespeare Theater's final performance. When Lucentio bounded onto stage, the audience applauded. When Anne-as-Katherina chased Bianca through the rows of seats, we yelped with laughter. When Anne smashed and licked empty plates in a hysterical display of mock-starvation, I lifted a Red Dog tall boy and toasted with the beards.

This was a Fairbanks evening at the theater: The sun was still up, the crew was drunk, the stage was crude. And, just two hours from now, we would begin the work of rendering the ersatz Renaissance villa back into firewood and outhouses. Audience, cast and crew would disperse and return to worry, work and winter.

Forward, I pray, since we have come so far: When Anne vowed her submission to Petruchio's strange whims and notions, she spoke also of our own willing submission to this moment at the Fairbanks Shakespeare Theater, the gratitude with which, for this summery second, we could forget ourselves, our place and our worries, and believe we were continents and centuries away. Back in New York, Fairbanks would seem almost as impossible and imagined as it had before I left. As a stubborn July sun in Brooklyn burned away the haze of THC and beery toxins, my memories would seem as unlikely as daydreams. But one thing I would remember perfectly, when I stopped counting words and finally started to write, was that kind of forgetting.

Pico Iyer is the author of two novels, *Cuba and the Night* and *Abandon*, and one work of nonfiction often misidentified as a novel (*The Lady and the Monk*). He has also published eight works of nonfiction, including *Video Night in Kathmandu*, *The Global Soul* and *The Open Road*. The first draft of his most recent book, *The Man within My Head*, was entirely fictional; the last draft was pure nonfiction.

When Things Make No Sense

BY PICO IYER

We'd met barely five minutes before, and already, insofar as I could tell, the bright-eyed young woman with whom I was walking through the leafy streets of Vedado in Havana was proposing marriage. This had nothing to do with me, I knew; I'd received several other proposals – propositions for life, in effect – already that week. Soon (I'd agreed to take this friend of a friend to a 'dollar store,' technically open only to foreigners) this highly eligible woman was telling me how she was going to set sail the next week for Miami; some friends of hers were about to oust Fidel – 'You know the C.I.A.?' – and things were going to be different, very different, soon. But I shouldn't tell a soul.

I couldn't, in any case, because a man was approaching us now – we were near the Malecón – and asking if I wanted to buy a turtle.

Fiction was impossible in Revolutionary Cuba, I quickly came to feel; even more than in Haiti, or India, or other of the tumultuous places of everyday chaos that I knew, so much was happening, so loudly, at every minute, both on the streets and in the overheated minds all around, that it stretched credulity in every direction. In part, this was a register of frustration, of course; the island had been condemned to thirty years at that point of strutting in place. In part it was a function of need: people had to have dramas, rumors and fantasies because they were not allowed much in the way of real lives. But as much as anything, it was a reflection of a passionate, theatrical, over-the-top culture where strangers on every side were sobbing and shouting and laughing in the streets, at all hours of the day and night, with operatic virtuosity, while also reminding me, under their breath, that my best friend here was probably an informer, and I should be careful of Lourdes, who would report even her sister to the neighborhood committee, and the proposal I'd just received had come from someone whose motives could not entirely be trusted.

As I began returning to the country, year after year, in the late 1980s, I realized that even a transcript of a typical day's activities – where a friend in prison came out to greet me with a smile (he had three guaranteed meals a day here, he told me, and security and quiet, everything he couldn't get at home); where the phone calls I was asked to make to loved ones who'd made it to the U.S. ended in static or stories of gang killings – would beggar a reader's belief; many of my friends outside Cuba lived in Jane Austen or Henry James worlds where it was hard to credit the desperation and suspicion that would make kids shoot themselves up with the AIDS virus, as I was being told they did in Cuba.

. . . .

One day I was sitting in an apartment on Calle 23, across from the university. I've told this story often, because it keeps going round and round in my head, and each time it gives off a different resonance. The Top 40 Countdown was coming in from some radio station in Florida, and copies of Sartre and Dostoevsky were all around us. A rooster called Reagan, in honor of its squawking, was clucking across the rooftop outside. And inside, thanks to our conversation, I might have been in an apartment in the 5th arrondissement, or one of the loftier quarters in Madrid: the students around me seemed to know far more about many aspects of the world, not least Oliver Stone's latest acts of insurrection, than I did.

'Where do you come from?' one asked, inevitably.

I knew the answer; I'd been to Cuba several times before.

'California,' I said (though there were many other places I could have named). California was the place these kids occupied as squatters in their heads; it was everything Cuba was not, as they saw it, and many, many had sisters, uncles, even wives who'd made it there, so that one part of their lives was now situated in Gardena – or Daly City – though out of reach, it might seem, forever.

'I have a brother in California,' one of the worldly-wise students said, not unexpectedly. 'He lives in this place called Tamal. You know it?'

I didn't.

'In this big house. He's got swimming pools and tennis courts. Four or five cars, I think.' I didn't need to hear what came next: please, please, please could I take a letter to the brother – the postal service between the neighboring enemies seldom worked, and e-mail had not really arrived in 1989 – so that he could get the stranded prisoner now talking to me out of Havana?

I said yes, of course, though earlier trips to Havana and ten or twenty letters collected on each one had made me sad about the likely outcome: the letters came back to me unopened, or disappeared into some black hole containing Cubans who, having left Cuba, no longer wanted to think of it or were no longer alive. I had to take the letter, but I was skeptical about the value of committing it to the heavens.

I was wrong. As I was about nearly everything in Cuba. Barely a week passed and a letter was in my mailbox in Santa Barbara from this town, Tamal, I'd never heard of. He was so happy to hear from his brother, the brother in California wrote; he couldn't tell me how he missed Cuba. But did his brother know that he was in San Quentin Prison now? On Death Row?

Could his brother in Cuba do something – anything at all – to get him out and back to the Cuba he missed so much? This was a big building, and it had all kinds of facilities, but he would rather live with nothing in Havana, free, than amidst all these locked cars and barred recreational facilities.

I conveyed the message to the brother in Havana, though the mail between the two countries was so uncertain, I couldn't be sure my letter ever reached him; I looked for him the next time I flew down, but he, like so many, seemed to have disappeared into the ever-shifting anarchy that was daily life in Havana. Perhaps he'd even made it to America by then.

I made contact with the brother on Death Row, too, and then realized I should go no further; I was already out of my depth and any subsequent letter I sent would only excite hopes that could probably never be fulfilled. I came to think, too, how my very trips to Cuba likely did the same, which is maybe one reason why, not long thereafter, I stopped going down there.

I'd told myself no one could write fiction about Cuba; through my trips, I'd collected notes, 800 pages of them, for a non-fiction book on one friend I'd met who'd finally schemed his way out of the island. It would be a sequel to the two books I'd already written, on the way cultures dream of one another and on one woman, in Japan, who'd taken the first steps towards making her dreams real life.

But then a forest fire swept through the hills of Santa Barbara and reduced my family's house, and with it every last note (in those pre-computer days), to ash. I had to write about the country by which I was possessed, but I knew I could not begin to put most of what I'd experienced into the entirely fictional novel I now made up. Two brothers in countries separated by only 90 miles of water: neither knows the first thing about the other's circumstances and each, more poignantly, longs to be rescued by the other.

In a novel who'd believe that? It would seem too pat, too easily ironic. In life it was as humbling as every heartbreak is. The story keeps going around and around in my head, even as more and more of our screens sing brightly about how we're living in a small, small world.

Jan Morris was born in 1926. After graduating from Oxford, she spent ten years as a foreign correspondent, first for *The London Times*, then the *Guardian*, and was the only reporter with the expedition that first climbed Mt Everest in 1953. Since then she has written some forty books of travel, history, memoir, biography and imagination. The *Pax Britannica* trilogy evokes the climax and decline of the late British Empire. The memoir *Conundrum* concerns the author's change of sexual role in the 1970s, and *Hav* is a fictional account of an entirely imaginary European city. Morris has also written literary studies of Wales, Spain, the USA, Canada, Venice, Oxford, Sydney and Hong Kong, and unorthodox biographies of Abraham Lincoln and the British admiral Lord Fisher, who died in 1926 and with whom she proposes to have an affair in the afterlife. She is an ardent Euro-Welsh patriot, standing for a sovereign Wales within a British federation, a European confederation and eventually a conciliated World, and lives with her life's partner, Elizabeth, and her Norwegian forest cat, Ibsen, in the top left corner of Wales, in frequent contact with their four children.

The Way to Hav

BY JAN MORRIS

Years ago, feeling that I had written quite enough, and more than enough, about the great cities of the world, I decided to invent a brand-new metropolis of my own. I called it Hav. I imagined it, imprecisely, as being somewhere on an eastern Mediterranean coast, and I wrote two books about it. The place was totally fictional, all out of my head.

To my surprise, however, I found that many of my readers took it to be a real city, and wrote to ask me how to get there. How to get there indeed? How to get to Hav? The more I thought about it, the more clearly I realized that I had indeed made a long, long journey to reach my imaginary destination, a journey in the mind as well as in the body, through history as through geography. It was my life's journey, really, mirrored in fancy, but I sent my readers there by a convenient short cut. 'I made it all up,' I told them.

Of course that was no more than a half-truth, because to my Hav books, as to all fiction, there was a sub-stratum of fact. There never was such a city as Hav, but the experiences that created it in my mind, the emotions and the illusions that swirled about my prose, were not made up at all. Real places were blurred in my mind, sometimes only in my subconscious, and things that had happened in reality to me, during half a lifetime of travel, were transmuted willy-nilly into experiences of Hav.

In my books I imagined the geographical and historical circumstances of Hav ranging from the Middle Ages to our own times, and I see now in retrospect that I drew them from my acquaintance with half a dozen real cities. There was Gdansk, for instance, sometimes a city-state, sometimes a fief of one empire or another. There was Trieste, all alone at the head of the Adriatic, where cultures, languages and histories overlapped. There were the queer little Åland islands, only half subject to Sweden; Cetinje which was once the capital of the Montenegrin monarchy; and pockets of minority cultures like the Yezidis of Iraq or the Karaim Jews of Lithuania. And in the later pages of my Hav books brazen new cities of the 21st century insidiously suggested themselves, tinged with greed and tourism ...

All, every one, old and new, northern and southern, occidental and oriental – all lay along my route to Hav.

Many encounters on my life's real journey, too, have found themselves metamorphosed into Hav's imagined scenario. Have you heard the trumpeter of Krakow, whose heartrending hourly call from the tower of St Mary's has always seemed to me a very epitome of Polishness? Well, no doubt his call was sounding in my mind when I invented the trumpeter, traditionally an Armenian, whose call has for several centuries awoken Hav each morning to its work and its proud memories. The Electric Ferry which swims silently across Hav's harbour has surely chugged there, more noisily, directly from the waterfront of Bergen, and I first heard the characteristic banging of its slatted seats upon the Star Ferry in Hong Kong. The Conveyor Bridge across the Hav Narrows is undoubtedly related to the grand old Transporter Bridge that carries cars backwards and forwards across the mouth of the Usk in Wales. The strange Chinese tower of Hav owes something to the tomb towers of Iran.

I think images of Michael Jackson may have influenced my evocations of Nijinsky, who had come to Hav with the Diaghilev Ballet in the 1900s. No doubt the Circassians I met long ago in Amman, guarding King Hussein of Jordan, were related to the Assyrians who attended the exiled aspirant to the Caliphate in Hav. Only now, though, as I scour my subconscious for this essay, do I realize the genesis of the self-righteous ex-Hauptsturmfuhrer, exiled in his old age to Hav, who so insistently tried to persuade me of the Holocaust's redemptive justice – 'tragic millions', as he saw it, 'in pilgrimage to their own Calvaries'. Did I not draw him, all unwitting, from my memories of the trial of Adolf Eichmann at Jerusalem, when the ultimate mass murderer in his glass cage suggested to me 'an elderly pinched housewife in a flowered pinafore', priggish and petulant in his self-justification?

Much of my own life's pilgrimage has taken me through the shadow of the lost British Empire, and I felt its presence also in Hav, which was British for a time itself. The ambiguous grandeur of that once-majestic dominion has always haunted me, not least in the crumbling memorial slabs I have stumbled across from Tasmania to Alberta. It is not surprising that I discovered a moving specimen down by the waterfront at Hav, commemorating an officer of the Royal Engineers who had 'Left this Station to Report to the Commander of a yet Greater Corps'.

But then again I have always been subject to the seductions of Araby, and Hav in the old days was marvellously endowed with mosques, caravanserai, quarter-tone music and sensual lyrics – *Ah* (as one of the best known Hav poets put it) *what need have we of mosque / Or learned imam, / When into the garden of our delights / Flies the sweet dove of Allah's mercy, with her call to prayer?'* Where did I first hear the gentle cadence of that verse, or did I make that up too?

I am an old Welsh patriot, but I have a taste for the cosmopolitan. Between the wars Hav had been a ward of the League of Nations, governed jointly by the French, the Germans and the Italians, and I found myself delightfully at home hearing about the thriving multicultural Hav of the 1930s, when the night-clubs flourished and people like Benny Goodman and Maurice Chevalier were pleased to perform in them. I spent happy evenings myself, too, in what remained of those old night-spots, and it's an odd thing that while all my life I have preferred to go to bed early, in Hav I often found myself carousing the night away to the blast of jazz and the thudding of drums, until the Armenian trumpeter up on the hill alerted us all to the coming of the day.

Much of all this, this correlation between fact and fancy, the dream-journey and the actual, has only come back to me now, as I write this piece. I have always been more aware, though, that I have travelled my life itself in allegory, as it were. Mine was an allegorical journey, minutely reflecting grander motions of humanity, and the Hav books that properly represented its destination are literary symbolisms themselves.

They are built, I now realize, around a great defining moment of our times, the destruction of the World Trade Center in New York in 2001, which more or less coincided with the virtual destruction of Hav itself. The first book describes Hav as it was before that epochal calamity – a city rooted in the long historical past, reflecting and

glorying in the whole kaleidoscopic variety of an ancient
European city, rich in quirks and anomalies and references
and contradictions, messy, colourful, funny, endlessly
surprising. The second book, though, reflects the world,
and the city, that has evolved since 2001, and its rebuilt
Hav is far less engaging. Now the place is without bumps
and laughter. It is governed by dubiously fundamentalist
theology, and by a particularly greedy kind of capitalism.
Its architecture is loveless, its freedoms are muffled, and its
old sense of intriguing mystery has hardened into
something more sinister.

So do you still want to know the way to Hav? Probably
not. Better to think of the old place as pure make-believe ...

Alexander McCall Smith is the author of over eighty books on a wide variety of subjects. He has lived and worked in Africa, the setting of his well-known series of books, *The No. 1 Ladies' Detective Agency*. He has travelled extensively and now makes regular tours of the many countries throughout the world in which his books are published. He lives in Scotland with his wife, Elizabeth, a doctor.

A Tango with Freud

BY ALEXANDER MCCALL SMITH

Most of us, I suspect, have a list within ourselves of journeys we would like one day to undertake. The more organised among us go on to make these journeys, ticking them off one by one. Mongolia, riding horses by day and sleeping in yurts by night: *done*. The train journey from Singapore to Penang: *done*. And so on. Neither of these happens to be on my list, although both might be, if I had the time. My list, like many such things, features odd places that bear no real relation to one another, but that have for some reason caught my imagination.

I would like to get to Bolivia some day to speak to people about the Bolivian navy. Why? Bolivia is a landlocked country and it interests me that a country that has no access to the sea (they lost that a long time ago) should feel so strongly about having a navy. The fact that one has no sea should not inhibit one unduly, of course: they have a lake and that's enough of an excuse to have a large number of admirals – and an immensely popular Navy Day. And the kindly Argentineans allow them to keep a ship in one of their ports. I can imagine long conversations in cafés about the importance of having a navy and the difference between brown-water navies (lakes and rivers) and blue-water navies (the sea).

Bolivia remains unvisited, but then there is Mobile, Alabama, that I have visited on more than one occasion now. The name is what attracted me: *Mobile, Alabama*. What sheer poetry! What lovely, mellifluous, feminine sounds! And I had read that Mobile, by long tradition, is said to have more ghosts than any other town. Why, I wondered? When I went there I found the answer: the streets are shaded by oaks that form a natural canopy across the road. Ghosts, as everybody knows, like shade – and a slow, Southern life-style.

Alice Springs, in the middle of Australia, was ticked off the list only last year. Alice is an unexceptional town – apart from being in the middle of the immense waterless heart of a continent – but it had the good fortune of being in the title of Nevil Shute's great romantic novel, *A Town Like Alice*. It was because I had read that as a teenager, and loved it, that I knew that I must go there.

Casablanca was on the list for the same reason, and I shall never forget the sense of satisfaction, mixed with excitement, as my battered Mercedes taxi drew out of the airport at night, its headlights sweeping through the darkness to illuminate a road sign that said, simply and enticingly, *Casablanca*.

But the journey that I really wanted to make above all others was to Buenos Aires. Now, many people want to go to Buenos Aires because of the tango and the bars and cafés with which the dance is associated. The Argentineans say that they invented the tango, and that claim is widely accepted – except by the Uruguayans, who argue that it originated there. To most dance pilgrims, I suspect, it is no contest: Buenos Aires is the place.

The tango was not what drew me there, however. My interest in Buenos Aires is tied up with my interest in Freud and psychoanalytical theory. That in turn stems from a reading, in my early twenties, of W. H. Auden's poem *In Memory of Sigmund Freud*. This poem, written at a time when Auden still believed that psychology, and science in general, could provide us with the solutions to the problem of human evil, is a beautiful and moving tribute to a man who changed the way in which humanity looked at and understood itself. Auden's tribute inspired me to read more Freud, and over the years that followed I dipped into a wide range of Freudian literature. Some of that, of course, stretches credulity to breaking point; some is quite frankly funny (the *tennis as a substitute for sex* school of Freudianism); other parts contain profound and valuable insights. Overall, I felt that Freud liberated us in just the way in which Auden suggested.

Then I came across an item in an issue of the late lamented review, *Encounter*. A boxed snippet caught my attention. Buenos Aires, it suggested, was the epicentre of contemporary Freudianism, more so even than New York, where psychoanalysis was becoming a bit *passé*. Streets were named after prominent figures in the Freudian movement, it revealed, and the conversation in cafés was as likely to be about neuroses as it was about sport or politics. I filed this information away mentally, thinking that it would be interesting one day to visit the Freudian quarter in Buenos Aires and see just how Freudian it was. It struck me as remarkable that a city, outside the dreary example of the Communist world, could be so in thrall to what, after all, was a secular religion as to celebrate it through the naming of the streets. It seemed to me that this was an alternative, parallel world of the sort dreamed of in fiction.

Imagine a city, for instance, where the delivery of flowers is sufficiently important to merit the equipping of florists' vans with flashing blue lights to allow them through. Nowhere like that exists, but it could. Imagine a city where what is important to people is not commerce and the making of money, nor fashion, nor power, but the analysis of dreams ...

Over the years, Buenos Aires remained on the list. I got close, but did not actually make it. On one occasion, we travelled round the coast of South America on an ocean liner, calling on Tierra del Fuego along the way, but going nowhere near Buenos Aires. Then my wife and I received an invitation to spend a couple of weeks with a friend who was then the European Union's ambassador to Uruguay. Montevideo is but a hop on a plane from Buenos Aires and I decided that this was the time to make the trip. I wrote to the representative of the British Council in Argentina (a cultural diplomacy body) and asked for assistance in finding an interpreter and guide who would arrange for me to meet and interview psychoanalysts in Buenos Aires. They readily agreed to do this, and went further in offering to host a dinner for writers in the city to coincide with my visit.

Travelling somewhere with a purpose is so much more rewarding than travelling somewhere with no purpose beyond looking at the usual sights. I could not wait to see the Freudian quarter, and was taken there soon after arrival by my guide. The quarter is known as Villa Freud, and is centred on the Plaza Güemes in the Palermo area of the city. My guide no doubt had her views as to the sanity of a visitor whose preoccupation is seeing psychoanalysts, but if she did harbour such reservations, she did not reveal them. I was taken first to a street in which every second door seemed to have a small plate outside it announcing the presence of a psychoanalytical studio. There was a bookshop, too, that had nothing but psychoanalytical texts in its window and on its shelves. And there, as I had hoped, was the Café Sigi, named after the man who had started the whole process. The coffee seemed normal, although I imagined that most of those drinking it in the café that morning were not long out of their hourly encounter with their analyst, or perhaps on the way there.

We visited two psychoanalysts, chosen from opposite ends of the spectrum. One was a man who practised from a very modest office in Villa Freud. He spoke quietly and with passion about the difficult days he had experienced during the time of the generals. Psychoanalysis had been suppressed during those years, he explained, and its teaching in universities had been discouraged. I was not surprised: Auden's poem on Freud has something very pertinent to say about how psychoanalysis threatened what he called the 'ancient cultures of conceit' and how it would lead to the destruction of their 'lucrative patterns of frustration'. Exactly. Generals do not like psychoanalysis, and they had made those days very dark for its practitioners.

The other analyst operated in the higher echelons of Argentinean society. She received me in an extremely elegant penthouse flat, the glass walls of which afforded a striking view of the city. Her practice was made up of wealthy people and it kept her, it seemed, in considerable style. 'I spend part of the year in Paris,' she announced. That, again, should be no great surprise: Argentinean psychoanalysis was heavily influenced by Lacan's theories and continues to look to Lacanian leads.

The dinner took place that night. About fourteen people were around the table, mostly writers and journalists, but there were also a few university students. That, of course, is hardly a representative sample of the population, but nonetheless it struck me as quite remarkable that all except one or two of them were undergoing or had undergone psychoanalysis. This was revealed when my conversations of the earlier part of the day were mentioned. 'But of course I've had analysis,' said one of the guests. 'Who hasn't?'

The trip was brief. The following afternoon we left Buenos Aires to return to Montevideo. I had hardly seen anything of the city, but I had found what I had come to find. On the plane on the way back, looking down on the sediment-heavy waters of the River Plate like a tabletop of brown, I reflected on how the national obsession with Freud had come about. The historical explanation was clear enough: a national newspaper had started a dream analysis column back in the first half of the twentieth century. That had been popular, and readers had written in to describe their dreams and get advice on their meaning. Then the universities' psychology departments had appointed professors versed in psychoanalytical theory and in this way the whole process of proselytism had started. Soon everybody was aware of Freud and of the possibilities of psychoanalysis.

Yet that in itself is not enough to explain the extraordinary popularity of a theory and practice that is no longer widely supported in other countries: Freud survives elsewhere, but only in pieces, and as a distinctly minority interest. There must be something in the Argentinean sense of identity that compels them to seek self-understanding in this way. Is the obvious explanation the real one – that they are a nation of people from elsewhere, from Italy and other countries in a distant Europe from which they feel cast adrift? It is, after all, a remote country, far from its European cultural roots. Perhaps they need to find mother. Perhaps they need to find out where, and how, it went wrong, if indeed it has gone wrong. Perhaps their national dance has something to do with it, although even the mere asking of that question tips one over into the territory of Freudian parody.

There is a final question to ask. Does the fact that I felt I needed to make this journey in the first place tell me something about myself? It is possible that the making of any journey is revealing in that sense; we do not go to places *by accident*. Personally, I'd prefer not to know.

Born in South Africa, **Bryce Courtenay** was educated in Johannesburg and the UK. He arrived in Australia in 1958 and became an Australian citizen the following year. He entered advertising and over a career spanning thirty-four years was the creative director of McCann Erickson, J. Walter Thompson and George Patterson Advertising. During this period, he was invited by the Chinese government to give the first series of lectures on the subject of Advertising and Free Enterprise. He has also lectured in Asia, the UK, the USA, New Zealand, South Africa and Canada, in addition to his own country. However, he is best known as Australia's top-selling novelist, with titles such as *The Power of One*, which has been translated into twenty-one languages and is the subject of a major movie of the same name. His other books include *Tandia, The Potato Factory, A Recipe for Dreaming, Jessica, Smoky Joe's Café, Whitethorn, The Persimmon Tree, Fishing for Stars* and *The Story of Danny Dunn*. His most recent book is *Fortune Cookie*. In 1995 Bryce was awarded the Order of Australia AM, and in 2005 he was awarded the honorary degree of Doctor of Letters from the University of Newcastle.

Getting Travel Dirt Under Your Fingernails

BY BRYCE COURTENAY

On May 29, 1953, a British Expedition sent to reach the summit of Mount Everest finally succeeded with the Union Jack planted 8848 metres up on the world's highest mountain by New Zealander Edmund Hillary and Tenzing Norgay from Nepal. To the world at large it was a stupendous achievement by two men not far short of being regarded as physical giants. Hillary's comment upon reaching base camp, 'Well, we knocked the bastard off,' is now a part of the English language and a metaphor for extreme physical achievement.

Almost 60 years after the initial conquest, approximately 3200 mountaineers, male and female, have collectively summited the highest mountain on earth some 5000 times. This is not to suggest that Everest has become a mountain for a novice to undertake; all of these people have been fine climbers. Andrew Lock, by no means a household name and from my own country, Australia, has summited all fourteen of the world's 8000-metre peaks and has reached the top of Mount Everest on two separate occasions.

The point I make is not intended to detract from Hillary and Norgay but to illustrate that between that first remarkable undertaking 59 years ago and today, personal adventure travel has come of age. For a great many of us, our travel mindset has largely changed from seeing to doing or from observing to participating.

This participatory aspect has become increasingly necessary in the latter part of the twentieth century and the beginning of the twenty-first with the advent of television and the various portable mass communication systems we employ. It could be claimed that they have overpowered our visual sense. We have, for better or worse, vicariously entered a virtual world where we are constantly mentally and visually transported everywhere and, depending how you look at it, gratuitously assailed or rewarded by most of the planet's wonderful surprises.

We've observed the view from the highest mountains, travelled the endless deserts, crossed the seven seas while breasting the highest waves, explored the rivers, heard the thunder of great waters, traversed the boiling rapids, hacked our way through the densest jungles, seen the chaos, misery, joys and wonders of the world's great cities, viewed the monuments, buildings grand and ancient, eaten thousands of imaginary meals set in exotic locations, all of this and much more through the eyes of the ubiquitous camera lens that prowls and snoops and records every small and large creature and detail to simulate the actual experience of going.

The result of all this is that I believe we are in danger of becoming visually overloaded. We've seen but not been to *feel* the personal thrill and sense of achievement of standing on the top of the mountain or some similar experience, alone or with a group of friends, where all our senses are employed and are rewarded.

Of course we will still flock to Europe to see the historical monuments and be inspired by great art, historical sites and the continuity of cultures we mostly learned about in history and geography lessons at school. These secular pilgrimages along with religious ones will always remain a significant part of the purpose of travel.

However, the great addition to going somewhere familiar to our hearts and minds is the adventure of traversing the wildest unknown way, a way of travelling for the masses that started in earnest in the 1970s. This was when Europe and the United Kingdom no longer became the usual and often exclusive great travel destination for those of us who lived in countries where the imposition of European culture after conquest was still relatively recent. And when young Europeans and those from the British Isles first began to travel in large numbers to countries beyond the traditional nations close to them.

We began to understand that when we set out to go where the people are culturally or demonstrably different, strange, unfamiliar – even alien – to our normal expectations, then we do so on local terms. Or that when we do something physical or requiring mental stamina in unfamiliar and often frightening surroundings, our personal Everest, in both instances we become the recipient of a psychological change, small or large, but where we are rewarded with a meaningful contribution to understanding ourselves. I guess some may even refer to a trek to the Everest Base Camp, a voyage to Antarctica or an archaeological dig somewhere in the Near East as 'life-changing'. Equally, for many ordinary folk, both young and old, volunteering to work for small N.G.O.'s, using a professional skill or simply helping on a project to benefit the less fortunate becomes a truly meaningful and rewarding way to travel to far-flung places such as Vietnam, Nepal, Africa or South America, to name but a few.

The Ndebele are a small Southern African tribe who have a saying, *People are people because of other people.* Translated, this simply means that we only recognise and get to know ourselves, who and what we are and may become, by the presence, experiences and observations of other people. While we may worship nature and other life forms, for most of us the ways of people assume the central place in our lives.

And so for me experiencing and observing at close quarters the beliefs, habits, lifestyle and wisdom of people other than those from more or less my own cultural background is the supreme reward of travel. Good travel is returning home a slightly bigger part of everyone and not quite the same person as when you set out. The ultimate reward is arriving home with a sense and understanding of who we are mutually as members of the human race. If I could nominate a supreme evil in our world it would be xenophobia. It may well be the greatest curse the human race has imposed on itself.

It is this need to know who we collectively are, our similarities and differences, anxieties and joys, habits, values, beliefs and actions that has made me a writer. My job and ongoing fascination is to attempt to explain the human condition, the good and bad we share in common, love of family, the universal need simply to put bread on the table and some kind of roof over our head, this taken together with the pain and suffering others cause us or we bring upon ourselves, the differences, fears and instincts that make us quarrel, even kill each other in the name of a particular God or strip of land or doctrine or simply for greed or acquisition.

The novelist is said to thrive on conflict, the eternal struggle between good and evil with the good guy winning out in the end. But if my personal travel experiences are any indication, I am forced to conclude that individuals of every race, creed, colour or secular sophistication, if given half a chance, are willing and even anxious to share courtesies, laughter, generosity and joy with an open-minded traveller who is curious and anxious to learn about and to understand their culture without necessarily having to embrace it.

As I write these words, in 2012, setting out to travel has at times become a somewhat tedious and difficult process and one predominantly motivated by caution and fear. The constant onslaught of bad news from the media would have it that the world is a frighteningly dangerous place. In turn, governments routinely issue stern no-go or extreme-caution warnings for major parts of the planet we share. We have collectively allowed a handful of fanatics and zealots who by no means represent the values of the various races to which they belong to effectively deny travellers access to large parts of the world. Nowhere is said to be safe. Airport security, where everyone is a potential suspect, has become a huge and growing universal preoccupation where paranoia is the officially required psychological approach.

When I was recently embarking overseas from my own local airport, the universally and now routinely common X-ray of my carry-on luggage took place, and the nail file from the gentleman's manicure set I'd been given as a prize as a young schoolboy more than 61 years previously and had inadvertently tried to take aboard was confiscated. By the time I returned to Australia, having deliberately repeated carrying the manicure set on every flight through several countries, only the leather case and the nail buffer remained. The loss of the first grown-up possession I was ever given is obviously of no importance. But the concept that a nail file or a pair of nail clippers is a lethal weapon and constitutes a potential terrorist threat aboard a 747 jet indicates a state of universal caution, suspicion and fear that means the sheer adventure of travel, those wonderful freedom-seeking journeys into the unknown where you end up finding out as much about yourself as you do of others, may be coming to an end.

My greatest fear is that the few with agendas big and small can pull down the shutters and slam the doors to those of us who wish to explore the many joys and adventures available to young and older travellers. That my grandsons will be forced to return to the xenophobia and Euro-centric world that formed the travel conventions when I put my first furtive foot forward in the 1950s.

My most recent reason to leave Australia was to visit Israel. My government warned me that the destination was potentially dangerous and a number of friends looked askance when I told them my major purpose was to visit the walled city of Jerusalem, a location that for twenty-two centuries those of us in the Western and Near Eastern side of the world have regarded somewhat arrogantly as the true centre of civilization. It is here that three of the world's great religions have taken turns beating each other up in the name of the same God in various disguises. At this particular moment in time, eighteen-year-old Israeli males and females in military uniform walk around wielding automatic machine guns and yet another wall to keep one of the three religious factions at bay has been built to cut off potential suicide bombers coming into Israel from the Gaza Strip. Nothing new, nothing different, the same twenty-two-century-old conflict continues with one of the three doctrines acting as top dog for the time being. Despite all this, having actually walked on the same cobblestones that have paved the path of twenty-two centuries of history was a memorable, remarkable and compelling experience I cherish.

I have had the good fortune to travel widely in my life. In terms of destinations I have experienced the familiar and the utterly strange, sophisticated and primitive, joyous and frightening. Among the lonely but hugely exciting places have been the tropical jungles and mountains in South America and Central Africa and the extravagant wildlife and primal ice and snow of the Sub-Antarctic island of South Georgia, the latter, despite the lack of human habitation, one of the truly great travel adventures. I have loved living in and exploring the teeming cities and countries of South East Asia and the Indian sub-continent. I've seen and been to many of the world's great locations and yes, of course, gawked with everyone else at the enduring treasures to be found in Europe and Russia. I've sometimes suffered a little hardship and inconvenience, and on one occasion in Peru, altitude sickness where I was convinced I was going to die. Corny as it may sound, I've been charged by a Cape buffalo and have stepped on a well-concealed sleeping crocodile while trekking along the Tsavo River on foot in Kenya. I have been on a camel safari in Somalia. Of course, there have been mishaps and near disasters, mistakes and misunderstandings, but I've for the most part enjoyed several truly grand body- and mind-expanding adventures, just one of many being allowed to run a section of the Great Wall of China.

Taking all this together, it would be impossible to choose the one travel experience that most profoundly moved, delighted, taught and in small or larger ways challenged and changed me.

At the risk of sounding over-sentimental or Pollyanna-ish, in almost every travel destination I've undertaken it has been the caring, kind, generous, giving individuals I've met along the way – and not any particular people at any particular location, or doctrine, superstitions, dogma or God or Gods worshipped – who have brought both new insights, fresh thinking and stimulus to my life. It remained the same this time in the old city of Jerusalem, where Jewish, Arab and Christian individuals, despite their conflicting interests, co-exist with what appeared to me to be a minimum of sectarian fuss and where my wife and I were treated with great kindness and consideration.

Finally, I've purchased a new pair of nail clippers and placed it beside the nail buffer in the small, much-scuffed and -travelled leather case. It occurred to me at the time that I couldn't remember ever once in 61 years putting the buffer to use. In the travel sense, getting your fingernails dirty is what it's all about. Furthermore, I am comforted by the notion that one of the truisms of travelling is that as one door closes, another window opens. I read recently that eight private citizens have each separately paid for and been to and returned safely from the International Space Station. Now that is surely the final great travel frontier that sadly I will miss. Damn! Damn! Damn! Can you imagine looking back at our small quarrelsome blue planet, a tiny dot in the vast universe? Now that would be an awesome out-of-this-world experience.

Charles Finch is the author of a series of historical mysteries set in Victorian England, the most recent of which, *A Burial at Sea*, was described by the New York Times as 'so fascinating it's a shame it has to end'. His first literary novel, *The Last Enchantments*, will be published in 2013 by St Martin's Press. He has written essays and criticism for the *New York Times, USA Today* and many other publications. Finch lived abroad for several years before returning home to New York in 2011.

A Small World
After All

BY CHARLES FINCH

With every week that passes there are another few square inches of the atlas that I can cut clean away: Time is always shortening, and in all likelihood I will never see the places they map with my own eyes. Sometimes I'll catch a name and think, goodbye, Cuenca, or Ashgabat, or Indianapolis. I genuinely wish I could come and learn about your beloved municipal celebrities and terrible art museums and novel ways of cooking chicken, but instead I'll probably go to London another half-dozen times.

Of course it's that way for everybody; each of us knows only a few pockets of the world intimately, a few dozen casually, the rest not at all. Such is the sadness even of the traveler – perhaps especially of the traveler.

And yet. In the summer of 2010, with a group of fellow Americans, I spent a month living along the waterfront of Cape Town, South Africa, and during that time it seemed as if the world had reduced itself approximately to the size of the city. The occasion was the World Cup.

During our first few days in Cape Town, we spent our time primarily with the staff of the U.S. Embassy, where we had a friend. (Sample quote, from a young, pretty Ole Miss

grad: 'Mexicans are dorks.') In fact the Americans and Brits
all seemed to cling together, haunting the same few bars and
plazas, a lack of enterprise that is hard to understand in
retrospect. Perhaps it was the simple astonishment of being
in Cape Town, with the great flat mass of Table Mountain
curving the city in toward us, the clouds above it moving
unhurriedly during the blue days, then quickly during the
bright, hard, moonlit nights. The weather was sultry.
Everything was cheap.

Things changed on our fourth day, when we went to a
liquor store to pick up beer. What I remember most vividly
about the shop is that its chief decorative adornment was a
small, autographed picture near the cash register of
Republican Senator Bill Frist, in which he looked as if he
badly needed to use the bathroom.

Behind us in line was a group of five men. I was standing
with my old college roommate, Bernie, and we deduced,
through careful analysis, that they were Chilean – which is to
say that they were wearing Chilean football shirts and had on
enormous felt top hats patterned after the Chilean flag.

They were singing a song.

'Maybe we should get a picture with them,' murmured Bernie.

The Chileans were delighted to pose with us. In the picture
one of them is making a peace sign with a cigarette between
his fingers, another is gesturing toward the camera ('Take it
already!'), and a third, though I didn't notice it at the time, is
wearing the same sneakers I had back at the apartment.

That evening we sat on our balcony along the waterfront,
drinking the Castles we had bought and discussing the
encounter. I don't remember whether we made a definite
decision to take more photos like that, but the next morning
we stopped a Brazilian fan for a picture, and an hour later a
group of Paraguayans, and soon enough we had a mission: to

get a picture with fans from each of the thirty-two nations at the World Cup.

It's funny: The principles for which the Cup is lauded, such as international goodwill, global understanding, even peace, are admirable, but their incessant repetition has a deadening effect. In fact I would argue that in general soccer receives credit for a great deal of aspirational nonsense and then, in practice, engenders primarily bitterness. Nearly all the teams lose a lot; the fans hate each other; it encourages various cities to despise each other.

But once we began to take these pictures, those principles slowly began to feel real. We encountered fans in bars, in parking lots, at games, locked out of their hostels late at night on Long Street, and these aleatory connections started to fulfill – to exceed – the World Cup's ambitious imaginative responsibilities. In other words, you really do feel more together there. People really are all the same. The world really does feel smaller.

. . . .

So who did we meet? Our holy grail was the North Koreans – but more on that momentarily. First, a brief and unscientific taxonomy of the fans we met in Cape Town.

The Friendliest - The Netherlands.
They were friendly to the point of possible derangement – other than our one Dutch acquaintance, who always greeted us, mysteriously, with 'Here come the homosexuals.' All the Dutch fans had vuvuzelas, those terrible plastic one-note horns that you've probably half-forgotten about, but by way of apology the ones we got a picture with handed us orange earplugs.

The Saddest - Paraguay.
I would attribute this to the biblical rainfall that arrived just before their opening game against Italy, but on later, sunnier days, they still looked sour. And they won their group! Not to mention having the breakout star of the World Cup (non-player division), lingerie model and fan Larissa Riquelme, who achieved international fame by keeping her cell phone in her bra! Maybe Paraguay is so beautiful that only the depressives leave.

The Coolest - Brazil.
But not, to our surprise, with a samba vibe. They were more like Europeans, wearing complicated metallic blue jeans, with hairstyles we would see six months later in the States. We got a photograph with a guy who looked like a fat Robinho.

The Best Looking - Algeria.
An attractive people. The lovely and very affable girl with whom we took a picture appears, upon review, to have been holding her middle finger up in the direction of the camera. Hopefully that was unintentional.

The Most Popular - Uruguay.
Easily spotted (their pale-blue shirts) and very cheerful. Our photo is with a large family of men from different generations of the same family; my eyes are closed in it. They were karmically rewarded for their attitude by a great run in the tournament.

The Grumpiest - France.
They were not pleased with the quality of coffee in South Africa. Or the quality of their team. Or our photography project. They were probably the nationality that most conformed to their international reputation.

The Worst - England.

As an avowed Anglophile, I am pained to write this. But the English fans booed their team, turned lobster red under anything other than the mildest sunlight, wore Manchester United shirts to high-end functions, sang 'England 5-Germany 1' at any perceived provocation, and were always half of whatever fight was going on. Alas.

The Best - South Africa.

At every Olympics and World Cup the host nation collects praise for its hospitality, but South Africa was – at least I believe – actually different. Everyone, *everyone*, black, white, rich, poor, seemed filled with an almost impossible sense of goodwill and joy. Nearly all of them felt it was a chance to redefine their country.

But did it succeed? Shortly after we arrived in South Africa we went to a Springboks rugby match. During the national anthem we noticed that the people near us sang only half the song. It turned out that the anthem is a hybrid of several Apartheid-era songs, and almost always the black fans sing the parts in Xhosa, Zulu, and Sotho, while the white fans take the parts in Afrikaans and English.

On the other hand I saw both white and black people openly weeping when Mandela appeared for the first time, frail and beaming. 'While he is alive, no man is an orphan,' someone said.

And this: After the rest has fallen away, the one thing I'll remember about this World Cup is the first goal of the tournament. South Africa was playing Mexico, and in the apartment where we were watching, it was tense. The score was nil-nil, and there was an almost desperate edge to the optimism of the South Africans who were with us – this all had to be worth it, the preparation, the hope. Then someone

named Siphiwe Tshabalala struck as pure a ball as you'll
ever see across the goalkeeper – and across all of Cape
Town, ongoing for what seemed like twenty minutes, came
waves and waves of cathartic and joyous screams.

The Weirdest - North Korea.
If you remember the North Korean team's presence at the
2010 World Cup, it's most likely either because you remember
when they lost 7–0 to Portugal in their second group game –
which led to a lot of uneasy jokes about the players and
managers being reeducated – or because you heard that Kim
Jong-Il was giving the team 'regular tactical advice during
matches' using invisible mobile phones...of his own design.

If you're surprised at this technological breakthrough, you
really ought to consider the dictator's other accomplishments,
such as: inventing the hamburger, circa 2004; controlling the
weather based on his mood; never defecating; and shooting
eleven holes-in-one in a single round of golf – the first round
of golf he ever played, in fact.

These facts are funny; but are they funny? Especially
after Kim died, it was common to recite them to friends and
laugh. But then, at least for me, some of the actual facts
would come to mind and depress me. There was the
predictable megalomaniac's lavishness (waterslides at all his
houses, $650,000 a year on Hennessy Cognac) and madness
(rounding up short people to exile them to an abandoned
island, forcing waitresses at his favorite restaurant to have
Westernizing plastic surgery) and above all the famine, the
$900 that the average North Korean lives on annually.

So, yes, the North Korean team got beaten – but maybe it's
better to pause and remember what they achieved. They had
no business being at the World Cup. Almost none of their
players play in international leagues, they had a coaching

staff of limited experience, and they came from this weird magical realist hellscape that Kim Jong-Il created.

And then when they *did* make the World Cup, they had the terrible misfortune to be drawn in the group of death, with the teams ranked first, third, and twenty-seventh in the world.

We went to their game against the third-ranked team – Portugal – full of hopes for a picture with a few grinning North Koreans. Almost immediately we heard the rumors, still unsubstantiated, that in fact the North Korean fans were hired Chinese actors, the DPR government fearing defections.

For their part the Portuguese fans were in riotous good spirits as they pooled into the stadium; by contrast the North Koreans walked in small battalions, very nearly in formation, each with an identical red hat, shirt and scarf, like an alien's interpretation of the erratic and festive outfits you see at the World Cup.

'Go up to them,' said Bernie.

'No, you.'

'I've got the camera.'

If I were North Korean, no matter how ardent my affection for Kim Jong-Il, I think my eyes would flicker upward if a big American came toward me, making a bear-hug motion and saying 'Photograph! Photograph!' in a loud voice. Nope. They flowed around me as unconsciously as water. We tried the next group. Same thing. The next group after that. Same again.

Then the game. There are two traditions in soccer that match the sport's outsized reputation for sportsmanship: kicking the ball out of bounds when an opposition player is injured, even if it means sacrificing an advantage, and exchanging jerseys at the end of the game. The North

Koreans did neither. And the gulf in class between the two teams was unbearably obvious.

But there was a kind of stupid heroism to their performance, even in abject defeat. They ran harder than the Portuguese – the absurdly gifted Portuguese, led by Cristiano Ronaldo, who might as well have been a cyborg designed to play the sport – no matter what the score was, their faces impassive, their inward spirits a mystery. What would be the consequences to them? How many of them believed fully in Kim Jong-Il, and if so, how distraught must they have been to fail him?

It risks condescension to describe what I felt at the end of the game, the mixture of admiration, pity, revulsion, curiosity, gloating, and arrogance, none of it very nice. The North Korean fans near us sang continually and ceaselessly, irrespective of the match's events. On the way out we attempted, while making sympathetic faces and noises, to get them to pose for a picture. In the end we had to settle for one of them walking around us two grinning monkeys, their eyes forward, their pennants still in the air.

Actually it's the photo I look at most often from the whole trip. No traveler wants to hear this – it militates against the almost spiritual amplification we ascribe to travel – but sometimes going out there, away from home, doesn't make you feel closer to other people, or make the world feel smaller. It makes you feel more estranged from other people, and it makes the world feel bigger. Even at the World Cup.

. . . .

In my experience there are three kinds of trips that have a lasting effect on a person.

First, there's the trip that confronts you with the natural world, forcing you to see yourself very small, as if from a great distance; second, there's the trip that comes at a crucial time in your life, after you just got your dream job or someone has left you, and it doesn't matter where you go, Quebec, Montserrat, whatever; and third, there's the trip that shows you other human beings who are different from you, how they live, what they do. That third kind of trip was the World Cup for me. It sounds stupid, but even if I never go to Uruguay, I kind of went to Uruguay, for ten minutes or however long we chatted with the Uruguayans we met.

On one of our last nights in Cape Town we sat in silence on our balcony, gazing out at a ship until at last it dipped below the horizon, birds looping loosely against the pink of sunfall. (Maybe it was that first kind of trip, too, now that I think about it.) There were four of us, a doctor, a sportswriter, a mystery novelist, and a businessman.

'Rio in 2014?' someone said at last.

For sure, we all agreed.

But who knows. I turned thirty in Cape Town, and I had just realized that I would probably get married very soon. By 2014 I would be thirty-four, and though I know that if you look for endings everywhere you'll find them, I had a sense, on the balcony, that a window was closing, that the future was uncertain. I've found that life is less recursive than I imagined it would be when I was younger, and the same faces seemed to pop up every month or two; now I know that I might never get to Rio, or even back to South Africa.

Maybe it was all three kinds of trips.

In the end we got pictures with fans of twenty of the thirty-two nations that were represented at the World Cup. There was Ghana (delighted with his team's run in the Cup),

Mexico (a family in Heathrow wearing enormous sombreros), Cameroon (we spotted him because he always held his scarf above his head), Italy (genuinely distressed at their team's performances, or perhaps just uniformly sullen).

Unfortunately we never got Nigeria, Denmark, or Japan, among others. It's a shame because I heard later that the Nigerian fans were the best. I guess the lesson is you can't go everywhere. You should still go everywhere you can.

M. J. Hyland is the author of three multiaward-winning novels. *How the Light Gets In* was shortlisted for the Commonwealth Writers' Prize; *Carry Me Down* was shortlisted for the Man Booker Prize, and was winner of both the Hawthornden and Encore prizes; and *This is How* was longlisted for both the Orange Prize and the Dublin International IMPAC Prize in 2009. Hyland's short story 'Rag Love' was shortlisted for the BBC National Short Story Award in 2011. Hyland is also a lecturer in the Centre for New Writing at the University of Manchester and cofounder of the Hyland & Byrne Editing Firm: www.editingfirm.com and www.mjhyland.com.

The Thieves of Rome

BY M. J. HYLAND

From August 2006, until June 2007, I lived, alone, in Rome. In August, most Romans move their olive bodies closer to the cooler sea and leave the city. They leave behind boiling days and packs of Roman and Roma thieves. The Roma are Romanian, not Italian, and many live in migrant camps, their tents and mattresses spread out on the roadside, along the dry, concrete outskirts. There are thousands of Roma pickpockets, many of them children under fourteen – too young to prosecute – and some get trained in Naples. The Roma children make the lion's share of their living working on the 64 and 40 buses, which run tourists straight to the Vatican.

I lived in the B.R. Whiting Studio in Trastevere as an Australia Council for the Arts Writing Fellow. My first Italian friend (I'll call him 'Stefano', not his real name) was a member of Italy's elite police force, the Carabinieri, the national gendarmerie of Italy. I asked my English friends, who lived in Rome, to recommend an Italian language tutor, and one of them, an artist, referred me to Stefano, a young friend of his, who'd recently told him he wanted to improve his English.

Stefano was twenty-eight and had high hopes for himself; he thought maybe – in about fifteen years – he'd achieve the highest rank in the Carabinieri, become a Comandante Generale. He came to the studio to meet me in late August. When I opened the front door, he said, 'I think you are the daughter,' and what he meant was, 'I want to have sex with you.'

We sat at the kitchen table and started our English and Italian lessons. Over the next six months, we met once or twice a week. He used gifts, and lobster dinners, to try to seduce me, took me to restaurants where he seemed never to be asked to pay the bill, and volunteered to become my 'protector'. I learnt the word *'padrone'* (boss) and that's what I called him, and I called myself *'bradipo'* (sloth) because I was so floored by the heat that I went to bed most afternoons, to sleep through the hottest parts of the day. Stefano and I met after dark.

Sometimes Stefano would take me out on his cop motorbike. One night we got off the bike near the Trevi Fountain. Stefano saw a Roma boy moving between the legs of American tourists.

'A thief,' Stefano said, and he told me about the ways of the Roma thieves.

He told me about their tricks and techniques: the 'drop' baby, street bumping, razor blades for slicing handbags, the scooter steal, the squirted mess of mayonnaise on the victim's back, the fake 'tourist' police officer who asks to check I.D., and the little girl selling roses.

'I know all those,' I said.

'No,' he said. 'You don't know all. Listen all of this!'

He told me about the lost and returned wallet trick. In this routine, after the thief has snatched your wallet – using the bumping method – he returns it, seconds later, pretending he's an honest man who happens to have found it. If the 'victim' is happy enough, they pay a reward.

'That's pretty good,' I said.

'It is no the best. Listen this.'

He told me about the routine used by Roma thieves on train platforms, a con used mainly in summer because the trick requires an open window: You are alone in a first-class train compartment. The train is on the platform, due to leave in a few minutes. An Italian man taps on the window of your carriage and you stand at the window. He's frantic and needs directions, but you say, 'I don't speak Italian. I am English.' He goes away. You sit back down in your cushy seat. A moment later, a good-looking, well-dressed man taps on the window. He speaks beautiful English and needs help, something about airport trains, where to buy tickets. You stand at the compartment's open window and answer his questions and forget to pay attention to the bag and the suitcase on the floor behind you. The first man, the one you couldn't help, is on the train now, and he's helping himself to your things.

'They also ride mopeds on the footpath and grab women's handbags,' I said.

'No. That is Italian thieves,' said Stefano. 'I show you a Roma technique. *Aspetti.*'

Stefano went to a nearby tabacchi and returned with a newspaper.

'You must walk back and then you walk forward me, you come me, and I show you.'

I put my satchel down. 'OK.'

'No. You keep your bag in your person.'

'You should say "*on* your person,"' I said, 'or you say just "keep it with you". Or just "hold your bag". *Capito?*'

'*Va bene.*'

I walked back about ten paces and then forward. Stefano walked towards me holding the newspaper. When I was near him, he held the newspaper under my chin, just held it there, no aggression, a strange, non-violent, unnerving interference, and as he did this, he looked at me and said nothing.

I said, *'Vai via!'* (Go away) and he pushed the newspaper up, and with this new force, my chin went up. I used my hands – both of them – to stop him, to pull the newspaper away.

He withdrew and said, 'I finish.'

'I see,' I said. 'When I let go of my bag, you snatch the bag from me.'

He laughed. 'You not understand the story how it ends.'

I reached into my satchel. My wallet and phone were gone.

'That was quick,' I said. 'Fucking hell.'

'You are not a woman who says "fucking hell". You say *"mio dio"*, *d'accordo?'*

Stefano would never get the sex he wanted, and he knew it, I think, and his frustration came out when I was in any way vulgar, not lady-like. This strange combination of sex-addiction and moral propriety, and an insistence on women being gentle and soft and respectful of the Virgin Mother, is common in almost all Italian men.

'Yeah, boss. I get it.'

· · · · • • • · · ·

In September 2006, I was at Termini Station, waiting for a train to Fiumicino airport. I was due to appear on stage at the Edinburgh Festival the next day and I stood straddling my suitcase, my satchel's strap tight across my chest, and watched the electronic departures board. There were dozens of tourists on the platform. A young man, about thirty-five, very handsome and tall, wearing a pin-striped suit, probably Armani, stood close to me, but not too close.

'Do you know if this is the platform for the airport?' he asked.

He spoke impeccable English and he smelt like soap, and his teeth, which he made sure I saw, were straight and white and had been near some good dentists.

'I think so. Yes.'

'Thank you,' he said.

He said nothing else, stayed just where he was, standing, like me, watching the departures board. There was a station announcement in rapid Italian, and I recognised the words cancellation, airport, change and platform. Like most non-Italians, I checked the board again. There'd been no change, and though I felt nervous sweat beading on my back, I didn't move.

The man in the pin-stripe stood closer now and looked up at the board, which was directly above my head. I didn't move away. People who smell like soap are good people.

'Excuse me,' he said, 'but I think the train is cancelled and we must move to platform number seven.'

'Really?'

I looked round: none of the other tourists was moving, and if what he said was true, none had understood.

'I think we must change,' he said.

I looked round at nothing in particular, the kind of redundant stalling which marks the early stages of panic.

'I don't know,' I said.

'I will find for us the answer,' he said.

I didn't wonder why he had no luggage, not even a briefcase. He was handsome and kind. He was an executive and not a dumb, male-model kind of handsome; he had one of those strong, uniquely beautiful faces we assume belong to smart, moral people.

He began to move away in search of a station official and while I was busy feeling looked-after, another man ran down the platform, a messy, short, greasy, criminal-type with craggy skin, and this filthy man crashed into me, hard. I stumbled and my Armani friend held my elbow.

'Are you OK?'

'Yes,' I said. 'Thank you.'

'I find for us the correct train for the airport now,' he said.

'Thank you.'

I waited.

The train was due in a few minutes. I opened my bag to check my ticket and, for no reason I can remember, I also reached for my wallet. It was gone, and so was my phone.

. . . .

Stefano and I were going to a crowded marketplace the day I told him I'd been robbed, that I'd lost €300 and my phone, but that I was happy, because I was on the Man Booker shortlist. He ranted against the Romani. He said they were gypsy scum, 'The way they breed and live like animals in all the tents in the motorways. Everywhere they are. Like stupid animals.'

'There are plenty of Italian thieves, too,' I said.

'Be careful for the thieves.'

I agreed I'd be careful, but he wanted to tell me more about the cons used by Roma pickpockets.

'I tell you now what they can do.'

He was showing off, of course, but I was having fun.

'OK,' I said. 'Tell me what I need to know.'

He told me to be on guard for: (a) The pickpocket who falls or trips and grabs your shoulder, then fleeces you (a

classic trick, sometimes known as Misdirected Pressure).
(b) The pickpocket who hangs posters near crowded tourist cafes with warnings such as, 'Thieves are at work in this area'. In this con the victim, who sees the warning poster, pats his wallet and this gesture tells the pickpocket where to aim. (c) The pickpocket who drops a briefcase and documents fall out: The 'victim' and another pickpocket stop to help and the victim is 'dipped' (in casinos, buckets of coins are used to cause the distraction).

Around the time of our day at the market, then Italian Prime Minister Silvio Berlusconi had proposed a law requiring the fingerprinting of all Romani children and another regulation requiring Romani prostitutes to 'wear jeans' when they touted for business, especially the ones who are '11 or 12 years of age'. This was one of several of Berlusconi's deranged attempts to control child prostitution and the 'vast uncontrollable illegal migrant population'. He would rid the country of Romanians, he said, even if this meant starving them.

When my Australia Council residency ran out, I wasn't ready to go back to England. I moved to an apartment in Monti and lived on Via del Boschetto for six months; my home was a one-bedroom flat on a cobbled, narrow street, not wide enough to let a Range-Rover through. I was happy. I understood, of course, that Italy is hell for its thinking natives; for the gentle, patrician and wise, Italy under Berlusconi's demented rule was a country of ever-worsening chaos, its major cities anarchic and its politics corrupt, racist, sexist, puerile, a bureaucracy jammed with nepotistic favours.

Rome is a stunning city, but it's also a dirty and disorganised shambles. Still, I'd never felt so alive, or so at home. The way Italians live for pleasure, so quick to love and hate, and are not so much interested in work; the way the air caught my skin, the way people throw their hands about, the way ancient ruins are unearthed whenever city engineers try to finish building the subway – all of these things made me want to go out at four a.m. and prowl like a wolf. For the whole year I lived in Rome, I did little else but write, and eat, and walk, and ride on a scooter in the beautiful streets, and drink espresso, and eat and talk. In that kind of way, I was living a life without interference from Italy's messes and I was, I suppose, and still am, stupid enough to think Rome is perfect.

I had just a week left before my money ran out, a week before heading back to darkest Manchester, and I was sitting outside a café, half a block from my apartment, two blocks from the Colosseum, smoking a Marlboro and drinking espresso. A Romani boy, about eight years old, came to my table. He said nothing and put a piece of cardboard on the table on which was written, *Por Favore. I am poor and hungry.* I gave him some change and he left. As he left, he picked up the cardboard, which he'd put on top of my phone, and as he lifted the piece of cardboard ... I didn't realise it was happening until it'd happened.

'Shit!'

When he was about a body-length away, I lurched at him, grabbed him by the wrist, and threw him down. He hit the cobbles, hard, and I got my phone. As he bounced up from the cobblestones, he called me a pig, bastard, bitch, and walked away, slow, watchful, hunting for another idiot.

I was back in Rome about three months later. I'd been living in Manchester and lecturing in Creative Writing at the University of Manchester, and I was invited to a writers' festival in Bologna. After Bologna, I stopped for a few days in Rome.

I was at Fiumicino airport, in the airport's two-platform train station. It was early morning, the quietest time. I bought my ticket, then went into the kiosk, a tabacchi, to buy a bottle of water and six packs of Marlboro Lights (fags are half the price in Rome).

There was a wad of cash on the shop's floor, resting there, still and crisp, right in front of the cashier's counter. The notes were folded neatly in half, perhaps €500, at least that much, probably more, straight out of an ATM. I bent down, pretended to adjust the zip on my boots, picked up the bundle, paid for the fags, and went out to the platform. I decided that I would find the owner myself. I didn't trust the polizia who patrolled the station, and I didn't trust the old man in the tabacchi.

I walked along the platform. I'd taken just a few steps when I saw him, a boy running down the platform toward the tabacchi. He was about eighteen, tall and blond, and he wore a short-sleeved rugby jersey. I moved back, closer to the tabacchi, and listened. The boy asked the old man if he'd found any money.

'No, no, no.'

'Are you sure?'

The boy was American, a clean-skinned optimist, well-educated, from somewhere like Wilmington, Delaware, that kind of place.

When he'd given up on the tabacchi, he spoke to the policeman guarding the one-man polizia booth. 'No, no, no.' The policeman had nothing.

I waited for the boy to walk down the platform and when he was near me, said, 'Excuse me. Have you lost some money?'

'Eight hundred euro. I just got it out of the bank!'

The boy looked down the platform. He had friends waiting for him, three of them, just like him: healthy, tall, fair-skinned. Now they were coming down the platform, wheeling their suitcases, 100 percent leather, unscuffed. These were boys on a gap year: next year, Harvard, Yale, athletics scholarships.

One of his friends called out, 'Did you find it?'

The boy shook his head.

'I have it,' I said. I pointed to the tabacchi. 'You dropped it on the floor of the shop. I just wanted to be sure it was yours.'

'Jesus,' he said.

Then he shouted out to his pals. 'I've got it! This woman's got the money.' His friends heard what he said and walked back toward the other end of the platform.

This woman.

The boy looked at my bag and said nothing. Not 'Thanks', not 'What a relief', or 'You've saved me'. Nothing. He looked at my satchel, waited for me to reach for the money and hand it over. He didn't look at my face. I was his money.

I fetched the bundle of notes and I separated some, loosened a couple, freed a few, two or three (I wouldn't know how many notes until I was on the train), and handed him the rest.

'There you go,' I said.

He snatched the money and said 'Jesus!' again and waved the money in the air for his friends to see – though they weren't looking – and as he walked away, he put what I'd given him into the front-right pocket of his shorts, and up the platform he went.

'You're welcome,' I said.

Chris Pavone is the author of *The Expats*, which hit the New York Times bestseller list immediately upon publication in March 2012. Chris grew up in Brooklyn, graduated from Cornell, and was an editor at a variety of book-publishing houses that included Doubleday, Crown and Artisan, most notably as executive editor at Clarkson Potter. He spent a year and a half as an expat in Luxembourg, but once again lives with his wife and children in New York City.

Arriving in Luxembourg

BY CHRIS PAVONE

I.

I'd seen them before in my life, many times. Departing from Mexico City and Beijing and Paris, with their giant suitcases and their terrified children and their passports of a different color than my deep American blue. And then on the other ends of their long-haul flights, arriving in New York or Miami or Houston, spent, exhausted, yet not even close to finished with their epic journeys.

Now I'm one of them: an immigrant, immigrating. With my mountains of cheap mismatched giant suitcases, and a dog crate with a nervous dog inside, and backpacks and computer bags, teddy bears and two small children and a calm, composed wife. I am leaving home, the place I've lived my entire life, for a new life, somewhere else. I don't know when – don't know if – we'll ever again live in New York City.

II.

My oven in Tribeca offered a wide choice of numbers, in Fahrenheit. This one here has no numbers.

I am fully aware that things will be different in Luxembourg; I want things to be different. I am prepared – I am eager! – to embrace the new. For example, to do my cooking in Celsius. I've long admired the neat roundness of water boiling at 100 degrees.

But this dial offers no numbers, Celsius or otherwise. What this dial offers are *Beleuchtung, Ober-Unterhitze, Unterhitze, Grill, Grill klein, Auftauen, Intesivbacken, Umluftgrill, Heißluft plus* (inexplicably, there's no plain-old *Heißluft*, without the *plus*), and *Schnellaufheizen*.

I speak no German, and I keep forgetting to buy a German dictionary. Sometimes I bring the laptop into the kitchen to use online dictionaries, attempting to translate my appliances. But I often mistype, especially the likes of *ß*, and anything with an umlaut. And I suffer from attention fatigue after four syllables. So I end up with the very unsatisfying 'your search term yielded no results.' This sounds like the recap to a disappointing night of unsuccessful carousing.

I stare at the dial. I'm attracted to the sound of *Intensivbacken*, which, like so many German words, seems to have at least one built-in exclamation point. But this probable idea – Intensive! Baking! – sounds too powerful for the task at hand, reheating the little chicken I bought from the farmers'-market truck that sells three things: little rotisserie chickens, big rotisserie chickens, and sliced potatoes that cook in the fat that drips from the rotisserie chickens.

Grill seems like a better choice, if only for the dimwitted reason that it's the most familiar of the words. As I turn the dial, I am actually thinking to myself: you are being an idiot.

A few minutes later I catch a whiff of something, and glance at the oven, from which smoke has begun to slink. I open the door to billowing puffs, and my head darts around in a panic, searching for a detector to disable. If there's one thing I don't want, it's to infuriate neighbors we haven't even met yet. But there's no smoke detector here, in this sleek hyper-modern kitchen. And if not here, there's probably no smoke detector anywhere. I'm relieved for the instant, disappointed for the long term.

The chicken is now extra-crispy, but salvageable. I tentatively lean my head into the oven, and see that the coils on top are glowing bright red. *Grill*, I now know, is the broiler. I will learn, one mistake at a time.

III.

My wife has started going to the office every day, but school has not yet begun. I am alone with my four-year-old twins, all day every day, in this foreign place. We go to playgrounds and markets, cafés and gelaterias. When we purchase things in small shops, the women at the *caisses* give candy to the boys.

But it is frequently raining, and not as warm as I'm accustomed to for early September. We need an indoor activity. So we gather bathing suits and goggles and towels, and walk over to the public pool. Where we find out from the sign on the door that today is the *hebdomadaire* closing. This undams a torrent of tears from my bored and disappointed and semi-scared children.

We return the next day. We pay our fee, and use our paper tickets to pass through an unmanned and irrelevant turnstile, and start to wander through what I realize – just a second too late – is the women's locker room. We scurry to the gender-appropriate area. We figure out, eventually, that we must use our tickets to release a door to secure a locker. Later, we'll have to use the same tickets to exit through those turnstiles. The children start referring to these multifunctional pieces of paper as credit cards, which are later described in a fashion that makes it clear they're the highlight of the expedition, which is otherwise what you'd expect from a public swimming pool.

But while paddling around, I notice that off to one side of the big pool is exercise equipment, and more of it up on a balcony. I need regular exercise, and I'm not sure how to go about finding a gym. Perhaps this swimming-pool setup will serve.

IV.

I return to the pool, buoyed with confidence that I know about the bi-weekly closing, and about the tickets, and about the soft demarcation between the locker-room zones for semi-naked women and those for semi-naked men.

An unmistakable sign – pictogram as well as words – expressly forbids shoes in the pool area. So I carry my sneakers to the machines, where I assume I'll be able to wear footwear. But the three people exercising are barefoot. Damn.

I step barefoot into the elliptical machine, and start the Sisyphean climb. My soles are immediately, painfully imprinted with the bubbled Braille of the footpads.

The other barefoot exercisers trickle away. Two new women show up, and I watch them closely. They're carrying their shoes across the tiled surround of the pool, then . . . they do it! They pull on their sneakers and climb onto the machines! Hurrah! I too will wear mine, as soon as I work up the courage to dismount and lace up.

But oh no, what's this? A lifeguard shows up, literally wagging his finger. He engages the women in a spirited conversation that begins in German, then turns to French, and fluctuates between simmering resentment and withering hostility. At one point, he gestures at me, and says something about what Monsieur is doing, and they all look at me, the women with suspicion and resentment, as if I'd betrayed them.

I give a weak smile, trying to communicate to the women that I'm on their side, but without signaling to the lifeguard that I'm against him, at least not personally, it's just that I too would rather be wearing my sneakers. That's a lot to pack into a single smirk; I probably look like I'm experiencing intestinal discomfort.

Upstairs, then. The strengthening machines are a bewildering hydraulic system. The disappointed shoeless women join me. Then two guys. All of us are trying to figure out these machines, and not succeeding to anyone's satisfaction. After I use the stomach-torturing contraption, one of the men asks me a question in rapid-fire French, the gist of which appears to be whether it's *supérieur* or *antérieur*. I feel my own stomach to try to pinpoint where it hurts. '*Supérieur*,' I answer.

'*Merci*,' he says, but I don't think my answer is what he'd hoped.

In the shower room, I can't get the hot water on; I assume there isn't hot water here, in the cavernous bath of this public facility. So I take a quick cold shower. As I'm toweling off, a female lifeguard enters the male shower room. '*C'est chaud, ou non?*' she asks, with neither prelude nor apology.

I'm pretty naked. I shake my head. '*Non.*'

'*Froid? Seulement?*'

I nod.

She shakes her head in frustration, maybe disgust. Just as abruptly as she arrived, she hurries away.

V.

'*Maintenant*,' one of the movers says, '*on attend le camion.*' He watches through the window as the last load of our rental furniture and furnishings descends on his crane,

then he pops a cigarette in his mouth, and walks out
the door of the apartment.

The elevator in our small building is minuscule, and off-limits for moving. As apparently are nearly all the elevators
in this country. So movers come equipped with their own
little cranes, sort of like cherry-pickers, on which everything
comes in and goes out, through the windows.

Our four-year-old twins are at school, a miniature version
of England called St George's International School, presided
over by silver-haired British Islanders. My wife is in the full-sized version for a few days, working in London. Her job is
what has brought us here, to live in Europe, for an
indefinite period.

So I am doing what the mover instructed – waiting for
the truck – while sitting on the floor of the almost entirely
empty apartment, on the cheap Ikea rug that sheds like a
sickly cat, spewing red tumbleweeds all over the place. Up a
flight of stairs, then down a hallway, then around a corner,
and under the bathroom vanity, I find red fur.

It was just a month earlier that I was sitting on the
floor in New York City, watching the last of our furniture
go out the door of our loft. I seem to spend a lot of
time alone, on the floor of my empty apartments. It's a
melancholy pastime.

I pick up the children from school, in a swarm of
other expat parents, 99 percent of them women. The boys
and I hurry back to the *centre ville* to rendezvous with the
orange container arriving to rue de l'Eau. The big metal
box was released in the late morning from customs at the
port of Antwerp, a city which I didn't even realize was
on water.

The massive trailer is slowly negotiated into our narrow
curving street. Then an unmistakable mood of

disappointment settles as the movers discover that
the container is padlocked.

'Avez-vous le clef?' one asks me.

I try to smile, probably unsuccessfully, and put my hands
in the 'what are you, kidding?' gesture, combined with a
beseeching 'please don't tell me you can't open this
goddamned thing, because I have two children and NO
furniture here' look on my face. He shrugs.

That's how it comes to pass that the police show up.
Because at that point, the four movers start taking turns
beating on the lock with wrenches, with hammers, with
pry-bars. They're making an unbearable racket – and to
all appearances committing a crime – right here beside
the grand duke's palace, the monarch's residence. A
motorcycle cop stops by to investigate – a woman,
unexpectedly, shaking her hair out of her helmet – and
starts asking questions, but without much apparent
concern or conviction. Then she lights a cigarette and
watches, half-amused.

The lock finally falls apart, clattering impotently to the
ground, a sound greatly disproportionate to the god-awful
racket that preceded. The container is pulled open, the
crane restarted, and the furniture – our furniture – begins
coming through the window at 4:30.

At 5:59 and 59 seconds, the movers leave. Everything has
managed to make it into the apartment. Nothing – *nothing*
– is unpacked. Couches are standing on end, boxes are
piled to the ceiling. It is anarchic and dark, and
surprisingly awful.

We go out to a restaurant for dinner, the boys and I. We
come home, and I set up their beds, and kiss my tired
children goodnight. Then I sit on the cold floor, alone in the
dark, and cry.

VI.

In the morning I drive the kids to school. In the hallway I smile and shake hands and chat with a few acquaintances. I still have no proper friends in this country, but not everyone is a total stranger, now.

I go to my French class – three times per week, studying every day – where I feel decent about my progress. I no longer begin every single interaction with the humiliating *'Parlez-vous anglais?'*

I return to the spectacularly messy apartment. But in the light of day, it's not nearly as bad as it was last night. I begin to unpack, box by box, day after day, until all our vases and pillows and pans, clothes and bureaus and toys, are where they should be. Then I look around with satisfaction, at this duplex apartment across the street from the grand duke's grand palace, in the middle of Western Europe.

I sort of like it here. Which is a good thing, because I live here. And little by little, challenge by challenge, this semi-permanent travel is turning into home.

Stephen Kelman was born in Luton, England, in 1976. *Pigeon English*, his first novel, was shortlisted for the 2011 Man Booker Prize, the Desmond Elliott Prize and the Guardian First Book Award. He lives with his wife, Uzma, in St Albans, England, where he is currently working on his second book.

Mumbai: Before the Monsoon

BY STEPHEN KELMAN

Ask anyone who's been there about Mumbai and they'll all tell you the same thing: that it's a City of Contrasts. They'll most likely be using capital letters when they say this, and their eyes will probably be glazed over, recalling some profound event or other that befell them on their visit, one of those clay-baked epiphanies that tumble from the shelves of tourist souvenir stands like bloated monsoon raindrops, something prone to rouse a latent spiritual yearning or to recalibrate a person's sense of what's important or just or worthwhile in the world. Their stories will probably include a combination of the following: blind children playing cricket in the acrid trickles from a crumbling sewage pipe, beggars outside the Bentley showroom, dough-eyed babies hanging from toothpick hips, the smear of kohl on saffron robes.

Orchids shivering in the shadow of a McDonald's billboard. Waiters with white smiles and white tunics, doormen with blunted ceremonial swords, auto rickshaw drivers with dreams of making a splash on *India's Got Talent*. An elephant in chains. Food that tastes like weather. A bomb scare and funny toilets and gratitude for a life lived in the lap of literacy.

I thought all these things were just for the brochure or the coffee table, a bright thread to be unpicked over grey Western mornings, a way for travellers to stretch out the myth of having been somewhere that can change how a human heart works, somewhere you can carry with you long after the bump and squeal of tyres on cool Heathrow asphalt.

Then I saw for myself and it all turned out to be true.

. . . .

I went to India to meet a man I was going to write about, a man whose life I'll summarize in my next book. He lives in Navi Mumbai, a satellite colony separated from Old Bombay by a creek bridged by two strips of clean highway and a proactive city planning policy, and as well as freelancing as a newspaper sports reporter and martial-arts instructor, he enjoys breaking concrete slabs over his genitals with a sledgehammer. More on him later. I spent ten days holed up in a business-class hotel in Vashi, Navi Mumbai's commercial centre, compiling research notes and trying to decide if I could go on living without the love of a good woman, and in between I took bashful meals with my new friend and his family, wandered around Vashi's two malls – one dishevelled and sparse, one all new and populated by aspiring Hilfiger models, both guarded by x-ray machines and body-scanners, unfortunate legacy of the terror attacks of 2008 – and accompanied my host on his assignments, covering amateur power-lifting trials and regional cricket matches, trekking into the hills to interview ping pong-playing monks. But it's my one night in Old Bombay that I remember most vividly, that I turn to in my quiet moments as proof that the world is as weird and sad and beautiful as I would have it be, and that my place in it is as inevitable as the wind in the trees.

It starts with a near-death experience, one that lasts the length of my journey into the city: Bibhuti, my new friend, drives like Mr Magoo on happy pills. He wrestles his mid-segment – it's what they call a hatchback – through the skittish traffic, often taking both hands from the wheel to clap gleefully at the retelling of a funny story, laughing with his whole body while I gouge fingernail furrows in the dashboard and mumble silent prayers for the stray dogs skipping the lights, the sunglasses-sellers three-deep at every intersection, rolling with the punches as we nose our way to the coast, the dusk streaking our windows like oil. The rear ends of every jam-packed fruit truck and weekend jalopy bear the hand-painted slogan 'Horn OK Please', an invitation that everyone is all too happy to accept, a cluster bombing of indiscriminate parps chasing us through the dust until we make the affluent suburb of Worli, the streets widen and the air slows, the naked children crossing the road have tidy hair and there are fruits hanging from the trees that look like lanterns.

It's not just me and Bibhuti in the car, his wife and son are along for the ride – she silent and placid like a lake, he chirruping away in dogleg English, reading aloud the brand names from the billboards, Cadbury's and Rolls Royce and Wayne Rooney, sucking on the words like he's gently tearing mango pulp from peel, hounding his father with plaintive requests for 'A/C, A/C!' We've already bonded over soccer and my groundless fear of snakes, and when our eyes meet in the wing mirror it's always my own ghost I see, that part of myself that's long lost and buried in the ash of living.

We pass a clapperboard church wedged between peeling mansion houses; the sign outside reads 'People are so often lonely because they build walls instead of bridges.' I feel like crying. I tell myself it's jetlag, but I'm not fooling anyone.

Travel isn't something to be done alone if you can help it, at least that's true in my case. This far from home I thought I could be anyone, but my own peculiar loneliness has followed me across the continents and sits patiently on my shoulder, a crow picking at a kerbside rubbish fire. I don't like myself enough to make leaps into the unknown, I can't forget who I am long enough to relax into a spirit of adventure, but Bibhuti is all smiles and I think that maybe I shouldn't leave the world before I've worn a moustache like his, that there are more flavours still left to be tasted. He points out the sights to me as we drive: colonial statues on roundabouts prodding at the sky in obscene salute to an imagined past, bereft citizens sleeping top to tail on the manicured lawn opposite Victoria Terminus, safely corralled behind wrought-iron spikes and the empty promises of progress. Then the lights all come on at once, and we hit festival traffic, a trail of pilgrims as far as I can see all shuffling, shuffling towards a temple guarded by machine-gun nests. We park and get out of the car to graft ourselves onto the limbs of the devoted. I see my first holy cow quietly shitting by the side of the road as a restless convoy of buses disgorges more souls into the mix.

So many people all waiting to give thanks, to pay homage to something invisible. All stepping softly around the toes of their neighbours, careful not to disturb the sleeping dogs. The elephant-headed one or the monkey one or the one that rides a chariot of flames, whatever it is that inspires a multitude to swarm so sweetly I can't argue with it; there's a force that compels me to breathe in, to alm myself with something lowlier than a tourist's silver dollar. I may not want to believe in what they believe, but I'm gripped by a sudden immutable desire to believe in

something, and when I spot a baby sleeping soundly among
the sidewalk dogs, cradled in a garland from the flower-
seller's castoffs, her mother entrusting her to the
benevolence of this sea of strangers, I feel protected. I
think India is finally working its stuff on me, and I've got
little choice but to go along with it.

. . . .

I spoke before of loneliness, and of love. I'd left a woman
behind in England, a woman for whom I was falling
but had for various reasons been unable to tell. Looking
back, I think my trip to India was in part an attempt to
cleanse myself of the need for her, to find an alternative
route to peace or else a definitive reason to give up the
search. This was a tall order, and it didn't work, thank
God – that woman is now my wife. But at the time, May
of 2010, in the middle of a heat wave that was killing
people, awaiting the cooling release of a monsoon that
I wouldn't be around for, I was convinced that life and
death – my life and death – hung on the discovery of
answers to questions I'd never dared ask before, if only
because to ask them would be to admit that I was just
as hungry for happiness as anyone else, and that I'd
probably take it any way it came. No, it's really not a good
idea to travel alone when you're as weighed down by the
pale blues as I was then.

So to epiphanies.

A sleeping baby and a man who derives the purest of
pleasure from being kicked in the testicles by his friends.

Bibhuti Nayak holds fourteen world records for various
highly specialised feats of masochism: inflicting suffering
upon himself is what keeps his powder dry. He broke his

first record in 1998, when he enlisted four of his martial-arts students to kick him in the groin, forty-seven times in a minute and a half. No padding or protection, no numbing agents or anaesthetic solutions. There was no existing record at the time, so he could quite easily have elected to stop at one kick, but Bibhuti doesn't do things by halves. He is a proud man – proud of his physique, which is wiry and whippet-lean, product of a harsh training regime which includes a thousand sit-ups a day and two hours' sleep a night. Proud of his family, who tolerate his hare-brained pursuits with noble equanimity. Proud of his moustache and his lustrous head of hair, which he combs precisely eleven times a day, at regular intervals. What Bibhuti does, he does to promote a message of peace and love. It's all for the good of his countrymen and of his eternal soul.

'God is not one form, he is all around us,' he tells me as we wander the park next to the temple, averting our eyes from the shyly courting couples strolling untouching beneath the benign canopy of the banyan trees. We've left his wife and son to pay their dues at the temple, something Bibhuti doesn't feel the need of. 'I give thanks to him by achieving peak physical condition. I feel his love by always being aware of the love in the people, be it my family and my friends, the children I teach or the new visitor who comes to me from across the seven seas.' He means me. I think he's saying he loves me, and when he invites me to kick him in the balls, I'm touched. I don't share his philosophy or necessarily approve of the extreme methods by which he expresses it, but there's something about being in the presence of someone who holds a conviction, really holds on to it like a parent to a child – with fingers splayed and supple, not so tight that

the imprint he leaves is indelible yet not loose enough to
risk a spill – that makes me want to give the world and
everyone in it the benefit of the doubt.

India working its stuff again. Signs and wonders and all
that jazz.

The place is warm and beautiful and later, when the
pujas have ended and the darkness has bedded in, I'm
taken to stand between the feet of the Gateway of India, a
photo op for my hosts, the Arabian Sea whispering at my
back and thoughts of scale predominating. What's big and
what's small. I'm small and the world is big. I'm too small
to make much of a mark in my departure and the world is
too big to walk alone. It's wedding season here. Marine
Drive sparkles with white horses, their heads bowed under
festive plumages, neon carriages pulling the laughing newly
married; how happy and nervous they look, how heavy
their investment in a future whose gifts and trials are
guesses to be carried pebble-like in pockets, to be rubbed
smooth in daily acts of faith and charity. I wish them the
best of luck. Warm and beautiful mean nothing without a
kindred flare to light them by.

The doormen at the Taj Mahal hotel really do wear
swords and when you look carefully you can see the
patches on the walls where holes from terrorist bullets
have been filled in. Bibhuti insists on paying the bill for
supper, won't take my money, and as the evening winds
down and talk of the book to come fades into contented
silence, I turn my mind to home and the woman who will
bear witness to whatever changes my brief stay in Mumbai
have wrought in me. Shortly after my return I'll meet her
for the first time in twenty-five years. A year later we'll
be married. When she asks me about Mumbai I'll tell her
it's a City of Contrasts. A city with a heart, and big ideas.

A city that makes you seek answers to those questions that pick at the stitches of lonely Western nights. I'll tell her it was Mumbai that pushed me when I needed pushing, and that the leap of faith was her.

I never got to kick my friend in the balls. I politely declined the offer.

Aliya Whiteley was born in North Devon, England, in 1974. After spending a few years living in Germany, she has returned to the UK and currently lives in Bedfordshire with her husband, daughter and dog. Her first two novels, the black comedies *Light Reading* and *Three Things About Me*, were published by Macmillan under their New Writing imprint, and she also writes short stories in many genres. Her first novella, *Mean Mode Median*, is available as an ebook.

An Alpine Escape

BY ALIYA WHITELEY

The cheapest flight is to Munich, so that's where we go. We withdraw some euros from a cash point and sit in one of the airport cafés, drinking coffee from small white cups, listing all the reasons why running away four days before our wedding is a really good idea: the alterations of the dress aren't finished, the florist has lost our order, and our closest friends suddenly aren't able to attend. Lots of little problems are coagulating to form a big puddle of mutual nerves. Being someplace else seems like the right choice. When we return, everything will have magically sorted itself out, we tell each other, as we hold hands over the table.

If we return in time.

We buy a pen and a map, and draw a shaky line, following the motorway that runs alongside the Alps, and ends up in Salzburg. At that moment, I know only two things about Salzburg:

- Mozart was born there
- *The Sound of Music* was filmed there

That's it. I also have a suspicion that Austrians like sausages and beer, and I'm partial to those things too, so we hire a two-door Jolly Car from a rental company and buzz off, feeling tiny and tongue-tied in the shadows of the mountains.

We drive all afternoon, stopping at a sparkling clean service station for a pork and Gouda sandwich, and find ourselves amidst the tall straight houses of the outskirts of Salzburg, crisscrossed with tramlines and power cables, just as the sun is setting. There is no music, no dresses made of old green curtains, no nunneries. People are striding, heads down, walking home after a long day at work, no doubt. The first drops of rain hit the windscreen. We move slowly in traffic, take a sudden turn, and find ourselves crossing over the Salzach River on an ornate iron bridge, the water high and choppy underneath. Above us, the castle rises up from the skyline: massive, morose. So Salzburg is not all Mozart and Maria von Trapp. I shiver at that brooding outline, and Ray turns up Jolly Car's noisy heating and drives onwards, through quieter streets, until we find a likeable sign for a hotel.

Hotel Jedermann is in the middle of a terrace, with a red front door flanked by mini fir trees. Inside, in the warm, a teenage girl with milky skin takes our one suitcase as if we are expected, and shows us to the third floor, and a bare, clean room with twin peach duvets.

Breakfast is between seven and nine, she tells us, in a clear, strong voice. She must have grown up in the hotel business; how easy she finds it to herd strangers into rooms and demonstrate the shower. I envy her. Later, sitting side by side in the first brauhaus we find, I tell Ray that I wish I was more like that girl, or like Maria von Trapp. If only I had Salzburgian confidence in myself. How easy would it be to conquer one wedding, when I can walk over mountains?

Maybe it springs from the beer and sausage, says Ray, so we order large amounts of both. The brauhaus makes its own wheat beer – Dunkelweiss, heavy and chewy and a delicious meal in itself, but when the sausages arrive we make a good job of them too. They're pork sausages, split and filled with cheese, served with sauerkraut and heavy black bread; the long bench we occupy fills up with friendly locals eating the same thing. It seems there's only one dish and one beer on the menu, but everyone wears the same calm smile, nodding as we all munch away.

After an indeterminate amount of beer, we wobble back to the hotel, past a tribe of young men who are taking it in turns to breathe into the breathalyser machine on the wall and congratulate each other for their levels of inebriation. The rain is stronger, and it soaks us through, but the peach duvets are soft and warm, and the unadorned white walls spin round, drawing close, keeping us still and sleepy.

Amazingly, we don't have hangovers. We eat alone in the immaculate dining room: more black bread and a tough, nutty cheese. Then we head out, into the town, and walk around as if we have just woken up with amnesia, oohing and aahing over the normality of trimmed hedges and shop windows.

In the centre of Salzburg, over one of the iron bridges, there are tiny crowded cafés and restaurants, piled on top of each other. In a cobbled square a string quartet wear penguin suits and play chamber music under a stripy tarpaulin tent.

Mozart! I say to Ray with delight, and then we find, around a corner and down an alley, Mozart's birthplace. The tour of the house takes an hour and thirty minutes, the guide speaking very slowly, in three languages, with that sureness of tone that means she thinks everyone is enthralled. The house is practically empty, apart from a portrait of Mozart's father and a harpsichord that apparently Mozart never used. But still, I can feel his bullishness and brilliance stretch across the centuries to me, and back outside I begin to catch moments of his music everywhere: street singers, antique shops, supermarkets. And there are hundreds of small boutiques selling Mozartkugeln – chocolate balls filled with marzipan, with his face and signature stamped on the red and gold foil.

I wish I was more like Mozart, I tell Ray. He smiles, and says he would not be marrying me if I was. He's more of a Beethoven person.

Are we really not going to go back for the wedding?

He stares at the pyramids of Mozart's beautiful balls. *Let's just do this, now. Let's just do Salzburg,* he says.

So we do. We spend the next two and a half days exploring the Alpine zoo with the family of sleeping, snoring otters, knotted together like a rubber-band ball; the falconry display high in the mountains, with enormous eagles swooping down, so close to our heads that we flinch from their claws and laugh at each other; the Augustinian brewery, serving tankards of beer and thick slices of hot meat all day to the students who line the long benches and play cards; Salzburg Castle, dominating the town, with its maze of dark rooms filled with suits of armour, glass cases of swords and guns, and audio guides describing the rise and fall of the fortunes of the state; and the gold of the churches, and the steps down into the basement record shops, and the hill that leads up to the monastery where the rain turns to snow and all of Salzburg is below us, green roofs and white walls, domes and steeples.

I'm in love with the place. *Can we live here?* I say to Ray. And he doesn't say no. But we both know that's not going to work. We're going to have to go home at some point. The only question is when.

On the morning of the day before our wedding we walk slowly into town, and decide to step into the art gallery opposite our favourite brauhaus. They are holding an exhibition – the work of Bernhard Vogel. We walk around the paintings, taking in the soaring skyscrapers of New York and the perfect arcs of the bridges of Venice, each scene textured with deliberate messiness that speaks of the gleeful unpredictability of travel. I want, at that moment, to keep travelling. I want to go with Ray, to see it together, to make sense of it through both sets of eyes, both tongues tasting. I realise it and speak it at the same time:

I do want to get married. I just don't want a wedding.

I think of all the things back home that are going wrong: the dress that won't fit, the people that can't come.

We wander back outside, and sit on a bench next to a hot-dog stand, in a mess of fine drizzle. We talk it through. Who cares if the dress doesn't fit? I've probably put on half a stone through pork-munching and beer-guzzling, anyway. And flowers are just window dressing. As for the friends that can't make it – well, we can send them a copy of the video. We can watch it together, one evening, and have a good laugh at our monumental case of nerves.

I don't have to be Mozart or Maria von Trapp to get through this. I don't have to raise six kids or write a symphony. I just have to be there, in front of the registrar, for a few minutes. And then I can be anywhere, with him: New York, Paris, Rome, the Rockies, maybe even back to Salzburg. Wherever we want to go.

We realise we're sitting outside the Mirabell Gardens, where Maria danced with six kids in curtain clothes. So we dance too. We run around the fountain and jump up and down the stone steps, singing that song about female deer and drops of golden sun. Then Ray turns to me and says, *Right. We can do this. Let's go home and get married.*

So we do.

When the day comes, I wear a white suit, picked off a rail at a chain store. I don't carry flowers, or wear my hair in complicated knots. I walk down the aisle to Mozart's Clarinet Concerto, and I walk back up it, with Ray, to the sound of Maria Von Trapp Climbing Every Mountain. Later, we play the DVD to our friends who couldn't make it, and we all sing along as we drink beer and eat sausages.

I catch Ray's eye and say, *Why were we so nervous?*

He shrugs, and gives me a smile filled with sunshine. It was stupid, that much is certain. But a random line on a map took us to a place where we could find the courage we needed. And I've begun to understand the purpose of travel; a few days of seeing the world in a different way gives us the confidence to face whatever waits for us at home. Even mountains.

The **Isabel Allende** Foundation (www.isabelallendefoundation.org) provides support to nonprofit groups that empower women and girls by providing healthcare, education and protection from violence, exploitation and discrimination.

Who Wants a Girl?

BY ISABEL ALLENDE

My daughter Paula died on December 6, 1992, of a rare blood disorder that nowadays should not be fatal, but there was negligence in the hospital, she was given the wrong medication, she fell into a coma and five months later, when the hospital finally gave her back to me, she was in a vegetative state. I brought her home and took care of her until she died, peacefully, in my arms. She was twenty-eight years old. She had been a smart and beautiful girl with a generous heart; her mantra was, 'You only have what you give; it's by giving that you become rich.'

Grieving for the loss of Paula was like walking alone in a long and dark tunnel. It took me a few years to reach the end of the tunnel and see light again. Those were years of confusion and sadness; at times I felt a claw in my throat and I could barely breathe. Without even being aware of it, I dressed all in black. I tried to write, but it was a futile attempt: I would spend hours staring at my computer or pacing my studio, blocked. For someone who lives to write, an internal drought is terrifying. I summoned the muses in vain, for even the most bedraggled muse had abandoned me. After three years of emotional paralysis, my husband, Willie, and my friend Tabra decided that I needed to fill up my reservoirs and proposed a trip to India, because according to them, India is one of those experiences that mark you for life, a land of great contrasts, of appalling poverty and extraordinary beauty where surely I would find inspiration. I accepted, although I had no desire to travel and even less to India, the farthest possible point from our home before starting back around the other side of the planet.

. . . .

Sirinder, our guide and driver in India, had the courage and expertise needed to navigate winding rural roads and crazy city traffic, dodging cars, buses, burros, bicycles and more than one starving cow. No one hurried – life is long – except the motorcycles zigzagging at the speed of torpedoes and with a family of five riding aboard. We didn't have safety belts, we had karma: no one dies before his time. Sirinder was a man of few words and Tabra and I learned not to ask him any questions, because the only one he answered was Willie.

One late afternoon, as we drove in the country, in a dusty and reddish landscape where the villages were far apart and the plains stretched forever, we saw a solitary tree, probably an acacia, and a group of four women and several children under its branches. We wondered what they were doing there, in the middle of nowhere, far from houses or a well. The sun was beginning to go and brushstrokes the color of fire streaked the sky. We asked Sirinder to stop, and Tabra and I walked toward the women. They started to back away, but their curiosity overcame their shyness and soon we were together beneath the acacia, surrounded by naked children.

The women were wearing dusty, frayed saris. They were young, with long black hair, dry skin, sunken eyes made up with kohl. In India, as in most of the world, the concept of personal space we defend so fiercely in the West doesn't exist. Lacking common language, we greeted each other with smiles and then they examined us with bold fingers, touching our clothing, our faces, Tabra's red hair and the silver jewelry we had bought the day before. We took off the bracelets and offered them to the women, who put them on with delight. There were enough for everyone, two or three each.

One of the women, who could have been Paula's age, took my face in her hands and kissed me lightly on the forehead. I felt her parched lips, her warm breath, her smell. It was such an unexpected gesture, so intimate, that I couldn't hold back the tears. The other women patted me in silence, disoriented by my reaction.

From the road, a toot of the horn from Sirinder summoned us: it was time to leave. We bade the women good-bye and started back to the car, but one of them followed us. She touched my shoulder, I turned, and she held out a small package. I thought she meant to give me something in exchange for the bracelets and I tried to explain with signs that it wasn't necessary, but she forced me to take it.

It weighed almost nothing, it looked like a bundle of rags, but when I turned back the folds, I saw that it held a newborn baby, tiny and dark. Its eyes were closed and it smelled like no other child I have ever held, a pungent odor of ashes, dust, and excrement. I kissed its face, murmured a blessing and tried to return it to the mother, but she ran back to the others while I stood there, rocking the baby, not understanding what was happening.

A minute later Sirinder came running and shouting. He snatched the baby from my arms and started toward the women, but they ran away, terrified at the man's wrath. Then he bent down and laid the infant on the dry earth beneath the tree, while the women watched from a safe distance.

By then Willie had come too, and he hustled me back to the car, nearly lifting me off the ground, followed by Tabra. Sirinder started the engine and we drove off, as I buried my face in my husband's chest.

'Why did that woman try to give away her baby?' Willie murmured.

'It was a girl. Who wants a girl?' Sirinder replied with a shrug.

There are stories that have the power to heal. What happened that day beneath the acacia tree loosened the knot that had been choking me, cleaned away the cobwebs of self-pity, and forced me to come back to the world and transform the loss of my daughter into action. I could not save that baby girl or her desperate mother or millions of women like her, but I could at least attempt to ease the lot in life of some of them. I had an account with untouched savings that I was planning to invest in something that would make Paula proud. In that moment I remembered that when she was alive I would often call her for advice – my life as a new immigrant in the US and as stepmother of Willie's drug-addicted children was rather stressful – and her answer would always come in the form of a question: 'Mother, what is the most generous thing to do in this case?'

'Now I know what to do with my savings,' I announced to Willie and Tabra. 'I will start a foundation to help women and children.'

And so I did as soon as we returned to California, never imagining that through the years, that seed would become a large tree, like the acacia.

Nikki Gemmell has written six novels, *Shiver, Cleave, Lovesong, The Bride Stripped Bare, The Book of Rapture* and *With My Body*, as well as several nonfiction books. Her work has been critically acclaimed internationally and translated into many languages. In France she's been described as a female Jack Kerouac, in Australia as one of the most original and engaging authors of her generation, and in the US as one of the few truly original voices to emerge in a long time.

Into Unknown Climes

BY NIKKI GEMMELL

'It will change your life,' the Antarctic old-timer proclaimed two days before I flew to Hobart to board the icebreaker *Aurora Australis*. The man's expression was hard to read and I could not tell if his prophecy would be a good thing or a bad thing. All I knew was that he had a lot of living in his eyes and he never wanted to go back to the place. He would not say why.

I was not wanting my life changed. A radio journalist too fond of wearing black, I was just doing my job on this trip, nothing else. And with all the righteous zeal of youth, I believed the journalist's blazing function was to make trouble – with other people's lives, not my own. I was the outsider, the observer, and when on a job I was never meant to get my hands mucky in the mess of life.

The Australian government fully kitted us out army-style the day before sailing. Almost everything we were given, from thermal underwear to padded jumpsuit to steel-capped boots, was bloke-sized. I had little idea what I'd be getting myself into but these early signs weren't promising.

The hull of the *Aurora Australis* was flattened so it could ride up on top of slabs of floating ice as big as

Olympic pools and crack them with its hefty weight. 'She's great in the ice, but she bobs like a cork in the open water,' said a seasoned expeditioner just before departure. This was not good because I'd been spectacularly seasick in the past, so within half an hour of sailing, a seasickness patch was firmly behind my ear. 'It's the last great sea voyage in the world,' the captain told me with something akin to awe. 'It's to the wild side of Antarctica, the bit where no one can fly and land. And it's across the Great Southern Ocean, the roughest ocean in the world.' Oh God, I thought, oh God.

Our ship was the first to reach the continent after the long, dark winter hibernation, the only one out of all the Antarctic nations so far south at that time. 'No one else is as mad as the Australians,' said Steve, a sailor. 'All the rest of them wait til later in the season, but not us.' Most of the people on board, apart from the crew, were scientists and trades people being dropped off at Australia's bases for the summer. There were few women. There were a lot of beards. I set about my task of ferreting out narratives with the zeal of a forensic scientist. I had a job to do and I seized it.

· · · · · • · · · · ·

'Antarctica,' the prophesising veteran had told me, 'is a place of vivid mateships.' And so it was that I stumbled across Martin, a historical archaeologist sent down south to assess the heritage value of the buildings at Australia's Mawson Station (established 1954) and Davis (1957). We both wore seasick patches, were both vaguely dissatisfied with our jobs, wanted to write books. We would stand on deck in the early hours of the morning and watch auroras like giant scribbles of moving light in the sky and talk endlessly of lives we didn't lead, and most likely never would, of what we would do when we got back. How we'd finally have the courage to do what we really wanted to. It all seemed possible down there.

In the daytime there were icebergs that looked like pool tables or Cambodian temples or Walt Disney castles or Uluru, some so blue it was as if the ice had trapped a piece of the sky. We stood on the bow as the ocean changed around us from open sea to water like heaving marble with long veins of white through it. One morning there were frozen pancakes of ice with their edges kicked up, an ocean of severed ears. Over the days the ears changed to huge waterlilies of ice, then oblong chunks twenty metres across, then vast sheets, ice-rink sized.

On the ice chunks were seals and their blood – it was the pupping season and there were many births. There were penguins that scurried in a panic away from the ship and left tracks in the ice like lines on a hand. In the channels between floes were minke whales, their backs breaking the surface in a stately arc. And circling around the *Aurora* were snow petrels soaring and dipping like hundreds of angels watching over us, such a fragile craft in such an unknown world.

Martin was contemptuous of the voyagers who spent most of their time in the video room in the bowels of the ship. 'Some of them haven't seen daylight since we left Hobart. They live in a world of virtual darkness. Maybe they're acclimatising themselves to twenty-four-hour darkness in winter, but no one has told them that they're going down in summer.' There were 300 videos on the ship, it took five weeks to sail from Hobart to Davis, and by the end of the fourth week, the video-heads were so bored they weren't fast-forwarding through the previews any more.

'I feel so alive in this place,' Martin laughed in vivid contrast, exhausting me with the ferocity of his enthusiasm. He was 37, the age of reckoning as we career into middle age, and he was gulping this world like a gleeful boy. He said that we must live differently after this trip, do all the things we really wanted to do. He was constantly dragging me up on deck to seize the light, the sky, the ocean. One day I forget my special-issue sunglasses but didn't care because I wanted to see unfiltered all the different shades of white around us, but then I got snow blindness like a thick film of milk over my eyes. It took me three days to recover and from then on I always wore my sunglasses, Martin made sure of it. He made sure of many things. That our lives would change after this voyage, they must. That they would veer from their proscribed course like an ocean liner heading off to unknown climes.

. . . .

A 'winterer,' helicoptered on board from another station, bit into an apple. 'That's better than sex,' he declared. It'd been a long time between apples. We, the 'summerers,' were delivering the first supply of fresh fruit and vegetables Davis had seen in seven months. Another newly-arrived winterer ate five apples in a row. There's an old Antarctic saying that Wednesday nights are wank nights and blizzards are a bonus. Apparently someone had a tape of the sound of a blizzard for when things got really rough.

Just before the ship arrived at Davis, the women were gathered together for a talk by the female ship's doctor. Women's business. We were told that in the strange and constrained social world of an Antarctic station, touching was often misconstrued. A veteran of several trips said she was a constant focus of attention for the simple fact that she was female. That she was always being watched, even when she ate her muesli at breakfast, and after the initial gift of the attention, it was utterly exhausting. 'People are always wanting a piece of you. I had to go for ten-minute walks outside just to get away from it all.'

We were told that if an attachment was formed, then the absolute rule was discretion – because it was so hard on everyone else if it was flouted. Later the chef, an old Antarctic hand, told me that if there were two single people on a station then invariably they paired up, but it was not the done thing to openly fraternise because 'it wasn't fair on the people who weren't having sex.' I was single when I began this voyage. I was intrigued, by all of it.

. . . .

The *Aurora* sailed up an avenue of icebergs and cracked the sea's skin to within three kilometres of the coastal station, but could crack it no further. The ship parked by a line of 44-gallon drums placed on the frozen surface by a two-lane highway bulldozed freshly in the ice for the cargo operations to commence. The gangplank was lowered to the surface and we walked or skied the last joyous wondrous leg, across the surface of the Great Southern Ocean, to the continent. Tears pricked my eyes with the sheer monumental emotion of it all, the wonderful strangeness of it.

Davis Station was a scattered collection of brightly coloured buildings that looked like large shipping containers. 'Legoland,' it was dubbed. The Australian mainland was 'the real world.' I wanted to leave the real world far behind, drown myself in this brave new existence, so vulnerable and lonely and exhilarating and replenishing in the vastness of the unsullied continent.

Yet Legoland's decor was almost disappointingly plush. There were carpets and tubs of Tim Tam biscuits, Apple Macs, an electronic board with up-to-the-minute temperature and wind-speed readings and a daily newspaper of stories culled from the net. I thought I'd at least be doing it tough, but walking into the Legoland living quarters reminded me of a small airport lounge. The oddnesses slowly dawned. There was no money; it wasn't needed – the government provided everything from alcohol to shampoo to condoms. The milk was powdered; the eggs were up to a year old. They were oiled to preserve them, but the chef had to 'crack and smell' before he put them in an omelette. The rules were ferocious. No one was allowed to go beyond the station boundaries by themselves, and Martin hated that one. There was a surgery and an operating theatre and a doctor but no nurses. If an operation was required the diesel mechanic and the chef would help out; they had gone through a two-week course on the mainland.

Outside were utes and bulldozers and a small cement-mixing truck, all with government number plates. Tank-like vehicles called Hagglunds were so noisy you had to wear headphones when you were in them, assaulting the silence that felt thousands of years old, untouched. And at night, the vehicles in the open were lined up obediently and plugged into heaters to keep the oil in their engines warm.

The Legoland buildings were scattered because one of the biggest dangers was fire. You couldn't afford to have everything in one complex because if it burnt down in May and everything was wiped out, there couldn't be a rescue until October. Smoking was taboo, only allowed in one small and reeking windowless shipping container. I didn't smoke, but if I did, that shipping container would have made me quit. And always in Legoland there was the hum of the generator. Martin told me to walk Antarctica, to move beyond that hum, any way I could, to listen to the thick silence of the land. It's a silence that thuds in your ears.

. . . .

The Australians were rigorous about keeping their chunk of the world's last wilderness as pristine as they could. There were many rules. No souveniring rocks from the continent. No taking polystyrene balls from packaging and bean bags to the continent, because they didn't degrade and they got stuck in the throats of animals and choked them. No leaving anything behind in the field but footprints and urine (and if possible, urinate down a crack in the ice). Everything else in terms of human waste was to be removed because it would never rot. Plastic bags were handed out for defecating during field trips and women got an extra device, a FUD (Female Urinary Device), plastic and pink and shaped like a funnel. It meant we could go standing up like a man.

There was a lot of camping by scientists in the field when the light pushed out darkness for much of the time. There was so much to see. Coastal icebergs shining like white plastic in the sharp sunlight. A baby seal a day or two old, its umbilical cord still attached, snap frozen to its belly. Seal blood whose hotness had plunged it into the snow. Penguins, thousands of them, clucking and calling in a frenzy of hormones as the breeding season began. A strangely lunar landscape of rock and ice in the hills surrounding Davis. And always, the stretched sky. One day the strap of my camera froze into a stiff scribble. The flesh of my cheek stuck to the cold metal of the camera back and panicking, I pulled my skin away. I had been trying to take a photo of a woman's eyelashes dusted with ice. It looked like white mascara.

I didn't want to leave this place. Didn't want to go back to my cluttered, inner-city life. Didn't want to leave Martin. He had entered my heart, was riveted to it, the relationship sanctified by the shared wonder of this land. But he was staying behind, his work wasn't finished. As we said goodbye our cheeks felt like plastic as they lingered a touch.

. . . .

I smelt Tasmania before I saw it, smelt trees and soil on the breeze. Then I saw green, in all its exotic vibrancy. It had been so long since I'd seen that colour in nature after my strict Antarctic palette of white and blue and grey and black. When the *Aurora* docked, I stepped onto a pavement that was too hard and after two days I'd jarred my shins. There were too many people, too much noise. The only things I wanted from home were the sun on my skin and the dirt on my hands and the taste of bananas in my mouth. Apart from that I wanted to be back in Antarctica, achingly.

. . . .

Three weeks after I returned, I got a phone call from down south. I recognised the crackle on the line and instantly felt the tug in my belly I always got when I spoke to Martin.

But it wasn't him, it was the station leader. It was about Martin. He had been killed in a fall. He was climbing a bluff beyond the station boundary to read his book, *If on a Winter's Night a Traveller*, and watch a spectacular sunset over the ice and listen to the wondrous silence. At a midnight barely touched by darkness.

My world fell apart. I foundered. Just wanted to go back down south and wrap myself in the solace of the silence and not emerge for a very long time. The real world was too hard. Too complicated, back home, where Martin had a different life, a different world that I'd never been a part of. I had nothing of him now but a bundle of emails and a battered old paperback with his name written in it and the words of wisdom at his memorial service which I held onto tight – to always live life vividly and with passion.

It took a while but slowly, gradually, I began to feel weirdly euphoric at times, as if I was scrubbing my life, starting afresh. Martin's wish, for both of us. At the age of twenty-eight I grew up – it was like I was being hauled into adulthood. Grief gave me clarity, it stopped the silliness. I realigned my priorities. Martin's death taught me to grab at life with his enthusiasm and passion, and the importance of following your heart before it was too late. To not let people fool you into giving up. I lost the hunger for journalism, the observer's life. Learnt to live closer to the earth, to be still with it and to listen to it. I wrote a book about the experience, a novel called *Shiver*, which balmed me through the whole process of grieving. My gift to Martin and his gift to me. Because finally, in my late twenties, I was doing what I really wanted to do with my life.

Téa Obreht was born in 1985 in the former Yugoslavia, and spent her childhood in Cyprus and Egypt before eventually immigrating to the United States in 1997. Her writing has been published in *The New Yorker*, *The Atlantic, Harper's, Zoetrope: All-Story*, the *New York Times*, and the *Guardian*, and has been anthologized in *The Best American Short Stories* and *The Best American Non-Required Reading*. Her first novel, *The Tiger's Wife*, won the 2011 Orange Prize for Fiction, the 2011 Indie Choice Award for Debut Novel, and was a finalist for the National Book Award. She has been named by the *New Yorker* as one of the twenty best American fiction writers under forty and included in the National Book Foundation's list of 5 Under 35. Téa Obreht lives in Ithaca, New York.

Nuestro Pueblo

BY TEA OBREHT

I grew up visiting sacred places. Pilgrimage was a condition of my childhood, largely resulting from my family's nomadic existence following the breakup of Yugoslavia. Somehow we always managed to land someplace where the most remarkable history existed side-by-side with the everyday. By the time I was eleven years old, I had seen the Vatican and the great temple complexes of Luxor, Edfu and Karnak; I'd squinted up at the Pantheon, the Parthenon and Petra; I'd paddled around, for better or worse, in Seas both Dead and Red. In several family albums, my chickenpox-riddled face grins out from under a straw hat at the feet of Ramses the Second's colossi at Abu Simbel. Growing up surrounded by other children whose families were on the move, I had no concept of the great privilege of this existence, how lucky I was to have the Sphinx and pyramids in my backyard, or how unusual it was that my family (a Muslim, a Roman Catholic, and an Orthodox Serb) didn't care whether the monument we were visiting was a mosque, a church, or a pagan temple whose convoluted representation of Hell would throw me into a panic-stricken, afterlife-affirming identity crisis – as long as the *fact* that it was sacred got some awe out of me.

Now, years later, sacredness is more clearly defined for me. It is personal, intimate, something totally individual. I understand that its temples, whether manmade or wild, are havens of the self at rest, and it is the story of their respective origins out of which their sacredness is constructed. This is why I make a pilgrimage, whenever I can, to what is probably the most incredible and unlikely sacred place I can imagine.

In the middle of Los Angeles, nestled in one of the city's most notorious neighborhoods, stands a complex of structures built by a single man over a period of thirty-odd years: the Watts Towers. As with every site of pilgrimage, the way is labyrinthine and bizarre enough to confuse even the most steadfast devotee, confound the most sophisticated GPS. It meanders through tight alleys of low-roofed houses; dead-end streets and ramshackle shops; fenced-in yards where weeds that have squeezed through the paving nod absently through the day; tightly packed cars that, for want of use, have spent years trapped under a coating of perpetual L.A. dust that seems to have a life of its own, while the Towers themselves dart in and out of view.

Coming here, I am aware that I am as likely to drive these streets in reverse as in the right gear. Yet every time I visit, I am joined by at least five or six other pilgrims, strangers all. At first, we drift in like shadows and do not notice each other; life goes on around the Towers, and not everyone in the vicinity is there on pilgrimage. But inevitably, we wind up gathered around the iron fence, and from every angle a viewing of the Towers is like assembling a jigsaw puzzle of Alice's Wonderland: is that yellow hook sticking out of the mortar a cup handle? That huge, round, red thing – is that a bowling ball? From how many christenings and funerals, Sunday lunches and failed restaurants, weddings and broken homes, no-particular-reason parties and birthdays, have the thousands upon thousands of glass shards and bits of crockery that make up the Towers been culled?

I did not fully understand why this was a sacred place to me until I became a writer. As a student at the University of Southern California, I was reluctantly introduced to the Towers as part of a college art class, the aim of which was to better acquaint its students with Los Angeles. While I thought the Towers were 'cool' – and then, as time went by, 'really cool' – their emotional impact on me did not manifest for years. I was not thinking about death, or how everything in life tries so hard to work against it. I was not thinking about time, and how it is made up only of stories and memories. I was not thinking about the human spirit, and how its most triumphant compulsion is to make something out of nothing. Now I realize that the builder, Simon Rodia, was doing exactly what writers do: making a patchwork out of fragments, a whole out of disparate realities. Every object studded into the concrete of his Towers has a story connected with some other life, and together they make up a new story, the fabric of his experience, his own understanding of the world.

When I think of Simon Rodia, I always imagine him waking, sitting up in his tiny house on a plot of land barely bigger than a tennis court. It is dark, and he is alone. Decades and thousands of miles separate him from his hometown of Serino, Italy. Through his doorway, he sees what he calls Nuestro Pueblo, the monument he has built to remind himself of it: arches and spires and coils of steel and mortar, inlaid with seashells and bowling pins, glass bottle bottoms and broken pottery, a ragged tile mosaic culled from the household accidents and disposed debris of a community that is convinced he is insane. He will get dressed, assess the damage his unwelcome life's work may have sustained at irreverent hands during the night, then walk for miles, searching for more materials in the abandoned lots and garbage dumps of Watts. When he returns, he will climb the Towers and build on. When he abandons the site, ten years before his death, he will have no idea that his structures, built entirely by his own two hands, will withstand municipal condemnation and the devastation of the Northridge earthquake, or serve as a center of the very community that shunned him, or become a gathering place for dreamers.